CW01551744

Abstract

This thesis investigates the role of the term *pl*
architecture and narrativity. Examining orga
tion of real and virtual spaces, it identifies lite
resisted, or subverted, plot conventions in fictio
de Goncourt, Xavier de Maistre and Neal Stephenson), and introduces architectural spaces such as Thomas Edison's film-studio Black Maria, and the plotless productions of early cinematography, to juxtapose concepts of plot and spatiality in a study of the production and consumption of pre-digital virtual spaces. Plot here relates therefore both to *narrative sequentiality* and *spatial organisation* – from "storyline" to "ground plan". The "plotless" narrative structure of Huysmans, Goncourt and de Maistre focuses on the interaction between man – the "writer-in-residence" – and his domestic interior, functioning as an excitant or stimulant for the production of both material and imagined spaces. The media culture of late 19th century society saw the first significant attempts at *moving image technology* and its related spatialities – the Black Maria, the kinetoscope, the kinetograph, and the films produced by these, which had yet to find a narrative form. The architecture of the plotless novels and the proto-cinematic experiments of the late 19th century modulate between physical reality and fiction. They are ripe in their descriptive narrativity, expanding in the imagination of the consumer. Stephenson's imaginative transposition of book media into a "Primer" – a new form of narrative media that develops its narrative content directly from the environmental context of its reader – concludes the discussion of the thesis, highlighting interrelations between fictive and real space, influencing both writer and reader. The refusal of narrative plot deprives the reader of causality, but emphasises the fictitious spatial creation in which the reader becomes immersed. These spaces, by virtue of their disengagement from plot, allow us to revisit the possibilities of *virtual space* without common preconceptions concerning the creation or experience of digital mediating technology.

Keywords

Architecture, architecture theory, narrativity, virtuality, virtual reality, spatiality, plot, architectural representation, fiction, plotless, 19th century media culture, domestic interior, virtual travelling, narrative organisation, game, interactive environment, moving image technology, proto-cinematic, Black Maria film studio, kinetoscope, immersion, spectator, sensation, imagination, fin-de-siècle, representation technology, excitoir, artifice, experience, consumption, Joris Karl Huysmans, Edmond de Goncourt, Thomas Edison, William K. L. Dickson, Xavier de Maistre, Neal Stephenson.

Malin Zimm

Losing the Plot

– *Architecture and Narrativity in Fin-de-Siècle Media Cultures*

Malin Zimm
Losing the Plot
– Architecture and Narrativity in Fin-de-Siècle Media Cultures

© Malin Zimm
Akademisk Avhandling 2005
PhD Dissertation 2005

KTH Architecture and the Built Environment
School of Architecture / xakt Critical Theory in Architecture
Royal Institute of Technology
SE-100 44 Stockholm, Sweden

www.arkitekturskolan.se
www.xakt.nu

Cover illustration: Malin Zimm
Typography: Peter Gibson Lundberg

Axl Books, Stockholm 2005
www.axlbooks.com
Printed by Bookpartner, Copenhagen 2005
ISBN 91-975901-1-8

To Peter

Acknowledgements

Writing is not solitary work, and it is not stationary business. This text has taken me to many places and has put me in touch with many people. I wish to express my gratitude towards all those who have contributed to this PhD thesis. These are the people who have helped me not to lose the plot.

First of all, my warmest and most heartfelt thanks to my main advisor, Dr. Katja Grillner, for her brilliant mind and professional instincts, for her way to make things happen, for her courage and patience, and most of all, for her way to share all these qualities with such warm confidence. No one could have done it better.

Since my licentiate thesis presentation in 2003, Dr. Rolf Gullström-Hughes has been co-advising my PhD thesis work, adding skilled guidance and bright ideas on many levels to this work, not least concerning the art of putting words together to form a dissertation. For being my rock – but not a hard place, I want to thank you both specially.

I am very grateful for the support of Prof. Jerker Lundequist, my first co-advisor, who encouraged me to embark on this journey. He has been a great teacher and initiator. The research group xakt: critical theory in architecture, has through its first years developed from a seminar group to an important forum for researchers both within and without the *KTH School of Architecture*. I wish to thank my colleagues of the xakt group for their valuable feedback and energizing comments, Thordis Arrhenius, Pablo Miranda, Catharina Gabrielsson, Lars Raattamaa, Ulrika Karlsson, Jenny Wiklund, among others, and especially Katarina Bonnevier whose perspective is as fresh as our friendship is old, and Jonas Runberger who has just started his research trip, but whom I have shared the journey as a friend, co-tutor and fellow researcher since my Diploma year at the *Bartlett School of Architecture*, University College of London.

This work has benefited immensely from the reading and support of my guest opponent at the final PhD seminar, Dr. Charles Rice, lecturer in architecture at the *University of New South Wales*, Sydney, helping me to build this thesis from the solid support of his constructive critical comments. Previous readers of my work include Dr. Jane Rendell, *The Bartlett School of Architecture*, as guest critic for a higher seminar in 2002, and Dr. Robin Durie, guest opponent for my licentiate thesis presentation in 2003, whom I wish to thank. For bringing my work into a global research context, I would like to thank Neil Spiller, *The Bartlett School of Architecture*, and Prof. Roy Ascott, University of Wales College Newport, for inviting me to contribute to their publications, which has been very motivating, and thanks to, once again Dr. Charles Rice, and Dr. Barbara Penner whose session *Interiorities* at the 2004 *SAH conference* in Providence was published in *The Journal of Architecture*. My attendance at international conferences, for example the *Caiia-STAR* conferences and *Congress-CATH*, has been graciously supported by travel grants from *Knut & Alice Wallenbergs Stiftelse, Forskarstiftelsen Theodor Adelswärds Minne* and *FoFu-Arkitektur*. I am also very grateful to all the helpful staff at the *KTH School of Architecture*, whose efforts range from administrational support to serving capricious computers. In the last few weeks of intense work, Staffan Lundgren at *Axl Books* made an offer as unexpected as it was welcome, to publish this thesis. I very much appreciate his brave enterprise and immense patience and support in this project. I am grateful to Alan Gibson who has been very helpful with last minute proofreading.

My most beloved ones; my beautiful sister Tomasine, my mother Kim, my father Bengt and my grandmother Karin, are never far away and always helpful, supportive, full of energy and joy, in anything from accommodating the cats to stirring up a good stew and a good laugh, thank you for everything.

Lastly; closest to my heart, Peter, for your brightness and glow, where I always want to be, and Joel, my best co-driver and most trusted swordsman.

Finally, my greatest debt of gratitude is to Peter who has put so much skill, time and energy into the graphic design of this thesis, in the process of shaping it into the book in your hand. Here is where all the work put into this work, by all contributors, really matters – as it materialises. Enjoy!

Introduction

The plot is an invitation into a story. The plot offers entry to narrative space, structuring desire into a forward motion through the text. The plot is the instrument for navigation and organisation of any linear storytelling. As architecture aspires to organise space in time, the plot seeks to create meaning and order in narrative space and time. A significant semantic leap unites the dictionary definition of the modest bean plot to the great machinery of conspiracy. The ontological range from the cemetery plot to the control-instrument of the map is tantalising. It provides structure and progression in fiction, enabling the author to weave a web of intrigues and the reader to navigate the network of a story. In physical reality, the plot is a virtual instrument that brings together the field and its governing plan. To plot is to make a plan, map, or diagram of an existing object, as a portion of the earth's surface, or a building.[1] The plot signifies the measured piece of land, the planning or drawing to lay this down on a map, and the resulting plans or diagrams governing its delineation and temporality. Plot is a term that instantiates space, time and the course or result of any action or process to represent the potentiality of these in the form of actual or virtual reality.

Thesis Overview

Within the range of the various senses of the term plot, from a signifier of place to denoting storyline and intrigue, this thesis investigates the relations between narrativity and architecture, and brings the notions of plot and spatiality together in a discussion about the production and consumption of, in particular pre-digital, virtual spaces. It identifies a set of literary works (Joris-Karl Huysmans, Edmond de Goncourt, Xavier de Maistre, and Neal Stephenson) and architectural spaces (Thomas A. Edison's film-studio Black Maria), where spatial organisation bears a particular and curious relationship to plot-making. The three core chapters are built upon three papers, of which the first two have been previously presented at research conferences.[2] In the first chapter, the operations of text and image in narrative space are examined through novels by Huysmans, Goncourt and de Maistre. This analysis is followed in the second chapter by an investigation of the first major attempts at moving image technology and its related spatialities. The third chapter analyses a fictive technological evolution of the concept of the book into a form of media with virtual powers beyond the narrative qualities of both novel and film, developing into a personalised and spatially plotted game. A fourth chapter is distributed alongside the three core chapters, providing a lexicographical view of late 19th century media culture. By studying examples from literary fiction and architecture, the thesis attempts to problematise the use of organisational methods in the creation of real and virtual spaces, on the one hand by novelists who have resisted the conventions of plot in the text, and on the other in the "accidental" architecture of nascent film technology.

In the absence of the plot, these examples expose a particular kind of spatiality, bared to the imaginative perception of the reader and the spectator, and allow for a way of thinking about virtual spaces, not as a pre-history of digital virtuality, but as a product of the time and space in which they are created and experienced. The physical space of production is reflected, not to say doubled, in the spaces where fiction meets its reader or audience. The architecture of the plotless novels and the proto-cinematic experiments of the late 19th century modulate between physical reality and fiction, and are ripe in their descriptive narrativity, which expands in the imagination of the consumer. The refusal of narrative plot deprives the reader from the vehicular function in the story, but emphasises the fictional spatial creation in which the reader becomes immersed. These spaces, by virtue of their disengagement from plot, allow us to revisit the possibilities of virtual space without preconceptions of neither the creation, nor the experience, of digital mediating technology. The plot is the link and common denominator in the text, the game, the built and the performed. It serves as a hinge between narrative progression and spatial organisation. The examples enable us to target certain contemporary understandings of virtuality, by being simple accounts of spatial effects produced without the presence of the formal role of the architect.

Beginnings

The beginnings of this thesis can be traced to an initial interest in alternative perception and its possible implications for the architectural experience. In my diploma project *The Synæsthetic Mediator*, presented as design portfolio and as a theoretical dissertation at the Bartlett School of Architecture in London and at the KTH School of Architecture in Stockholm in 1999,[3] I explored the neurological condition of synæsthesia as a possible condition of physical and virtual space.[4] In the research phase of the diploma dissertation work, I came across Joris-Karl Huysmans' novel *A Rebours* from 1884. Huysmans' suggestions for synæsthetic architectural applications and fictive inventions of multimodal appliances inspired the design portfolio work as well as the theoretical diploma dissertation, but called for further analysis and closer examination. The novel was shelved for future use, and thus became the outset for this research project in 2000, resulting in a series of articles collected in the licentiate thesis *The Dying Dreamer – Architecture of Parallel Realities* presented in 2003.

The licentiate thesis examined architecture as a transgressive state between the virtual worlds of imagination and the domestic interior. Huysmans' novel *A Rebours* was investigated as a pre-digital virtual reality manifested as narrated architecture. Its protagonist, Baron des Esseintes, was introduced as the main representative of a particular method of negotiating material fictions in real space, suggestively termed "obsessive dreambuilding". This fictional character was placed in the company of similar creators of physical and spatial fictions, who share and develop the theme of an extreme form of individualistic architectural transformations: Kurt Schwitters, the dadaist painter and constructor of the Merzbau created in Hanover between 1919 and 1937, Sir John Soane, the architect and collector, who arranged his home as a Museum from 1790 until 1837, and the German artist Gregor Schneider, whose home in Rheydt since 1985 is slowly folding in on itself under the name Haus Ur. The licentiate thesis was completed with a website featuring interactive illustrations for each chapter of Huysmans' novel and interactive dialogues with the featured dreambuilders.

From the studies of applied synæsthesia and alternative perception in architecture, through a gallery of artificers of architectural dreams, to the doctoral thesis at hand, the line of investigation crosses many subject boundaries and reaches beyond architecture in the sense of the art of building. From the home waters of (critical theory in) architecture, routes of varying depths lead into the territories of literature, sociology, history, philosophy, psychology and media history. Breaking down the field of research from the most general definitions of architecture and literature, this introduction aims at outlining the plot of the thesis and plotting its position on a chart of related research.

Chapter Overview

The thesis consists of comparative studies of a selection of key persons and objects in the context of the time of their production. While the first part focuses mainly on the late 19th century, the concluding chapter extends the discussion into the present discourse on virtual reality. The distance created by time and by fiction allows for sightlines across the related fields of research, and facilitates the identification of critical points of development of concepts like virtual reality and its architectural and narrative expressions.

Chapter one: Writers-in-residence
– Goncourt and Huysmans at Home without a Plot

In the first chapter, the narrative architecture of Joris-Karl Huysmans' novel *A Rebours* (1884) is analysed in relation to Edmond de Goncourt's *La Maison d'un artiste* (1881) and Xavier de Maistre's *Voyage autour de ma chambre* (1795). These textual accounts, whose respective forms resemble an inventory list, a catalogue, and an internal travelogue, display a very close relationship between the spaces of their production and the spaces that they produce. With *La Maison*, Goncourt introduces the idea of a "memoir of things", in terms of a plotless narrative structure focusing on the orders of material objects and the construction of the subject among these. In Huysmans' *A Rebours*, the narrative serves to mediate between real and imaginary spaces in the house and life of the Baron des Esseintes. The writing method of Goncourt involves his residential interior as an *excitoir*, in a similar way as the fictive narcissistic architecture of *A Rebours* stimulates the reveries of the hyperæsthetic Baron. The excitoir, an interior enabling the invention of other interiors, both material and imagined, is discussed in this chapter in terms of its radical mediating function.

These novels, whose inventive narrative form is devoid of action and social scenes, focus exclusively on the interaction between man – the "writer-in-residence" – and his domestic interior, potentially expanded by inert travelling and extensive book-collections. These writers-in-residence are involved in an exchange of impulses, where the interior inspires narrative constructions and the text enables the production of space. The intersecting field of narrativity and architecture is here negotiated by the plot, a term that holds a variety of definitions equally applicable to action, space and text. The absence of the *plot* in these three novels brings about a discussion of its function as a framing device, allowing the inhabitant to merge with the interior.

Chapter two: Clockwork West Orange – Moving Images and Kinetic Architecture in Edison's Black Maria

Following up on the individualist creations and sensations of virtual reality in the novels, the focus of the thesis shifts in the second chapter to a study of the spaces involved in production and consumption of moving images. It presents an analysis of the Black Maria – the world's first film studio, and the introduction of film in the late 19th century, as medium and as formative of a completely unprecedented architecture. In 1892 construction had begun on what is said to be the world's first purpose-built film studio on Edison's laboratory grounds in West Orange, New Jersey. Its accidental architecture prompted the nickname "Black Maria" after the police patrol wagon used at the time. The tar paper-clad structure was designed purely from principles deriving from the camera housed inside it – the *kinetograph.* Revolving on rails, the daylight required for the camera could be maximised in the studio space. Constructed by Edison's assistant William Kennedy Laurie Dickson, this was the centre for development of audio-visual technique at the West Orange Laboratory.

Film is technically a sequential form of media, apt for the plot as a temporal unfolding of events, however in its first expressions, the possibility of plotting was diminished due to technical limitations. The films produced in the Black Maria had yet to develop a plotted structure, and the architectures of the production and presentation of moving images were at this stage still unformed. In the same way that the novels of Huysmans and Goncourt are opposing the notion of plot leading up to a closure of the narrative, the very short scenes produced for the kinetograph lacked a plot and were displayed as perpetual loops inside the kinetoscope. The Black Maria, a rotating, non-directional building, was designed without apparent architectural ambition, instead its form was derived from the functional requirements related to its function as a *camera.* The twenty-second-long filmstrips that the kinetograph produced did not contain any narrative material, only a kind of prolonged photographs, showing a couple kissing or a man sneezing. The isolated experience of novel-reading was reproduced by the viewing apparatus named the *kinetoscope*, developed by Edison. It allowed only one viewer at a time to see the looped captures of moving images. Having misjudged the mass market for projected cinema, Edison would eventually lose the race in film system development to the Lumière brothers, whose *cinématographe* patented in 1895 provided material for public screenings in cinématographe theatres or "cinemas" in major cities like London, Brussels, Belgium and New York in 1896. The immobility and isolation of the observing subject is studied by Jonathan Crary, whose investigation of "the visual culture of modernity" demonstrate how the spectator creates and is created by instrumented perception in 19th century image culture.[5] The history of media technology is complemented by Walter Benjamin who observes a beginning of a democratisation of media culture with the new technologies of mass reproduction, especially cinema, that at the time of his essay "The Work of Art in the Age of Mechanical Reproduction" (first published in 1936) had developed into an art fom in its own right.

"Black Maria" in this chapter is investigated as an extension of the camera space into architecture, upgrading the building to a media device, illustrating the relation of durational time to actual space. According to the French philosopher Henri Bergson, the film camera is an extension of our capacity of spatialization of time into a succession of images that disrupts the awareness of duration. Memory and imagination, according to Bergson, are tools that overcome this "cinematographical" operating mode of perception, restoring the notion of duration to consciousness, that is, a capacity to perceive reality without chronological or procedural limitations. Bergson's psychotechnological metaphor by which human perception is characterised in terms of a cinematographical mode of composition of space and time, suggests a possibility of liberating ourselves from the plot, the unfolding of reality in terms of a mechanical succession of images. The illusion of movement is depending on movement somewhere in the mediating process, as in the case of filmmaking, in the apparatus of the camera. The accidental architecture of the revolving camera-building challenges the framework of the building and contributes to an understanding of the possibilities of a virtual architecture yet to be realised: an inverted situation of animated building and static camera.

Chapter three: Shelf Life – The Primer of Virtuality

The third chapter looks into the possibilities of a cross-breed of architecture and narrative, based on the study of the proto-version of interactive architecture of Huysmans and the early efforts of capturing human activity in the first film studio. An example of the possible result of a plotted environment and an autonomous progressive device driven by interaction is presented in Neal Stephenson's novel *The Diamond Age* from 1995. The main character of this novel is a book, or rather an interactive device called *A Young Lady's Illustrated Primer,* created for the private education of a girl in the uppermost classes of a neo-Victorian society, and by theft gotten into the hands of a girl at the bottom of the highly enclaved society. With its ability to adapt to and grow with its reader, the book constructs a dynamic and continuous time-space, guiding the user through real and virtual environments for training and development, aided by "ractors", interactive actors who are real physical performers transmitted into the plot as avatars.

Stephenson describes a device with all the characteristics of a fully developed virtual space, which can take the proportions of an opera or a cabinet, formatted in the media that treats text as architecture. The plot is the development of the user herself, merging the role of author and reader into an interactive entity. The nanotechnological fiction of Stephenson takes on the character of a multimedial game, reminiscent of and bringing together the virtual qualities of the 19th century novels featured in chapter one and the adaptive time-laboratory of the Black Maria into a powerful interactive device: the architectural narrative. An investigation of some key concepts of perception and duration in Bergson is performed, where virtuality is a parallel concept and not an antithesis to reality – a double but not (yet) actualised reality rather than one split in half – constitutes the field where the narrative unfolds. The title of this chapter, *Shelf Life*, read as "use-by-date", alludes to the life of a book resting on its shelf, and to the question whether this format of narrativity stands the test of time. The media types of novel, film and game as narrative constructions are described in Janet Murray's *Hamlet on the Holodeck* which has become, together with Marie-Laure Ryan's *Narrative as Virtual Reality*, one of the most cited works in the field of virtual reality analysed from a perspective of narrativity. Their work guide the discussion about the constitution of virtual narrative spaces, bringing together the objects of study of this thesis as a critical (pre-)history of virtuality. Further speculations and observations on the theme are given in the concluding *Epilogue – Notes from the Excitoir.*

Distributed Chapter four:
Illustrated Notes on 19th Century Media Culture

Parallel to these three chapters is a distributed chapter, in the form of a *découpage* into illustrated notes. The notes describe the media culture of the late 19th century society – the society of Goncourt, Huysmans and Edison – that has been labelled the "Second Industrial Revolution" (1871–1914), "la Belle Epoque", and the "Troisième République".[6] The expanding sensation culture of this era saw a new type of consumer (spectator, listener, reader, tourist, holiday-maker) who partakes of sensation technologies ranging from the bearded lady to the Eiffel tower, from the wax cabinet to the roller coaster, from the introduction of global time to the universal exhibitions, and from the diorama to the department store, among other inventions and phenoma.

The illustrated notes expand media culture from film and print media to the *circulation* of film and print media in a wider cultural realm, for the production of certain effects and a certain subjectivities, perceptions and æsthetics. Significant technological innovations related to the media and entertainment industry was in progress during this time, forming a media that in turn created myths; celebrities as well as monsters. Thrill rides might be difficult to identify as an element of media culture, but the sensation culture fetishises technology alongside an infatuation with extreme individual existence, like the celebrity, the inventor or indeed the monster. In the development of media, different kinds of spectatorship are developed, of both individual and collective character. This duplicated being is the result of an emerging media culture that returns a mirror image of the process of individuation, and in which technology in general and the sensation industry in particular is separating the subject from the body. Communication in terms of both transport and information technology was in focus for much of the innovations made during this era, which reverberates in the development of information technologies today, especially with regards to the impression that the readers and consumers of contemporary culture share with the readers of the 19th century; that the speed and quantity of information in such a society is simply overwhelming. This era is the backdrop to the writers-in-residence, it is the ground into which the plotless novel fell as a seed.

The Plot – Definitions and Theoretical Concepts

This section discusses the use of the key term *plot* in this thesis and how the plot relates to the 19th century *media culture* that provides the main temporal setting for the thesis. The traditional sense of plot and plotting within literature theory may be accredited to Aristotle, whose conditions for the plot is of great influence to any producers of fictions since Antiquity. In *Poetics*, Aristotle provides us with a set of rules for the plot *(mythos)* as "the source and the soul of tragedy" and its most important scaffolding for completeness.[7] It should provide the story with the structure of a beginning, a middle and an end and thus make it a connected and self-contained series of events in a structure designed for closure.[8] The poetic plot deals with the actions (*praxis*) of a specific individual and his or her character *(ethos)*, not with everyday actions of the general public. Aristotle is also concerned with the "byte size" of the plot; it should be proportioned to our mnemonic capacity since memory is a prerequisite of understanding plotting. With regards to the unifying qualities of the plot, Aristotle rejects historiographic and biographic constructions of plot, which are forms for description of a single period of time, not of action and events towards an end.[9] Neither is the plot unified because it is concerned with a single person.[10] Aristotle demands of the parts of the plot to have effect, or it is not part of the whole. A relevance test could be performed in that a transposition or removal of a section of the plot would dislocate and change the whole.[11] The Aristotelian definition of plot is essential for the understanding of its function as a tool for construction of narrative progression and closure. The set of rules for plotting presented in *Poetics* is what the authors of the plotless novels studied in this thesis depart from. The Aristotelian criteria for a well-formed plot are not met by the authors of the novels analysed in chapter I of this thesis. Neither Huysmans, Goncourt, or de Maistre base their narratives on a progressive storyline in their biographical, or rather "spatiographical" accounts that the reader may enter or exit at any point without loss of continuity. The beginning or end of their respective stories are basically interchangeable, which deviates from the idea of opening and concluding of the story. This thesis advocates a different understanding of plot that we might call a spatial one. The idea of a narrative-based plot at the point of its loss becomes something that can be taken up spatially, and similarly, that the spatial conditions begin to loosen the narrative plot in particular.

The Plot as signifier of procedural thinking

In *Reading for the Plot*, Peter Brooks provides a history of the plot and its varying roles throughout literary history. From the Enlightenment through Romanticism and into the 19th century, scientific progress was reflected in the mode of its narration, that is, in a plotted form that suggests the readability of the world as a temporal unfolding of events. The intense development of the social sciences in the 18th and 19th centuries was presented in dynamic plotted form.[12] Whether making sense of history or rendering private life narratable in fiction, meaning and availability was achieved through narrative design. Brooks notes a culmination of fictional plotting in the 19th century with the development of mass-consumption literature and popular novels.[13] With 20th century modernism came an era of experimentation into non-linear narration, alternative forms of fiction and deviations from sequential storytelling, raising an awareness of the artifice of the plot and preparing the grounds for the creative use of storytelling within electronic media that facilitate hypertextual constructions. As consciousness developed about the narrative and linguistic constitution of knowledge about the world, further studies in narratology were presented by Russian formalists (like Vladimir Propp's morphological analysis of folk-tales and Mikhail Bakhtin's language analysis by the conceptual tool of the *chronotope*), and French structuralists (like Claude Lévi-Strauss' structural analysis of myths) among others in the middle of the 20th century.[14] These structural and linguistic analysts reduced stories to their constituent elements in order to trace a logic and grammar of narrative, related to the regularities found in the structure of language.

In this perspective, the plot as organising method for space, time and causality appear to be an inherent condition of external reality. The various meanings of the word plot fold the sense of architectural groundedness into the volatile desire machine of the narrative storyline and its extension in space and time. Plotlessness is a problematic, if not self-contradictory, term. Any reader willing to invest causality in a story, and any spectator capable of finding coherence in a sequence of actions, will find or fabricate a plot; in fact, that is how the creative mind operates. The refusal of plot as a control instrument of time and space within a story does not automatically cause a narrative void, but calls for a different form of organisation. Where the term plotless is used in this thesis, it is intended in the sense of a deviation from the plot as a temporal control instrument. The novel is a medium in which an exchange of plot is expected. The refusal of plot in the novels studied in this thesis resonates in the domestic isolation of the protagonist from the causality of society. The thesis thus departs from a negation of form – the absence of plot in a novel – an exception or literary experiment. In the first chapter, this thesis focuses on the hinge between a narrative and a spatial understanding of plot, by looking at some textual accounts in very close relationship to the spaces of their production and the spaces that they produce.

The Plot as continuous commodity

This section provides a brief overview of the social and technological discourses related to the production of narrative plots in the late 19th century – the era of the main examples used in this thesis. It relates issues of individual consumption and production of narrative plots, from the early days of market economy, with regards to its qualities of dispersion and suspension, to the development and conditions of narratives in contemporary media involving the Internet as a narrative forum.

In the final quarter of the 19th century, consumption became mass consumption and media developed into mass media. Many of the technological inventions in media were named after the principle of the process of recording; *graph-*

ein, or the inscription of "data", as in for example the telegraph, the phonograph, and all the various stages of cinematographical inventions. The visual entertainment establishments had previously been given the suffix *–rama*, as in the diorama or the panorama, from the Greek *horaein*, to see. The inscription of a strip of information organised the experience in a linear scripted, or coded, mode. With the fixed sequence of events, a linear story can be told to a large audience, who will share the experience and progressively be trained to share the same stories, and consider this an entertaining leisure activity, more a collective daydreaming than for instance an educational medium. Mass media did not just produce stories to be shared by many people simultaneously, it also made sure that the audience would come back for more of the same story. The single plot development of a film often reaches its conclusion, but the open-ended fringed plotlines of the feuilleton are elastically constructed to enable old plotlines to re-enter the story and used characters to resurface, forming webs of social complexity that would develop into the televised soap opera.

Successful plots may continue for years or generations, as long as the audience want to share and follow the story. The plot does not need to be fictional, or even entertaining, as the lives of celebrities and crime stories originating from news develop parallel realities just like the early plots of the age of the feuilleton. The plot is a dynamic engine, as reading is an activity where desire is directed forward, in anticipation. According to Herman Hesse, we are living in the "Age of the Feuilleton", a cultural condition he assigns to the 20th century in *The Glass Bead Game,* characterised by the shallow and cut-up nature of knowledge and information and the æsthetics of the media that transfer them.[15] Hesse's Glass Bead Game is a cross-disciplinary multiform game, set in a future that, leaving the "Age of the Feuilleton", where we were enslaved by the plot, for a cultural global game that is all about seeing patterns and making connections: it is a game in which the totality of human culture is combed precisely for the densest and richest connections between the most widely separated areas of thought. The *roman feuilleton* was a 19th century invention, a serial novel published in installments in the daily newspaper, keeping the readers tied to the "to be followed". It was a huge economic success for the newspaper; generating profits that helped to create modern mass-circulation journalism. The feuilleton shared the front page with the news articles, just like most media contain fiction and facts side by side. Many readers were so dedicated to the plot that they contacted the author and demanded alterations to the story when they were not satisfied with the development of the plot. The example of the feuilleton, not to mention Sheherazade's narrative skills, demonstrates the exchange value of the plot; sometimes to the currency rate of life itself.[16]

If the plot becomes difficult to follow, we break down the narrative in smaller units, or, if we lose the plot altogether, our interest fades away and the storyteller (storyseller) has lost the audience. The plot in itself is designed to be deciphered – to be interpreted, followed and understood – like the code; an executable form of understanding. The plot and the activity of plotting has been an increasingly attractive and efficient construction since the early days of the popular novel and through the last two centuries of increasing individualism and consumerism. The plot is what makes a story transferable from one medium to another, which indicates its dynamic autonomy. As we move further in this introduction into the role of narrative plot in representation of history and sociology, we will observe its correlation to social discourse and available media. Fiction, history, philosophy and the social sciences have used plotted structure as narrative mode, by virtue of its transferability of the notion of temporal causality. The plot is the most useful mode of telling us about global progress and universal causality, while maintaining its traditional format for the individual stories of the world.

Media Culture and Virtuality – Theoretical Context

Delineating an area of research that might encompass architecture, literature, film, and virtuality, studied at the end points of a temporal span of a century, the research context of this thesis can be broadly defined as *media culture*. This section proposes to position the issues of this thesis in relation to media culture by way of theoreticians like Marshall McLuhan (media historian), Friedrich Kittler (media theorist), Walter Benjamin (critic and philosopher), and Jonathan Crary (art historian). The notion of virtuality, in our days a notoriously fleeting term both within and without media culture, is in this thesis examined mainly through a reading of Henri Bergson as one of the most important theorists of the virtual paradigm. This overview of theories of media culture and virtuality concludes by a brief commentary on Bergson's pre-digital virtuality and a definition of the contemporary terms *virtual reality* and *cyberspace* as digital/spatial instantiations of virtuality.

Media culture

Media culture may for the purposes of this thesis be defined briefly as media and its applied narratological forms and how these affect and reflect the human mind and our notion of space and time. It includes, but is not synonymous with, visual culture, and proposes a model that connects popular culture and critical thinking. It is the cultural spaces we inhabit as consumers and producers of spaces, texts and images, whether these are realised in built form or under perpetual virtual construction within our minds, with whatever tools or instruments available for the construction, reconstruction or deconstruction of these environments. Media studies, media theory, or media ecology, relate to the modes of recording, storing and transmitting communication, and the materialities involved in this communication.[17] As a discipline, media theory is not easy to delimit. In effect, it could extend into areas as widely separated as print technology, textual criticism, digital storage capacity, archiving methods and theories of virtual reality.

The rise of *mass media* began in the final quarter of the 19th century, at the same point in history as the global unification of *time* by the Greenwich Meridian as a direct consequence of the desire to co-ordinate spatio-temporal means of communication, both of information and transportation. Incited by the growing international network of railroads, and the need for reliable timetables, the GMT was a crucial means of organisation as a first step towards the *information society*. A timetable is a plotted chart of visualised communications and the regularity one might expect from it, enabling the planning of a public and personal agenda of the late-industrial Western world, available at least to the one who can afford such displacement. The organising principles of time and space prompted by economic forces also included the separation of time into work and leisure, reflected in the emergence of what could be called a *sensation culture* with its related spaces and activities, early tourism in Victorian seaside resorts, mechanised amusement parks and fun fairs, casinos and an extension of visual entertainment including a range of establishments from kinetograph parlours to wax cabinets. The urban social density and visual culture, commented on in the daily press, created a particular form of individual. The dynamic development of individualist culture made celebrities out of entrepreneurs, inventors and other daredevils, along with entertainers and freaks. Fame was channelled into media, turning personal fate into a form of narrative, public stories in bourgeois society.

Friedrich Kittler, professor of media technology, maps a vast field of intersections of media technology and media contents, focusing on the 19th and 20th century media landscape. As a media historiographer and "genealogist", his studies aim to disclose the *discourse networks* specific to certain historical moments. "Mediality", according to Kittler, "is the general condition within which, under specific circumstances, something like 'poetry' or 'literature' can take shape."[18] Kittler analyses materiality, power, storage, transmission, training, reproduction methods and notation systems in order to frame the discourse network from the "outside" of technology.

In *Gramophone, Film, Typewriter* – a study of the machines that enable cultural memory separated from the human body – Kittler argues that the 1880s are distinguished by the technical recording of optical, acoustical, and written media: in his words a "media revolution".[19] Prior to the perfection of revolutionary media machines is the de-mystification of the human body and mind, by physiological and cognitive research. The last years of the 19th century diversified cultural expressions into different forms of media, like the phonograph, telegraph and film – each of these boarding a parallel technical development of modes of recording, storage and transmission. In Kittler's discourse analysis, "feature films take over all of the fantastic or the imaginary, which for a century has gone by the name of literature."[20]

This thesis examines both literature and film from a perspective that wishes to reveal the nature of the spatialities involved in the production of both media. Kittler's historical analysis of late 19th century media is important for this thesis in relation to its theoretical content and research method. As Kittler looks at production hardware as functions of the soft systems they serve, this thesis looks from the frame of architecture into fields where spatial production is a function of a narrative system, and not necessarily a function of an æsthetic system.

Marshall McLuhan's *Gutenberg Galaxy* belongs to the first generation of media studies, a creative and extensive report later revisited by Kittler in his discourse analysis, among many others.[21] McLuhan's work traces how form rather than content of communication shape the experience and perception in the situation of communication. His studies include social implications prompted by media, such as the development of individualism in writing cultures,and the subsequent effects on our mode of cognitive perception. [22] Written words become part of a visual culture, thus generating new media than the spoken word. The narrative content might be unaffected, but the printed story embarks on a different journey that differs from the mobility of the orally transmitted story. The change is a change of perception of the transmission. The credo of the western modern man, seeing is believing, reveal our dependence on visualisation of spatio-temporal relations: "the mechanistic sense of causal relations so necessary to the order of our lives."[23] The social form of the village and its enlargement enabled by electronic media, the global village, is a structure that depends on, and is best narrated by, an interplay of cause and effect.[24]

McLuhan points out that the alphabet, as a set of discrete phonetic signs, means a reduction of all senses into one visual code, or in spatial terms, the reduction of an interplay of many different spaces to one single space. He suggests that the invention of print technology, the *Gutenberg press*, would have contributed to a de-synæstheticising of the world; the result is a further separation of the senses and a specialisation of them to send and receive information. In our time we are able to translate a story between different media, which in turn can be characterised as different spatial forms.[25] The method of invention from this perspective is easy to trace down to a process deriving from the idea of a product, rather than a process leading up to a product. The 19th century was a period of time in which the method of invention was invented, and this is applicable even for the invention of the plot.[26] The detective novel, as Edgar Allan Poe identifies in his

Philosophy of Composition, is a plot suitable for reversed construction, that is, constructed from its desired closure, then designed backwards from the dissolvement of the plot, in all its turns and hooks that design the reading experience.[27]

McLuhan connects literacy to the acquired ability (perhaps disability), to perceive an image, or a text, in its entirety. Based on the anthropological research that was undertaken in the late 19th century, depth perception of a three-dimensional perspective is a convention of seeing that requires training and practice of the visual sense, in order to acquire the habit of accepting "flat" representations of three-dimensional perspective in photographs and moving images.[28] The literate spectator perceives the field of vision as a scene from which the spectator is separated, that is, the convention of a "point of view" is present, reminding us of the construction of the perspective image, constructed by a body separated from the perceived. Relating acquired literacy with the disciplination of vision as a fixed point of view to Euclidean space and the ability to read and represent image space by depth perception, McLuhan identifies the illusion of depth as it re-enters narrative space, exemplified by an analysis of Shakespeare's *King Lear*.[29] McLuhan touches briefly on the simultaneous invention of perspective and the chronological story, in emphasis of the dominance of visuality in writing cultures.[30] The illiterate audience, McLuhan claims, is unable to conceive the separation of the body and the perceived, why the objects in the image are "at hand" and not for the eye. The consequence of this sustained synæsthetic approach is that details and textures are brought to attention in a tactile manner, as if the body was present in the image, living the image by the body and not by the eye. To members of a tribal cultures dominated by auditive cultural exchange, Euclidean space is inconceivable, as is the idea of perspective and all other constructions following from that spatial and geometrical construction.[31]

Huysmans and Goncourt, the literary examples in this thesis, approach a similar mode of perception, ruled by objects, details and textures, in an effort to return to the lost synæsthetic dimension of writing and, as a consequence, of reading. Huysmans even ventures into the fabrication of synæsthetic machinery in his novel, while Goncourt in his *préambule* articulates his passion for the object and the solitary pleasure of collecting as a consequence of the education of the eye of 19th century man: "l'éducation de l'oeil des gens du XIXe siècle".[32]

Virtuality

By reading virtuality through Bergson in his own time, we are returning to the discourse of the 19th century fin-de-siècle, exploring the possibilities of a pre-digital perspective on space and time. As one of the first theorists of virtuality in the industrial era, Bergson has been reread in the late 20th century by, among others, Gilles Deleuze whose "Bergsonisme" continues on the theme of virtuality as immanent in the real. By consciously leaving out Deleuze's reading of Bergson, this thesis frames Bergson in his contemporal relation to the examples used for the present discussion. The Bergsonian model of virtuality is not technically oriented, but a virtuality intertwined with the relations between space and time, distinctly fundamental to later instrumental theories of the virtual. Bergson provides a "pure" take on virtuality, roughly defined as the "potentiality" of space to be actualised in time, by the powers of perception and memory as modes of access. This is precisely the perception that his near contemporaries Huysmans and Goncourt assign to their protagonists, narrativising the process of perception taking place in space, particularly materially organised to aid memory travels in durational time, extending and delinearising the concept of actual space as a present container of matter, to an immobile vehicle accessing evoked and revived places as alternative actualities. The linear plot in these authors is absent on account of this awareness of differentiated actualisations within the mind, and the virtualities that remain within each object and environment.

The scholarship on Bergson is today as extensive as the general scholarship on virtuality, often with mutual contributions. His studies on time and space are spread through the many contemporary readers of Bergson. However, this thesis emphasises his theory of virtuality in historical relation to the spaces created by Goncourt, Huysmans and pre-mature cinema. The concept of virtuality is in this thesis examined primarily from the point of view of a pre-digital era. A more accomplished discussion of immersive virtuality might be found within these works, where the experience relies more on the immediacy of perception than on the quality of illusion created by technology.

The contemporary definition of virtuality, or more specifically, *virtual reality*, is largely synonymous to "cyberspace" (William Gibson's term from his 1982 science fiction novel *Neuromancer*, drawing the prefix from Norbert Wiener's *Cybernetics* or the study of steering systems): a computer-generated environment in which not just images and objects can be virtual, but where the operational agency can be inserted in the form of a virtual interactor immersed within the virtual reality. The cultural theorist Margaret Morse's *Virtualities* focuses on the virtual relationships between people and machines in physical reality, and how these relationships create and affect subjectivity and social exchange. Morse characterises cyberspace as "the most inclusive term for the imagined, as well as the completely or partially 'realised' virtual environments which are capable of *interacting* with users to some extent or other and/or within which, to various degrees, users feel *immersed*, and, by extension, for the subcultural discourse loosely concerned with the future and technology." Further on, Morse identifies "the contemporary notion of virtuality as a subset of cyberspace /.../ an extreme example of the substitution of the material world for an immaterial and symbolic one."[33] Even though we might think of virtual reality as a substitute for the material world, this careful characterisation of cyberspace reveals the limitations of the present stage of development of virtual reality, revealed by the general expectations on virtual space as a mimetic, and not alternative *reality*, a space where we can expect to maintain control and remain within our habits of behaviour and communication. In the still very product-oriented evolution of media, much effort is invested in development of electronic extensions of the human body for the actualisation of interaction within virtual reality.

The issue of disembodiment in digital media culture has been analysed by N. Katherine Hayles in *How we Became Posthuman*. Her study concerns, among other things, how virtuality is taken up in new forms of media and how the body, subjectivity and perception are amenable to changes in technology that continually update the concept of virtuality. Hayles uses a number of literary examples to illustrate the development of a new model of subjectivity, the deconstruction of the liberal humanist subject into a posthuman body, defined by William Gibson as "data made flesh".[34] She concludes from her reading of Gibson that "cyberspace is created by transforming a data matrix into a landscape in which narratives can happen."[35] While our dreams of virtual reality are still largely technologically unfulfilled, it is the theoretical techno-cultural discourse that creates cyborgs, rather than inventors or technologists. This mythological construction in turn creates an illusion of disembodiment of information, and humans as embodied virtualities. However "information, like humanity, cannot exist apart from the embodiment that brings it into being as a material entity in the world; and embodiment is always instantiated, local, and specific."[36] Disembodiment is a powerful illusion, created by electronically mediated constructions, or, as in the first chapter of this thesis, created in narrative form by a material environment and the disembodied virtual travelling enabled by this space.

Control and navigation within a virtual environment have so far been achieved by whatever available means of wearable and integrated circuitry between human and machine – hot-wired or glove-clad, projected or suspended, helmeted or overalled, sensorised or gridded – for the translation into digital readability, then rendered into graphical or other possible forms of representation, at which point perceptive feedback is given. Paradoxically enough, the more advanced mediation technology used for interaction, the more contrived becomes perception and the more aware the user becomes of her mediated predicament. As a subdivision of virtuality and its environmental applications, cyberspace is also (to various degrees of technological sophistication) entering into actual space via smart devices: objects invested with a more or less ratified intelligence enabling them to communicate their or your needs within everyday environments. This is actually a step back from the immersion that Goncourt and Huysmans advocate, which takes place on another level of understanding of virtuality reinforced by Bergson's reliance on the powers of the mind to operate on time and space without the ambition to "enter" virtuality physically. Still, the computer has become the dominating machine for production and consumption of *virtual reality*, by force of its emulative qualities, that is, as a powerful tool of integration of existing media. The technological ambition is to reduce apparent mediation to a minimum, reaching a level of "naturalness" in interaction in the virtual world.

Related Research

This thesis focuses on the interrelations between real and fictive spatialities involved in narrative production, and this endeavour situates the thesis in a field of theory that provides, if possible, an even more elastic framing than do the general fields of literature and architecture.

Historical context

Walter Benjamin's critical essays are already mentioned in relation to the research field of media culture and history, and as a key reference in the discussion of film media. In his great odyssey in 19th century French culture, *Paris: Capital of the 19th Century*, a collage project that is a reinvention of the very form of historiography, Benjamin analyses the "phantasmagoria of the interior" and the æsthetics of private space in relation to changing conditions of urbanity in 19th century Paris.[37] Benjamin's unfinished script, by virtue of its simultaneous analysis of – and becoming – a passage work, allows for multiple readings where the reader might enter a portal from a proverbial point of departure, pass through an argument flooded in indirect atrium light and lined with shop-windowed theories, and exit by another portal to find that the passage gives to another street in the same textual superstructure, as a new point of departure. Cutting through the passage, the flâneur/reader is both within and without the city/text. The process of decay that haunts the environments that Benjamin is describing is also consuming his work, just to a degree that reminds the reader of the labour of receptivity in the effort of capturing an epoch in the light of its debris. The reader is able to read in the light of his text, not because it attempts to illuminate the entire history of the 19th century, but because history reveals itself as if animated by a flashlight, exposing objects, details and textures in a soft cone of brightness. Benjamin temporarily separates light from darkness in a work that perpetually reminds the reader of the shadowing of history upon history.

Two key commentators on Huysmans and Goncourt have informed the first chapter of this thesis. The alternative form of narrative organisation in Huysmans' *A Rebours* and in Goncourt's *La Maison d'un artiste*, that we may refer to as *catalogue style*, has been closely examined by Janell Watson in *Literature and Material Culture from Balzac to Proust: The Collection and Consumption of Curiosities.*[38] Watson's study concerns the bibelot, and how this trivial decorative object is rendered in 19th century French novelists whose literary works are dominated by material detail. From the perspective of literary history, Watson detects the dominance of descriptive style in late 19th century French literature, where authors like Flaubert, Zola, Mallarmé, Maupassant, Proust, and particularly in Balzac, Huysmans and Goncourt, all become bearers of consumption culture in narrative form. Goncourt and Huysmans are in her study representative of authors whose descriptive style is not merely a listing but produces a social commentary on the bourgeois interior. The reduction of the setting to one space only – the private residence – and the detailed commentary on this dwelling is manifested in extreme form in the work of Goncourt and Huysmans.

The history and psychology of possession is the theme for Rosalind Williams, who provides a reading of Huysmans and Goncourt as literary representatives of elite consumption in her historical study of private consumerism in 19th century France, *Dream Worlds: Mass Consumption in Late Nineteenth Century France*.[39] Her work focuses on codes and activities related to consumption, such as collecting and cataloguing, analysed through real and fictive domestic interiors. Among the narrative interiors studied by Williams, Huysmans and Goncourt are included by virtue of their extreme æsthetics and particular form of introvert, tacit luxury.

Both Watson and Williams analyse Huysmans and Goncourt, and make a similar observation of Huysmans as an amplifier of the narrative style presented by Goncourt, whose collection inventory *La Maison d'un artiste* preceeds "the founding novel of decadence" – Huysmans' *A Rebours*.[40] Like Williams, Watson identifies a significant elitist attitude in their work. Both references share the interpretation of Goncourt's and Huysmans' complex relationship to consumption, in that they are simultaneously opposing material culture as a mass culture, while celebrating material culture as individual expression. While these writers devote entire novels to a single private interior and the material existence within this space, they are distancing themselves from the general public's uneducated interest in collecting, made accessible by museums and galleries, and increasingly, by commercial establishments such as department stores, antique shops and auction houses. Watson observes that the authors who engage in the close observation of domestic decoration are "readers" of the house, visualising its contents and textures to the reader, which implies that the domestic environment is open for semiotic interpretation as a set of signs.[41] However, the same criteria of readability could be applied directly to any real or fictitious catalogue, which, however abstract and non-narrative, permits for substantial analysis following the postmodern interpretation of society as text. Watson's reading of Huysmans' *A Rebours* could be summarised by her interpretation of des Esseintes as "constructed not as a subject which creates an object world, but rather as a subject created by an object world."[42] From their respective fields of cultural criticism, Williams and Watson have contributed to the understanding of materiality in Huysmans and Goncourt.

In relation to their studies of 19th century consumption culture, Anne Friedberg traces the postmodern cultural identity back to the visual culture of the 19th century in *Window Shopping – Cinema and the Postmodern*.[43] Friedberg deduces the experience of virtual mobility in contemporary culture from the visual experience of photography, dioramas, department store shopping, tourism, or simple urban *flânerie*. These environments and activities created a modern observer, in anticipation of the postmodern virtualisation and commodification of space and time.

General historical documentation that has informed this thesis in the field of 19th century history and sociology, reflected in the bourgeois interior, is to a large part provided by the fourth volume of a series on the historical development of individualism, *A History of Private Life*, edited by Michelle Perrot. The social theorist and geographer David Harvey offers in *Paris – Capital of Modernity* a chronicle of social geography and urban capitalism in Second Empire Paris. In the field of art history, Deborah Silverman's work on *Art Nouveau in Fin-de-Siècle France* expands on issues of 19th century æsthetics by an analysis of the politics, psychology and style of the period.

The early history of cinematography includes Thomas A. Edison's inventions of the kinetograph, the kinetoscope, and the production studio Black Maria, in this thesis mainly read through Charles Musser's *History of the American Cinema: The Emergence of Cinema: the American screen to 1907*.[44] The Black Maria is, even in this thorough historical documentation, mentioned very briefly in the account of the West Orange years and William K.L. Dickson's assistance in Edison's kinetograph project. Resource material on the Black Maria film studio in sources of film history draw from the historical documentation, technical and biographical material in Edison archives, in which the image material of the original studio building is limited to three exterior photographs by Dickson, one drawing of the interior and two etchings of external views. Archive documents mentioning the studio building are limited to a few inconsiderable notations and a budget post. The kinetograph and the kinetoscope are to a higher degree (than the Black Maria) available in the records of film history archives. These appliances are included, along with a number of examples of kinetoscope film strips, in Musser and other film historians, for instance David Robinson in *From Peep Show to Palace: The Birth of American Film,* a comprehensive overview of the intensive years of motion picture development between 1893 and 1913.[45] David A. Cook provides an extensive overview of the origins, international expansion of, and technical development of film in *A History of Narrative Film*.[46] The film experimenter and physiologist Etienne-Jules Marey is portrayed in *Picturing Time* by Marta Braun, including his technical inventions and biographical details along with carefully preserved photographic material.[47] Braun incorporates accounts of the main figures of pre-mature cinema in her biography of Marey, as his achievements were made in competence with firstly Eadweard Muybridge, and would later be rivalled by Edison through the efforts of Dickson. The achievements of early French cinematographers like the Lumière brothers and George Méliès among others, are described by Maurice Bardèche and Robert Brasillach in *Histoire du cinéma*.[48] Alongside the above historical and technical descriptions of early cinema, a comprehensive account of the principles of narrative construction in film, is found in *Film Art: an Introduction* by David Bordwell and Kristin Thompson, describing the film plot as a narrative formal system, among other form concepts and conventions in film.[49] Jonathan Crary's influential theories of modernism and spectatorship are already mentioned in the chapter overview. His work *Techniques of the Observer* describes proto-cinematic optical instruments and the way these condition the eye. Crary's objects of study includes the camera obscura, simple handheld devices like the phenakistiscope, thaumatropes, the stereoscope, the kaleidoscope, and paintings to illustrate the phenomenon of fusion of optical instruments, the vision produced by these, the spectator and a resulting composite reality. His analysis is equally relevant to the technical appliances of moving images, since the analysis concerns the effects on the observing subject by image-producing technology.

Theoretical context

In the field of architectural theory and criticism, a few scholars have explored complex architectural narrative forms approaching a fusion of structural elements of building and the literary form. Jennifer Bloomer's *Architecture and the Text: The (S)crypts of Joyce and Piranesi* draws from the infinite readabilities of the creators of the title in pursuit of the evanescent and powerful "ghost of architecture".[50] The work itself deviates from formal expectations on objectivity and linearity in order to unveil the intuition and imagination in the process of (de-)construction of meaning of the writing reader and the reading writer of narrative architectures. Bloomer's hypertext in print operates on multiple levels of understanding of human constructions, from the minor elements of linguistic nomination to the arched powers of historiography. The present work draws inspiration from Bloomer's careful interweaving and layering of architecture and text, as well as the author's ability to embed the theoretical structure in a navigational form.

A recent publication in the field of architecture and text that explicitly studies narrative elements such as the plot and its relation to architecture is Roy Eriksen's *The Building in the Text – Alberti to Shakespeare and Milton*.[51] The author employs an analytical method termed topomorphology in order to study the design and distribution of places and themes within the structure of a text.[52] The study reveals similarities in the structuring of Renaissance writing and architectural design, not just in compositional terms but also in direct referencing to architecture within the texts. According to the author, the æsthetic composition of a building resounds in the internal order of a rhetorically shaped piece of writing, for example in terms of symmetry, ornamentation, sequential repetition, framing, and structurally balanced order, apart from the frequent architectural metaphors. Eriksen suggests that "the plot of a play or poem might simply have started out as something not unrelated to the plan for a building."[53] Eriksen's detailed study engages in the direct representation of architecture in text and the examples remain within Renaissance architecture and literature.

Given by the selection of objects of study from the literature and media culture of the late 19th century, permeated by their contemporary movement of ideas, the thesis is looking at concepts of virtuality from a pre-digital era, yet imbued with aspects of virtuality that are independent from their position in history. The examples presented in this thesis share the problem of narrativity, with unconventional relations to the notion of plot, for a reciprocal production of virtualities, within and without the narrative itself. In response to the intersecting theme of narrative and virtuality, two indispensable volumes are called into action: Janet Murray's *Hamlet on the Holodeck – The Future of Narrative in Cyberspace* and Marie-Laure Ryan's *Narrative as Virtual Reality – Immersion and Interactivity in Literature and Electronic Media*. Both authors are relevant to the synthesising discussion in chapter three, in order to deal comprehensively with the different aspects of combining the novel and film into an emulsive media form, that takes the form of a computer game while maintaining the form of a book: Stephenson's Primer in *The Diamond Age*.

These theorists approach the æsthetics of digital media from the point of view of narrativity, by using examples from both print culture and image-based culture and the more performative instantiation of these in the form of the game. Murray has achieved a highly approachable, yet theoretically advanced, reader of virtual narrativity that moves across various narrative forms that include the agency of the reader. She acknowledges that we are in "the incunabular days of the narrative computer"[54], in anticipation of a new type of storyteller who is “half hacker, half bard”.[55] Murray points out that narrative is a threshold experience and that it is sustained by our awareness of it as a transitional object. By virtue of the liminal condition, and thus limitations of any medium, all narrative artforms develop conventions to sustain the “liminal trance”.[56] These conventions are subsequently challenged in all forms of representational technology, why 20th century media (novels, films and plays) “have been steadily pushing against the boundaries of linear storytelling”.[57] With the introduction of the computer-based literary form, a new readership and spectatorship is created by offering interaction. Whether the interactivity takes place on the fictive holodeck or in the form of a hypertext, digital environments are characterised by four essential properties that make them suitable for new forms of literary creation: they are procedural and participatory (which makes them interactive) and they are spatial and encyclopaedic (which makes them explorable and extensive).[58] The combination of these qualities helps to create a sense of immersion. The æsthetics of the digital story-telling medium is threefold: immersion, agency and transformation produce readers and gamers endowed with the powers of the medium, while sustaining or creating a dramatic plot. Both Murray and Ryan address the issue of procedural authorship and hypertext as its most common form, and although this is an important development of narrative plotting or even plotlessness, this thesis remains within the form of narrative that allows a virtual immersion in and not an actual co-production of the narrative.[59]

In *Narrative as Virtual Reality*, Marie-Laure Ryan departs from the definition of virtual reality as “an immersive, interactive experience generated by a computer”.[60] With the ambition to “take a more critical look at interactivity, and a more sympathetic one to immersion”,[61] Ryan includes a number of examples from literature that has “already perfected the art of immersive world construction"[62] to explain how the concept of interactivity, still in an experimental stage, might develop. Ryan identifies three types of immersion; spatial, temporal and emotional immersion in response to setting, plot and character respectively.[63] This comprehensive structuring of the dimensions of immersive reading is driven by literary examples of how to place the reader in a scene, the various ways of creating temporal sense and suspense, and the sympathetic experience of fictional situations.

Ryan advocates the idea of text as potentiality, in conjunction with the philosopher Pierre Lévy's take on virtuality as potentiality (which in turn descends from Henri Bergson):[64] "As a generator of potential worlds, interpretations, uses, and experiences, the text is always already a virtual object. But the marriage of postmodernism and electronic technology, by producing the freely navigable networks of hypertext, has elevated this built-in-virtuality to a higher power."[65]

These two sources are overlapping each other, in terms of the subject of narrative virtualities in the forms they have already come into existence and in the forms to come, and to some extent also in the choice of objects of study in relation to that theme. Stephenson's "Primer" and its appended "ractor" are mentioned among the many examples in both Murray and Ryan, by virtue of its expansive narrative possibilities. In Murray, this cyberpunk novel illustrates the meta-nostalgia that takes the form of inclusion of pre-industrial themes and objects in the narrated futuristic setting with all its sophisticated forms of interaction and computation.[66] With the possibility of virtual reality, a strong narrative and not least embodied engagement will arrest desire at the limitations of technology, or be discontinued by the characters you are interacting with. In a film or book, the arrested development of desire is inherent in the medium and thus presupposed. Obsolete forms of media enter cyberspace as nostalgic elements of an era of passive consumption rather than "ractive" production. Ryan devotes a whole interlude to the "dream of the interactive immersive book", exemplified by the Primer in Stephenson.[67] Apart from explaining the vast array of neologisms in the book, her contribution is a contextual analysis of the complex plot of *The Diamond Age*, identifying informational structures in the "cybercultural dream of a collective intelligence".[68] The references to Stephenson in the work of these authors reinforce his intertextual influence in the field of future narrative forms.

Four of my objects of analysis are books, and one is derived from the nascent film industry. What they have in common as representation technologies is that they are challenging the conventions of narrative plot in different ways. The following chapters will examine, in order of the chapters, literature that deviates from the plot as narrative form, film as a media that has not yet found its narrative form, and ultimately, the Primer as a fictive invention of a device that develops its narrative content directly from the environment of a designated reader. On the one hand we discuss the organisation of the plot and its relation to architecture, on the other hand, how it might provide some kind of critical theory of virtuality. The architecture of the mind's eye is the resulting effect of the deviation from plotting. Once the medium is liberated from the temporal control-device of the plot, an unprescribed, contiguous and continuous space unfolds in all its potential, or shall we say, virtuality.

I

Writers-in-residence –*Goncourt and Huysmans at Home without a Plot*

Embarking on an Internal Journey

In 1881, Edmond de Goncourt published a minute description of the home of the Goncourt brothers in Auteuil: *La Maison d'un artiste* is essentially a catalogue of the exclusive art collections, furniture and interior details of the mansion.[1] The residence is narrated in order of appearance, room by room from the vestibule to the boudoir, the writer neglecting no details of its every material and surface, its texture and nuance, its maker and function, its origin and significance. The Goncourt residence was a nexus for the literary circles of Paris, gathering the most influential naturalist and symbolist writers, among them Joris-Karl Huysmans, who published the decadent breviary *A Rebours* in 1884.[2] Devoid of action and social scenes, and focusing exclusively on the interaction between man and interior, Huysmans introduces the hyperæsthetic Baron des Esseintes who has retired to an isolated mansion in Fontenay-aux-Roses outside Paris, where grand projects of domestic adaptations and transformations will take place.[3] In his quest for total immersion in alternative realities, the Baron surrounds himself with carefully selected art and literature, artificial installations and sensory augmenting devices, to trigger visions and dreams beyond nature itself. The insertion of a ship's cabin into the dining room, complete with fish tank windows filled with mechanical crabs, is intended to distract him from his dyspepsia (fig. 1). Des Esseintes does not stop at collecting and decorating; he ventures into advanced design projects against nature, like the hothouse where real plants are chosen by virtue of looking artificial, or the artificial embellishment of a tortoise, gold-glazed and encrusted with precious gems. Des Esseintes' ultimate individualist interior can be perceived as an interface where his interaction with any object could revive memories or project him into imaginative worlds.[4]

The domestic mode of travelling that Huysmans describes in *A Rebours* is shared by Goncourt, whose passion for rococo and Asian craft expands *La Maison d'un artiste* to the era of the Royal French Court and to equally remote exotic destinations. This particular form of travelling had been narrativised by Xavier de Maistre in the late 18th century, in the novel *Voyage autour de ma chambre* (*A Journey around my Room*), which takes place in one single room during forty-two days and nights. Although separated by a century from Goncourt and Huysmans, the inclusion of de Maistre in this investigation is motivated not only in respect to the theme of internal tourism, but to a kinship in the writing method that incorporates the space of its production, by necessity or for aesthetic reasons, into the novel and allow it to transform space in return. De Maistre wrote his novel during a period of house arrest, spent with pen in hand, deciding to exercise the expansive qualities of the mind in relation to his furniture and objects that share his enclosure. Without moving from their domestic spheres, the writers-in-residence rely on the interior and its objects set their memories and mind in motion, using space as a vehicle for immobility.

Fig. 1

A Memoir of Things

The literary form in Goncourt's *La Maison d'un artiste* and Huysmans' *A Rebours* could be described as a catalogue novel, its narrative structure an inventory list that is essentially plotless, focusing on the orders of material objects, most often in a domestic space.[5] The construction of the subject takes place within the narrative, which serves as a mediator between real and imaginary space. A radical example of the mediating function is introduced here in the form of the excitoir, an interior enabling the invention of other interiors, both material and imagined. The writing method of Goncourt involves his residential interior as an *excitoir*, in a similar way as the fictive interiors in *A Rebours* stimulate the reveries of des Esseintes.

The writer-in-residence is involved in an exchange of impulses, where the interior inspires narrative constructions and the text enables the production of space. The absence of the *plot* in these two novels brings about a discussion on its function as a framing device, allowing the inhabitant to merge with the interior. Among the objects collected and consumed in these narrative interiors, is the book itself, perhaps the most important item in the construction of the subject in these plotless novels. Both Goncourt and Huysmans provide extensive intertextual references and accounts of the library, as an element of the outside world and as an extensive function of the interior. The literary cross-referencing inserts a critical discourse into the novels while sustaining the notion of an inert and isolated *shelf life*.

Goncourt launches, in the short preface of *La Maison d'un artiste*, the idea of the "memoir of things", since things are associated "by the description in modern literature, with the history of humanity". In his search for a new kind of narrative, Goncourt needed to look no further than his own home to write the memoirs of "things, amidst which a man's existence had passed".[6] At the time, Huysmans was striving to escape from "a literature that had no door of escape" to create "a purely unpremeditated work, imagined without any preconceived ideas, without definite intentions for the future, without any predetermined plan whatever".[7] Goncourt's model was adopted by Huysmans, and the escape route from naturalism lead him to the fictive narcissistic architecture of *A Rebours* with its single resident.

Architecture in the Mind's Eye

In a bold suggestion, *A Rebours* is a novel about *space unfolding from a text*. Huysmans is well aware of the representation in the reader's mind reflected off the space in the text: the architecture of the mind's eye. In *A Rebours*, Huysmans displays his trust in the reader's ability to create such powerful virtualities from the experience of literature and art. The conventional structuring through plot is abandoned for the purpose of demonstration of freedom in time and space. Where the plot has come undone, the narrative experience extends into virtual space.

One of the main motifs in *A Rebours* is the mind's eye and its ability to create virtual architecture. This exercise depends on the complete isolation of the creator. The narrative environment is carefully limited to the interior, with few exceptions that only serve in the narrative to remind the reader of the undesirability of leaving the home at all. Instead of unity created by the forward motion of a plot, Huysmans focuses on a "real movement" produced directly by the senses.

Within a year of each other, two characters were born into the 19th century, both of whom would, literally, personify the era. Queen Victoria was born in 1819, crowned to rule over the British Empire in 1837 and her reign continued until her death, in 1901. Mary Shelley's *Frankenstein* was first published in 1818 and had become a widely-read and immensely popular novel by the time of the Queen's birth.

Goncourt and Huysmans shared a contempt for contemporary society and the prevailing yet anxious and unrefined taste of the bourgeoisie, and both created strategies to ward off the levelling of taste in their writings. Forever regretting being born a century too late, the Goncourt brothers dedicated their creative production both as artists and critics, to the 18th century and the social life of the nobility in Paris before the Revolution. The house in Auteuil was bought in 1868, in an area spared from the radical surgery of the Haussmannisation era. Their desire to identify with the aristocratic ideals and fashions of the Louis XV epoch inspired them as collectors, indulging in the Rococo revival and an interest in Japanese arts and crafts formerly reserved for the elite.[8] Ten years after the death of Jules de Goncourt in 1870, Edmond had completed the Auteuil house's interior design, after which he immediately restarted the project, this time in the form of the novel. *La Maison d'un artiste* was published in 1881, as a record of his collections but also as a kind of epitaph over his brother, whose chambers he had kept unchanged since his death. Edmond engaged the architect Frantz Jourdain to convert Jule's room according to the will of his brother, into the *Salon Grenier*, which opened in 1885, gathering the French intellectual elite in Goncourt's home (fig. 2). The artist's house in Auteuil hosted an influential literary forum and was also "an education of the eye of the nineteenth century man", where a "new kind of feeling" is discovered: "the almost human tenderness towards things".[9]

Fig. 2

In *La Maison d'un artiste,* the Goncourt residence is caught at a moment of complete serenity. The visitor barely stirs the dust in the air in this completely static and idealised moment of architectural bliss, which lends itself to an ordered walk in order of the house plan. Room by room, chapter by chapter, the reader experiences the result of many years of meditative arrangement of space. In *A Rebours*, the Baron has a more restless attitude, barely finishing one project before starting the next, like the exotic hothouse that consumes all his interest and passion until he collapses from over-stimulation, sedated by the intoxicating scents of his new room. The hothouse is left to decay after this hallucinatory incident. In *La Maison d'un artiste*, the interior is an accumulation point, while Huysmans' fictive interiors function as departure points: the completion of one project prompts the start of another.

The authors and their narrative personæ alike, are relating to the cultural force field of Paris. Goncourt primarily seeks to break away from Paris in *time*, where Huysmans' main concern is to avoid the *place* itself. Huysmans, in his disgust at the corruption and mass culture of the city, separated the Baron from the vulgarities of contemporary urban life by placing him under a glass jar.[10] The almost unattainable exclusivity and individual expressivity of des Esseintes' consumer habits is parts of this critique of increasing mass consumption and the establishment of department stores in Paris.[11]

The authors' escape strategies are further reflected in their modes of description, but in an inverse manner: in *La Maison d'un artiste,* the space is described in order of appearance, as the reader – assuming the role of a visitor and a rather patient listener – follows the narrator from room to room, thus pursuing a *spatial*, linear description. Conversely, in *A Rebours*, the reader follows a *chronological* description of space in the order of creation, implying the sense of time and inviting the reader to trace the creative process.

The Excitoir

The authors of these inventory novels use the text as the site of the domestic interior's (re-) construction, while depending on the interior space as a constituent part of the literary method. Goncourt declares this interdependence of text and space by admitting that to be able to write anything at all, he needs to spend an hour in the *Boudoir de l'Orient,* to "fill his eyes" by this "vision excitante" of the cabinet of Japanese ceramics, until he feels his pulse and that little "brain fever, without which I wouldn't be able to write a word".[12] Having meditated on the objects, he then retreats to write in a room "...which I prefer completely bare with chalk white walls". The *Boudoir de l'Orient* functions as a kind of *excitoir*, a space that is also a reliable method to summon poetic creativity. This *"excitory"* chamber indirectly generates other rooms, both narrative and architectural. Goncourt claims that the architectural design process requires the same "long meditation" as does writing: the mental preparations for each of the rooms in his house were "akin to the meditation for a chapter of a book".[13] Emboldened by literary production, the narrator embarks on a new design project as a treat: "Making a room in my house, that is what I almost always, after the publication of a book and the money it returns, the recreation, the reward that I allow myself".[14] The author confesses that had he not been a man of letters, he would have been an "inventor of interiors for rich people".[15] The profession of the architect does not seem to sufficiently span the activity that Goncourt is interested in, which is perhaps why he suggests the role of *inventor* of interiors.

A cardinal motif of *A Rebours* is artificial creation, and the Baron is an avid inventor of multi-modal stimulation devices, employing any kind of artifice to surpass nature and normal perception. The result is a mechanised interior that serves the Baron's hyperæsthetic mind as an excitoir, projecting him into imaginative realms that inspire him to yet other inventions and reveries. Des Esseintes withdraws into an existence of pure experience. Throughout the novel *A Rebours*, Huysmans lets the Baron des Esseintes challenge conventions of living, possessions and the body, positioning him in relation to the city, to nature and to the body itself, far off from the uneasy urban bourgeoisie, characterised by des Esseintes as conformists and followers. The Baron's life is carefully separated from any kind of media input, in effect he has distanced himself from all types of "mass" activities to the benefit of the collection of sensory-enhancing chambers, literature and artwork, keeping consumption at a highly elitist level of customised creation rather than mass production. Des Esseintes adapts his interior to electricity: a novel technology that will enable him to act against nature and to live his life in a reversal of day and night – any convention should be challenged. The "fantastic" elements of the physical space of the Baron des Esseintes are products of this freedom of movement: the open channels between imagination, dreams, memories, desire, and the actual space as the site for creation. He goes beyond embracing the machine: anything created by man is superior to nature. In his denial from taking part in any human or social system, he also desires freedom from his internal system, the subroutines of his being. The problem in this process of perfection of architecture, art and artifice in the service of imagination is that quite literally, the Baron does not have the guts to pursue his lifestyle. The final obstacle in his game is the body, suffering from the nervous condition of severe dyspepsia. In his efforts to manage his disturbed metabolism, the very transaction of nourishment is perverted into an artificial process. At the point where des Esseintes' begins to experiment on his own body functions instead of his external environment, he is finally forced to give up his "double life" and all efforts to separate himself from his bodily existence, and return to society.

Frankenstein's monster is a composite being, part science and part fiction, manufactured and brought to life through narrative. The monster and Queen Victoria both transcend humanity into iconography, superhuman in their respective symbolic roles and automated in their respective functions.

The instrumented and æsthetisized interior is common to the methodological approach of Goncourt and Huysmans, although the latter is constructing fictive spaces within the narrative and the former is creating and describing his domestic interior. The resident of the *Maison d'Auteuil* is the *artiste*, just like the sensation addict des Esseintes, a composite character of the resident and the collector, the inventor and the historian, the architect and the author.

An External Envelope

Oscar Wilde used *A Rebours* in a cameo role in *The Picture of Dorian Gray*, in order to probe the depths of Gray's moral descent: the young Dorian becomes absorbed by the "poisonous" book, this "novel without a plot".[16] The influence of *La Maison d'un artiste* on Huysmans was no less "poisonous" than the influence of *A Rebours* on Dorian Gray, giving Huysmans a push in the direction of experimental Symbolism. It was necessary for Huysmans "to do away with the traditional plot of intrigue" and pursue "the desire that filled me to shake off preconceived ideas, to break the limitations of the novel, to introduce into it art, science, history; in a word not to use this form of literature except as a frame in which to put more serious kinds of work".[17]

The narrative plot in the Aristotelian sense is, in these novels of Huysmans and Goncourt, reduced to the life of a single character in the setting of his own residence, the description of which will constitute the entire novels. No dialogue will unfold and no social connections will be made, but, aided by the "props" in the setting, virtual encounters and travels take place and memories of profound relationships will haunt or tickle the dweller in his retreat. Goncourt trusts the visual senses to produce these sensations, while Huysmans goes further and lets des Esseintes create entire sceneries, even industrial landscapes, in his perfumery, or has him play his *Mouth*

Organ, a bar played like an organ, to synæsthetically compose drinkable symphonies.

The plot operates as a framing device, in the construction of fiction as well as of buildings. Its outline decides the architectural layout, as the foundation, the ground framed for a building project. In fiction, it creates an envelope, a set of performance limits, for each character and space. The Goncourts referred to themselves as æsthetic spirits without a casing – "*sans enveloppe*", compensating for this skinlessness by the creation of the Artist's house, an external envelope.[18] Their acute sensitivity of observation is similar to that of des Esseintes, craving complex stimulating environments and limitless expansion of the mind. In 1881, the time of publication of *La Maison d'un artiste*, Huysmans stayed at Fontenay-aux-Roses, the mansion that would be the model for the Baron's mansion, to convalesce from nervous exhaustion and neurasthenia, possibly also a case of "lost casing". The two writers fit perfectly into Walter Benjamin's characterisation of the collector as the liberator of the object, himself and the interior becoming the case, the container, or the folder. The interrelation between a dweller and his material possessions has, apart from the plotless accounts of Goncourt and Huysmans, also inspired the almost opposite form of fiction, the plot-intensive detective novel, constructing the unfolding of the narrative around the traces left by man among his possessions.[19]

The *Difference Engine*, created in 1833 by Charles Babbage, is the mother of all computers. The mechanical calculator machine was later improved by Ada Lovelace, who was invited by Babbage in 1842 to develop the even more advanced *Analytical Engine* to which she created a computer code, the first programming ever made. Lovelace described its mathematical process thus: "The analytical engine weaves algebraic patterns as the Jacquard loom weaves flowers and leaves".

As the plot thickened in the domestic interior, the Haussmannisation of Paris led to the partial loss of meandering streets and irrational alleys, as well as many blocks of misery and layers of history and mythology. It was this loss of complexity that formed the urban and cultural backdrop of both Goncourt and Huysmans. Paris was changing from a constant source of hidden objectives and invisible goals, and the surgical opening of boulevards and monumental sight lines, caused, in short, the vanishing plot of Paris. In our novels we find that the artist's house in Auteuil and the Baron's Fontenay-aux-Roses, are carefully chosen locations in relation to the object to be avoided: the urban situation of Paris. Huysmans describes the Baron's satisfaction with his dissociation from urban society: "Thinking of the new existence he was going to fashion for himself, he felt a glow of pleasure at the idea that here he would be too far out for the tidal wave of Parisian life to reach him, and yet near enough for the proximity of the capital to strengthen him in his solitude."[20] There is both a manifest separation from and a tense vicinity to the city and its modernity, in order to maintain and measure the alternative lifestyle lived in the respective residences of the Goncourts and des Esseintes. There, in an environment that in Swedish would be described as *plottrig* – cluttered with objects – the writer's output will be the plotless novel, a rational catalogue in paradoxical refusal of the rational, broad lines that were simplifying the plot of Paris. The interior protects its perceptually skinless inhabitant, the artist without performance or perception limits, the author without a plot.

The Fetish Book

The passionate relation between des Esseintes and his library is clearly inspired from the lengthy sections of *La Maison d'un artiste*, where Goncourt gives a complete account of his entire library in great detail (fig. 3). In both cases, the narrative flow doubtlessly suffers from the disruptive accounts of what volumes occupy the shelves, meter by meter. There is no doubt of the efficiency in these accounts in terms of delineating the tastes and scholarship qualities that these men enjoy: the list has a meta-level, like a voice-over, that line by line etches an accurate portrait of the owner of these books, not only his academic merits but also his whims and fancies, his fetishes and (possibly) sense of humour, in short, his end of the human spectrum. The library serves as the friendship and microclimate that the soul needs, substituting social relations and public life. The only personal descriptions in *La Maison d'un artiste* are the descriptions of statues and figurines, most of them female, that Goncourt describes with great empathy and sentimentality. A particular fetishist transition is featured in *A Rebours*, in the description of the Baron's unique binding of the works of Baudelaire: "in a large format similar to that of a mass-book, on a very light Japanese felt, a bibulous paper as soft as elder-pith, its milky whiteness faintly tinged with pink. This edition, limited to a single copy and printed in a velvety China-ink black, had been dressed outside and lined inside with a mirific and authentic flesh-coloured pigskin, one in a thousand, dotted all over where the bristles had been..."[21] The description not only discloses the Baron's ironic allusion to mass culture, modified to suit his own eccentric taste, but also the transformation of the book into an embodied entity, virtually reproducing Baudelaire in the flesh. The tactile quality of the soft pages eroticizes the reading, and the leather binding – the skin of the book – becomes the outer skin of the reader himself, erasing the boundary between book and reader under his fingertips.

Fig. 3

The inventory of the study in Huysmans is mirroring the thorough descriptions of Goncourt's library chapter.[22] Texts, fiction and non-fiction, poetry and novels, all volumes are precisely declared, the chapter concerning his book-collection reads like a displaced bibliography. Résumés and reviews seem to serve a double purpose: they are simultaneously painting the portrait of the author and his character by description of his interests and identity, perfectly embedded in the titles and themes of his library. By the numerous intertextual elements, the confined social space expands to incorporate not only more names and figures, a gallery of ideal characters, fictive or real, contemporary or historical, dreamed or existing, to accompany the writer-in-residence in his perfected confinement. The critical impulse is also along the lines of the "selective" ambience of the space; many are called, few are chosen. The precise taste and preferences are cultivated in accordance with everything else; the *Gesamtkunstwerk* includes every item in the environment and exists in a holistic balancing act in this scaffolding of fiction supporting reality, and the other way around.

There is a strong element of intertextuality in the novels: large parts of both *A Rebours* and *La Maison d'un artiste* is occupied by extensive reports on books in the respective writer's libraries. Goncourt honours Huysmans with a position on the shelf of "young writers" in *La Maison d'un artiste* (fig. 4),[23] and similarly, in *A Rebours*, Huysmans introduces his readers to the contemporary section of the Baron's library, where Goncourt is represented by *La Faustin* and *Germinie Lacerteux*.[24] Huysmans' appreciation of Goncourt is communicated through des Esseintes: "This book of Edmond de Goncourt's [*la Faustin*] was one of des Esseintes' favourites, for the dream-inducing suggestiveness he wanted abounded in this work, where beneath the printed line lurked another line visible only to the soul, indicated by an epithet that opened up vast vistas of passion, by a reticence that hinted at spiritual infinities no ordinary idiom could compass."[25] Apart from this cross-referencing or reciprocal *homage*, the books play an important role in the construction of the narrative subject. The library inside the plotless novel allows for literary critique and a meta-discussion about the role of intertextual references. The accounts of the library in both Goncourt and Huysmans is plotting a diagram of literary discourses that allow them to accurately position themselves in terms of timeless and spaceless preferences.

Fig. 4

Space as a Vehicle for Immobility

Huysmans and Goncourt share the idea of inert travelling. The best known demonstration is in the famous chapter of *A Rebours* where Baron des Esseintes, meaning to take a trip to London, is satisfied by the experiences gained while waiting for the train, killing time reading a London guidebook and having a meal in an English pub while recollecting Dickens' characters in the faces around him. Crowning his condensed trip with a drizzle on the way back to the mansion, the Baron decides that a real journey would not be able to top his mental expedition. The Baron prefers the instant relocation capacitated by imagination: "Travel, indeed, struck him as being a waste of time, since he believed that the imagination could provide a more-than-adequate substitute for the vulgar reality of actual experience."[26]

The original idea of "inert travelling" could be credited to the French author Xavier de Maistre who introduced a new kind of journey in his travelogues *Voyage autour de ma chambre* from 1795, and the sequel published thirty years later *Expédition nocturne autour de ma chambre* (1825). Xavier de Maistre launched this method of extracting plot from acute observations of details in the confined space of his chamber, by expanding the senses to evoke a universe in mind from what is interiorised in matter. The journey begins by plotting the position and constitution of the space: "My room is situated on the forty-fifth degree of latitude, /…/, it stretches from east to west; it forms a long rectangle, thirty-six paces in circumference if you hug the wall. My journey will, however, measure more than this, as I will be crossing it frequently lengthwise, or else diagonally, without any rule or method. – I will even follow a zigzag path, and I will trace out every possible geometrical trajectory if need be."[27]

Photography steadily progressed from the time of the first picture taken by Joseph Nicephore Niépce in 1826, showing the urban roofscape seen from his window in le Gras, to the time of the development of moving pictures about sixty years later. With the invention of the movie camera, together with the development of cutting and montage techniques, film became an expressive visual media.

The observations were made during a forty-two day journey around the chamber where de Maistre spent a house arrest as punishment for duelling. He praises the possibilities of the journey he has invented, which could be exercised by anyone who lives in a room, independent of fortune, in fact "… there isn't a single one – no, not one (I mean of those who live in rooms) who will, after having read this book, be disinclined to endorse the new way of travelling that I am introducing into the world."[28] He made virtue out of necessity and used the time of his arrest to write a book, describing the ways his mind travels as it freely exits and enters the physical space, where his physical body, referred to as "la bête" (the beast) and "the other", remains grounded. The mode of travelling introduced by de Maistre is based upon on a controlled relationship between the two substances of the duplicated existence of human being: "Everyone is more or less aware that man is double; but the reason – they say – is that he is composed of a soul and a body; but quite irrelevantly, I can assure you, since it is just as incapable of feeling as it is of thinking. It is the beast that is behind it all – that sensitive creature, perfectly distinct from the soul, a real *individual*, which has a separate existence, its tastes, its inclinations, its will, and which is higher than the other animals only because it is better brought up and endowed with more perfect organs."[29] His confinement actualises the separation of self and other, two distinct halves closely fitted together, where man need to domesticise his beast in order to free himself of space: "The great art of a man of genius lies in being fully able to train his beast so that it can get along by itself, whereupon the soul, delivered from this painful contact, can rise up to heaven."[30] The idea of a double existence allows the mind a separate existence from the body, which is attached to the room.

De Maistre articulates what remains unstated in Goncourt and Huysmans, that is, the terms and conditions of the mobility of the mind, using physical space as a point of departure. His narrative personæ is, however, not the possessed collector and passionate consumer that we find in Goncourt and Huysmans, and the narrative is not constructed from a spatial order of appearance (as in Goncourt), or in the order of production (as in Huysmans). De Maistre does not travel in a straight line, the narrative consists of memories, poetry, philosophical passages, anecdotes, criticism, and all sorts of whims, all but a consistent plotline. The methods of the room traveller allow for any distractions and deviations, analogous to the narrative method of de Maistre. Consistent to the plotless disposition of the novel, the travelling is not goal-oriented: "And so, when I travel through my room, I rarely follow a straight line: I go from my table towards a picture hanging in a corner, from there I set out obliquely towards the door; but even though, when I begin, it really is my intention to go there, if I happen to meet my armchair en route, I don't think twice about it, and settle down in it without further ado."[31] His methods of displacement are not consistently non-physical: it also includes the mode of armchair ("this excellent piece of furniture")[32] travelling used "when I'm not in any hurry": the technique of wriggling the chair on its hind legs in order to slowly advance forward.[33] Distractions during the journeys are sometimes to blame on the body, which, when trusted to make breakfast, burns his fingers on the tongs while toasting bread, and sometimes on the soul, as in the example of reading: "When you read a book, sir, and a more agreeable idea suddenly strikes on your imagination, your soul straight away pounces on it and forgets the book, while your eyes mechanically follow the words and the lines; you come to the end of the page without understanding it, and without remembering what you have read."[34]

The chamber's set of furniture appears to him at times to represent a most unnecessary set of luxury: "Six chairs, two tables, a desk, a mirror – what ostentation! My bed in particular, my pink and white bed, and my two mattresses, seemed to me to rival the magnificence and the soft ease of the monarchs of Asia."[35] Apart from this opulence, de Maistre enjoys a library that would claim another forty-two days of arrest to present in its entirety.[36] The *Voyage autour de ma chambre* is a celebration of the art of distraction and far-flung associations, perhaps inadvertently it is a testimony of the human mind's impossibility to be confined, by walls as well as by form – in the words of de Maistre: "...it's a useful and pleasant thing to have a soul that is so independent of matter that it can send matter off on its travels all by itself..."[37] The dichotomy of body and mind is reinforced by the confinement of the chamber, in fact, it is even probable that de Maistre would not have reflected or articulated this dichotomy had he not been exposed to the situation of house arrest. Without any sign of regret for his misbehaviour, he swears to the reader that he would have set out on his journey earlier, regardless of this imposed confinement of what was intended as a punishment.[38]

The London *Colosseum* panorama, created in 1827, and the diorama both displayed dramatic but plotless scenes: they were merely rooms with an artificial view from an elevated position, liable to a fee. The panoramic painting could be complemented with a *faux terrain*: a space with three-dimensional objects. As a forerunner to the cinema, this visual experience created a market and an audience that was mentally, perceptually and socially prepared to embrace any new visual media and sensations.

Like Goncourt and Huysmans, de Maistre exposes the consumption of books in his text, not the activity of producing literature. In *Voyage autour de ma chambre*, the activity of writing, which is apparently the actual activity in this space during the period of confinement, is not articulated. It seems that the mind dictates the words to the "beast", whose narrative is thus eliminated by the stories of the mind. The stimulation of the mind is mediated by the senses, but paradoxically, the body seems not to be the experiencing site of the senses. The interaction seems to take place directly between the senses and the space, unmediated by the body. The body's main function is as an anchor-point in physical space, and most often an object of estrangement or discomfort. Where des Esseintes is plagued by escalating digestive problems and nervous symptoms, de Maistre also reproaches his body for interrupting his mind travels with metabolism-related issues. Sitting after dinner in his armchair, properly dressed in his travelling clothes (his night coat) awaiting the departure time, the vapours of digestion reaches his brain and "so obstructed the passages by which ideas make their way from my senses that all communication found itself intercepted..."[39] Aside from the interruptions caused by the body, the author/traveller has to beware of time as the most valuable asset of all, considering the unlimited access to virtual spaces (provided by the novels and the unlimited travel routes of the mind). De Maistre shudders at the prospect of the day of his release: "They have forbidden me to roam around a city, a mere point in space; but they have left me with the whole universe: immensity and eternity are mine to command. So, today is the day I am to be free, or rather the day on which I am to be shackled in chains once more!"[40] Compared to the social limitations that await him, his punishment is comparable to the "exile of a mouse in a granary".[41]

At the end of his life, de Maistre repeats his journey according to his word. He returns to his concept of the plotless "chamber travelling" and chooses his attic chamber on Rue St Thérèse in Turin, where he decides to spend a last night by himself before leaving Italy. In the *Expédition nocturne autour de ma chambre* (*A Nocturnal Expedition around my Room*), he abolishes the system of *l'âme et la bête*, the soul and the beast, and let them travel together "like a tradesman carrying his goods, to travel in unity in order to avoid trouble".[42]

Fig. 5

Paul Virilio claims that "to be" is "not to live" and tells us about the man who strived to make himself unidentifiable by never living anywhere, and more importantly, not to identify himself with anything or anywhere, to be a polytrope.[43] Virginia Woolf identified the minimum requirements for writing as "a room of one's own" and financial security. The authors studied here meet the requirements to such a degree that they prove the requirements of private space and means from the opposite direction: they depend on writing to maintain and furnish their material existence. Benjamin describes the relationship between the collector and his objects in terms of an existential dependence: "ownership is the most intimate relationship that one can have to objects. Not that they come alive in him; it is he who lives in them."[44]

After the death of Edmond de Goncourt in 1896, as one of the executors of Goncourt's will, Huysmans carried out its instructions which included setting up the eponymous *Académie Goncourt* in the house in Auteuil, of which Huysmans was the first president (fig. 5). The house in Auteuil provided a room to maintain a literary culture. Goncourt's objects came together to bear witness on the ever-lasting ideals of nobility and æsthetics, but objects as well as stories outlive us.

This chapter has pursued the connections between interior and text, negotiated by the writers-in-residence represented by Goncourt and Huysmans, developed through the mind travels of de Maistre. Their interiors, real and fictive, are invested with mediating and meditative qualities, as interfaces between the external world and interiorised representation: a mental, narrative and generative space. As dwellers and as authors, they weave architectural and narrative spaces into a dense web of objects and objectives, enabling them to act without a plot, without performance limits as constructors of fictive space and time lost, idealised and remembered. Their activity is reinventing the interior as an instrument of literary production, the product of which is not just the plotless, inventory novel, but also a new type of inhabitant: his mind, his material manifestation, his cultural context, or the loss of the same.

What these residential minds seem to wish for is a direct connection between man and space, unmediated by the body, the interface of the senses being unobstructed by the interface of the body. The ultimate form of existence would be to detach the mind from the body and allow the dweller to merge with the interior. The mode of existence of this new "spatial subject" would then be as a pure narrative form, unhindered even by the plot. True freedom is exercised in the idea of plotlessness; independent of what patch of land has been granted to the dweller, freed of the imposed sequence in time that the plot constructs, liberated of any worldly contrivances, conspiracies of social life, or human intrigues. The plotless mind is impossible to position on any charts, or fit into any diagrams. He evades any graphic representation and makes no plans.

The proto-cinematic experience developed from the panorama and the diorama through to the cyclorama, pleorama, sensorama, neorama, poecilorama, cineorama, physiorama, europerama, cosmorama, mareorama, and other variations of artificial vistas, like the "introspective" panorama shown here. Towards the turn of the century, however, all these visual environments were to disappear almost overnight, giving way to the motion picture experience industry.

We inhabit narrative space in very much the same way as we inhabit architectural space, as shown by the examples in Goncourt, Huysmans and de Maistre. The ideas launched in these novels have preceded an existence in narrative space, enabled by electronic media, making a social or for that matter, anti-social, life possible in digital environments, computer games, online communities, or any combination of these structures, deriving its form from both text and architecture.

The plot is however not a fundamental requirement for any of these textual and/or architectural activities, neither in the sense of organisational method of a story, nor in the sense of physical site, as in a “patch of land”. Still, the plot as a term enables a discussion about the production of, activities in, and architectural design of a narrative/narrated life. At a time where the grand narratives seem to have come to an end, anybody could enjoy the irresponsibility of his own story, in the privacy of his own narrative.

2

Clockwork West Orange

–*Moving Images and Kinetic Architecture in Edison's Black Maria*

The World's First Film Studio

In 1892 construction began on what was said to be the world's first purpose-built film studio on Thomas A. Edison's Laboratory in West Orange, New Jersey. Its accidental architecture prompted the nickname "Black Maria" after the police patrol wagon used at the time. The tar paper-clad structure revolved on rails, in order to maximise the daylight required for the kinetograph camera. Designed and constructed by Edison's assistant William Kennedy Laurie Dickson, this was the centre for development of cinematographic technique at West Orange. This chapter investigates the Black Maria as an extension of the camera space into architecture, upgrading the building to a media device, illustrating the relation of durational time to actual space. According to Henri Bergson, the film camera is an extension of our capacity of the spatialisation of time that disrupts the awareness of duration. The illusion of movement is depending on movement somewhere in the mediating process, as in the case of filmmaking, in the apparatus of the camera. The architecture of the revolving camera-building challenges the framework of the building and contributes to an understanding of the possibilities of a virtual architecture yet to be realised: an inverted situation of animated building and static camera. The Black Maria's ambiguity in space and time suggests an animated existence, like a literal instantiation of the words of Walter Benjamin: "architecture has never been idle".[1]

This chapter aims at expanding the field of temporal and spatial organisation from "the plotless novel" to the early efforts of cinematic production, embodied in a remarkable building liberated from architectural conventions to an extent that it becomes a camera itself. This curatorial approach continues the line of investigation of construction of realities, analysed through selected narratives and objects in the previous chapter concerning the writers-in-residence. The investigation of film production follows the line of investigation raised by the "plotless" novels: the possibility of virtual, in the sense of potential, architecture and mobility in the time and space created and mediated in that virtuality.

The theoretical reflection of perspective, mobility and technology in the architecture of the Black Maria is assisted by the French philosopher Henri Bergson and the cultural theorist Walter Benjamin. Both thinkers have incorporated the metaphor of film: Bergson in his critique of the mind and Benjamin in his critique of the mechanical reproduction of art. The art historian Jonathan Crary has investigated vision and its historical construction in 19th century modernity. His study complements the theories of Bergson and Benjamin with the embodiment of technology in the perceptual apparatus and in the body of the observing subject.

Henri Bergson (1859–1941) was contemporary to the most important era of cinematographic development. During his lifetime, film developed from crude technology to an artform in its own right. His ideas of duration, *la durée*, and the modes of perception and creation it evokes, are at the core of his critique of cinema, chiefly expressed in *L'Evolution créatrice* published in 1907, a seminal work on evolution and existence, from the order of nature and its various forms of intelligence, to forms of human thought and perception, briefly, a philosophy of the organism.[2] In this text, he uses the durational principles of film as an example in his exploration of the capacities of the human mind. Bergson famously used cinematography as a mechanistic analogy to the workings of human perception, associating the thought process and perception to the form of this, at the time, novel media. "The mechanism of our ordinary knowledge is of a cinematographical kind", Bergson writes in *L'Evolution créatrice*.[3] The constructed/reproduced mobility of animation reveal to us the workings of memory operating on duration, the constant flow of images among which the body is just one image.

Joseph Paxton's *Crystal Palace*, which housed the *Industrial Exhibition* of 1851 in London, was a commercial hothouse that was to set the standard for subsequent event architecture. The building encased the industrial world in a glass and steel structure, reducing the boundary between interior and exterior to a transparent membrane.

At the time of publication of Benjamin's essay "The Work of Art in the Age of Mechanical Reproduction" in 1936, filmmaking had developed to a stage where cutting and pasting of time and space created efficient narrative plots. In his essay, Benjamin argues that the mediation of the camera has consequences for the artistic performance of the actor, not just in the sense of distance to the audience, but in the elimination of the aura of direct appearance. Benjamin argues that film is the "most powerful agent" of the process in which a plurality of copies substitutes the unique existence of a work of art.[4] In the field of technical reproducibility, all claims of authorship and authenticity are obliterated.[5] The most important aspect of the detachment of the copy from the original is its possibility to transcend its presence in time and space. His investigation follows the introduction of recording and multiplication of art, from the printing process reproducing writing, to lithography, via photography to film, showing that the work of art becomes a creation with entirely new functions, and that human sense perception changes with the introduction of new media.[6] The visual culture of modernity is, according to Benjamin, focused on control and possession of the object, which is technically made possible by taking and reproducing images.[7]

Jonathan Crary argues in *Techniques of the Observer: On Vision and Modernity in the Nineteenth Century* that the relationship between the eye and proto-cinematic optical devices, from the *camera obscura* to the *stereoscope*, has prompted a "modern and heterogeneous regime of vision".[8] Vision, located in the observing body of the human being, has developed in relation to advances in technologies for seeing. In a process of "industrial remapping of the body in the 19th century", a separation of the senses takes place, removing physical engagement and tactility from the observation situation.[9] As observers become more and more immobile and less physically involved with the observed, they become better "fitted for the tasks of spectacular consumption".[10] The body becomes a component of the machinery applied for observation. Our technologies of representation have an enframing effect on perception, and are consequently circumscribing the possibilities of action. In the process of development of devices designed for illusory simulation of movement and optical depth, Crary identifies an increasing immobility of the observer. In the *panorama*, spectators were walking around on the observation platform, in the *diorama* they were seated on a circulating platform, restricted to movements of the head, while the organisation and control of time and movement of the spectacle was mastered by the machinery.[11] Crary analyses how "new modes of rotating, communication, production, consumption, and rationalisation all demanded and shaped a new kind of observer-consumer."[12]

The trajectory of this chapter will pass from a description of the architecture of the Black Maria film studio, to a presentation of the project that called it into existence on Edison's initiative and by execution of his assistant William Kennedy Laurie Dickson to a recaption of their place within the general historiography of pre-mature cinema, to the viewing device of the kinetoscope and the plotless films produced in the Black Maria. The analysis and the theoretical discussion revolve around the key concepts perspective, mobility and technology, with the recurring participation of Benjamin, Bergson and Crary. Since the documentation on the Black Maria studio is not as extensive as the historical records of the technological devices it would serve – the *kinetograph* and the *kinetoscope* – the analysis of the building draws upon different historical sources in Edisoniana, cinematography, and film history. The available images – three exterior photographs, probably taken by Dickson himself, two exterior drawings and one interior

Fig. 1

drawing – circulate within the different sources. In accordance to the general appearance of this "pieced-up" building, there is no drawing material or plans to be found in the Edison archives. The building seems to have been designed in an ad hoc-manner by Dickson, making adjustments along the way, while keeping within the modest budget.

A Phototropic Building

In February 1893, the world's first film studio was completed on Edison's laboratory grounds in West Orange, New Jersey. Work had begun in December 1892 and three months later, to a total cost of $637.67 (a quarter of the total budget for the kinetograph project), the construction was completed.[13] This studio was intended as experimentation space for the kinetograph, the camera device that was to provide the kinetoscope with filmed material. As soon as the confident team, led by Dickson, had perfected the kinetoscope viewing device, the studio would be the base for production of film material for the planned commercial use of Edison's nickel-slot kinetoscope at *The World's Columbian Exposition* in Chicago later in 1893. Despite all efforts, the kinetoscopes were not ready in time for the fair, to the disappointment of thousands of people who anticipated Edison's latest achievement, largely advertised in advance. Although the Black Maria was fully equipped and operational in May 1893, the delays of the kinetoscope project caused a standstill for the studio until later the same year.[14]

The Black Maria was the result of the efforts of the temporary architect Dickson, an interim assignment as part of the production of moving images. This intermediary role of architect was combined with continual development of the kinematograph capturing device and the development of the kinetoscope viewing device, which might have influenced and inspired the design of the Black Maria studio (fig. 1).

Fig. 2

The pragmatic design of the Black Maria studio building affects its readability in multiple ways: stripped to the bones of function and overlapped with cheap cladding, it is both revealing and obscuring to its character. The world's first (allegedly) purpose-built film studio was a riveted tar paper-clad wooden structure. Perhaps the most particular feature of the Black Maria is the rotational mobility of the entire building, like a windmill, as an adaptation of the architecture to the light requirements of film production. Dickson's main design idea was to centre the entire building on a graphite core, permitting a three hundred and sixty-degree rotation around its pivotal point. The wooden frame penetrates the sides where the core is, and wooden rails circumscribe the building as a support track. The revolving capacity renders the studio with the organic ability of phototropism (reorientation of an organism in the direction of light), or more correctly, it is a heliotropic building, able to follow the sunlight on its trail.[15] This function was however not automatic, but required the participation of a couple of men from the workforce to push it around. The choice of façade material would, apart from being cheap and weatherproof, have met the requirements to keep the building lightweight. The rotation was necessary for obtaining enough light for the kinetograph camera, a piece of equipment so big and heavy it was called "the doghouse" by the project staff. The camera was placed in darkness, facing the stage end, probably in a fixed position, as the experiments carried out in the studio interior were all done with a static camera view (fig. 2). The interior was one single room, blacked out by the façade material and with the stage end draped in black fabric, making the objects in front of the camera stand out against the background, lit by the flooding sunlight from the roof aperture.

Fig. 3

The building is divided into three sections with alternating saddle roof orientation, of which the middle part of the roofscape is dominated by a square-cut skylight, angled for optimal aggregation of daylight by an adjustable aperture. This shutter function is demonstrated by its different positions in the exterior photographs. The pole attached to the lower roof structure is part of the hauling mechanism for the shutter roof, and at the short end of the lower building part, there is a rack to rest the roof on, should the shutter be completely opened (fig. 3). The building's elongated asymmetrical shape corresponds to a mill or hangar of some kind, but some scale-giving standard elements help to restore the perception of a rather small structure: two entrance doors joined with hanging steps on each side of the central body, on one side with a regular window next to the door (fig. 1), and small windows on each side of the lower part of the building. A larger "barndoor" with a cut corner is excised into a slightly protruding portion of one side of the studio, to be able to enter stage props and set décor. Next to the barndoor, a ventilation pipe penetrates the wall (fig. 4), but is removed in the other photograph of the same façade, leaving a circular patched hole in the wall (fig. 3). This studio would have accumulated considerable heat with its black tar mat cladding absorbing sunlight, or alternatively, during the winter months, a heater stove would perhaps have been necessary for the comfort of workers and performers. The populated photograph, showing the barndoor and rooftop wide open, taken by Dickson in late 1894, also shows how the cladding has been patched by extra tar-mats vertically along the side of the middle section of the building (fig. 3). The building itself had more than its dark appearance in common with its namesake; the "paddy wagon" – a prison wagon built for transport of troublemakers (fig. 5), used by the police at the time – the mobility and the building's outline, with its varying roofscape and different widths along its body, certainly bear more similarity to a motorcar vehicle than to a conventional workshop building.[16]

Fig. 4&5

Edisonia

Edison's laboratory was a factory for inventions, a clockwork think tank renowned for solving every material problem of the civilised world. Edison kept specimens of virtually all substances and materials known, so that spur-of-the-moment experiments could be carried out without having to await delivery of the chemical compounds or the stuff required. "Edisonia" (see below) was moved from Menlo Park, New Jersey in 1884 to a larger estate in West Orange, where construction work began in 1886. The Menlo Park Laboratory was built in 1876, a two-floor wooden barn-like building that housed a research and development laboratory employing twenty-five men to work on the incandescent lightbulb, electrical power stations and distribution systems, as well as development of communication media like the telegraph, the telephone, and the phonograph. During the seven years at Menlo Park, Edison filed around four hundred patents, became a household name and was dubbed "The Wizard of Menlo Park".[17]

Fig. 6

"We went over to Menlo Park, New Jersey, the two of us, to see Edison and his wonderful inventions and make some discoveries and sketches for the Graphic. Menlo Park is not a park. It is not a city. It is not a town. /.../ Although it is on the Pennsylvania railroad /.../ it is not even a stopping place, except when the station agent flags the train to take on waiting passengers. It is composed wholly of Edison's laboratory and half a dozen houses where his employees live. It is, in short, Edisonia, and nothing else."[18]

The Edison laboratories were based upon the concept of team-based research for the production of marketable products; softening the authorship to the benefit of the "brand" Edison. The West Orange facilities employed approximately sixty workers, a workforce that Edison aspired to manage administratively himself, resulting in a rather modern company climate where personal initiatives were promoted, although maintaining a hierarchy where Edison's name was the brand and all credits and patents were registered to him. Edison's work force was on constant standby to assist in building the future: "Physical endurance, skill in draughtsmanship or workmanship is required for the always present three to four assistants willing to comply with his wishes".[19] The creative climate at the laboratory was governed by the efficiency of Edison "the workaholic" – enthusiastic though grumpy, methodical yet impulsive – and a master of powernaps. Playfulness was appropriate as long as it led to patent registrations. Edison was the self-made man without formal education or privileged background, who made the inventor the archetypal hero of modern society and who became the first corporate icon. Edison's mythological status reached into literature, as a subgenre of Victorian science fiction – the *Edisonade* combined pure fascination with technology with the heroism of the businessman and inventor.[20] A "fan fiction" portrait was published in 1884 by Auguste Villiers de L'Isle Adam, who assigned the invention of a female automata, *The Future Eve* (*L'Eve future*), a woman whose artificial perfection put nature to shame, to the genius of Edison.[21]

Fig. 7

A Phonograph for the Eye

The Edison kinetograph project was incited by the spirit of the pioneers in chronophotography. Edison's contact with photographic inventors using film technique for mainly scientific purposes, like Eadweard Muybridge and Etienne-Jules Marey, is well documented. Muybridge was installed in 1883 at the *University of Pennsylvania*, where his outdoor research studio on the campus had been in operation since 1885 (fig. 7).[22] Edison attended one of Muybridge's *zoopraxiscope* demonstrations and lectures in New Jersey on February 27, 1888, at which point Muybridge suggested to combine his moving image apparatus with Edison's *phonograph*.[23] Edison declined the offer as his mind was set to develop his own "instrument which does for the Eye what the phonograph does for the Ear".[24] The meeting incited Edison's interest in moving images, mainly because of the commercial possibilities of joining the phonograph, his most cherished invention, with visual technology, as Muybridge had suggested. Edison was convinced of the advantages of using the same technical principles for image-recording as applied in the phonograph: on a cylinder. Edison was never passionate about moving images, yet his sense of business told him to go ahead with the idea of adding a cylinder covered by images to the wax cylinder for sound. The apparatus, in his mind a commercially exploitable single-viewing machine, was at this stage named the *kinetophonograph*. From the beginning, Edison resisted the idea of projection, as his vision was of entertainment units gathered in arcades or parlours, possibly also adapted to domestic use, with a profit made from both the viewing device and from an expanding market of cylinders.

Dickson had been working for Edison as an assistant since 1883, when he was made responsible for the motion picture production at West Orange in 1888. The young Dickson was an amateur photographer and an aspiring mechanical engineer, devoted to a career in invention business. He had already in a keen and passionate letter to Edison in 1879 applied for a job – "the lowest place in your employment, until you find me worthy of something higher" – but was rejected due to a full work force.[25] Not taking no for an answer, he set off to the United States from London that same year, and was finally four years later brought to Edison's attention by a letter of introduction from an artist friend, expressing Dickson's interest in electricity studies, along with his drawing and language skills.[26] Edison found use for him as his official photographer from around 1884, due to his skills and interest in the subject.[27] In 1887, Dickson was engaged for Edison's prestigious but unsuccessful ore-milling project, but was relocated once again to realise the "phonograph for the eye" and a matching viewing device, a project that was not assigned more time than what Dickson could spare from other projects.[28] Dickson stayed faithful to the cylinder idea until 1889, when Edison got back from Paris with new directives.

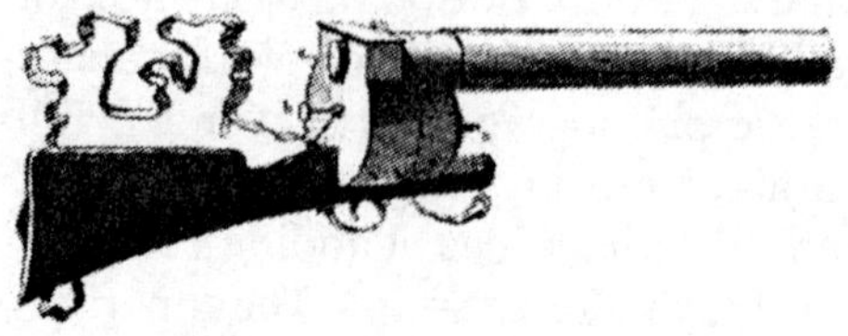

Fig. 8

Edison had spent August in Paris that year to attend the *Exposition Universelle*, where all his most influential inventions were shown to a European audience. When in Paris, he had taken the opportunity to work his PR and visit colleagues, among them the famous physiologist and animation experimenter Etienne-Jules Marey who demonstrated his *fusil photographique*, the revolving film-gun-camera developed already in 1882.[29] The revolving gun was a technological revolution in itself, with a fast mechanism that Marey made use of by modifying it into the chronophotographical gun (fig. 8). This was the first truly mobile film camera, with which Marey captured the flight of a bird on a circular set of twelve exposures, which ingeniously replaced the cartridges of the revolving magazine.[30]

Fig. 9

The revolving principle also governed the layout for his open-air studio, to which Edison paid a visit in 1889. The *Station Physiologique* in Bois de Boulogne, with its outdoor film facilities and workshop, was established by Marey in 1882 for the study of animated physics (fig. 9). The "field laboratory" was complete with a kiosque-size mobile camera wagon (fig. 10) placed on a circular rail track (fig. 11), alongside which a white and a black hangar was placed, providing neutral background for experimental motion photography of people and animals.[31] Marey gave a convincing account of the sequenced filmstrip camera, compelling enough to Edison, who upon his return called a halt on all efforts with the cylinder idea for the capturing of moving images.[32] Possibly Edison also brought with him the impression of the facilities of the *Station Physiologique*, and thus considered investing in a "revolutionary" studio for Dickson and his kinetoscope film team.

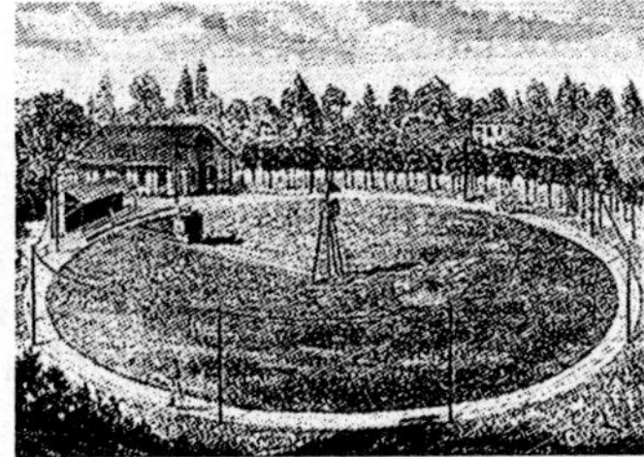

Fig. 10 & 11

The Black Maria "building-automaton", chronicled as the first purpose-built motion-picture studio, or "dream factory" as the Hollywood film industry would call the centre of film production some fifty years later, was intended for film recording in its *interior*, in contrast to Muybridge's outdoor studio and Marey's *Station Physiologique*, which functioned more like outdoor "shooting galleries": roof-protected sheds opened on one long side for the camera view. All references to shooting in the cinematic context, still lingering in the expression "shooting a film", "film shot" etc, have more than circumstantial literal roots in these appliances. There is, from the very first moment, an unspoken powerplay built into the act of filming: one individual selects a viewpoint, aims and shoots, controlling the scene and choosing a time-space for recording.[33] In the mechanical principles of early film technique, the idea of rotation, or rather closed revolutions, seem pervasive: from Marey's chronophotographical gun, to the circular railtrack on his studio grounds in Bois de Boulogne, to the closed loop of the filmstrips in the kinetoscope, perpetually reeling the pictures inside the box, and finally, the Black Maria itself: revolving around its centre to feed enough light to the static camera inside. Instead of succeeding the novel as a medium to tell and experience a linear story, the idea of a *perpetuum mobile* of imagery was strangely persistent.

Moving Images in Progression

Although film would develop as a medium for fiction mainly, the first motion pictures were distinctly non-fictive – more like a photograph with an animated motif. The three-dimensional depth illusion of a photograph existed already in the form of the popular *stereoscope*,[34] and the development toward movement had a history of more than a hundred years of motion perception devices: toys like simple flip books and magic lanterns, the *phenakistiscope*, the *zootrope* and the successive scientific ambitions of contraptions like the *praxinoscope* and the *zoopraxiscope* etc.[35] In the evolutionary process of film media, depth illusion was developed before motion, non-fiction preceded narrative fiction, and synchronised sound was developed to meet the market (the audience) before colour film. Drawing from the progress in electric lighting and photography, the Victorian artificers were keen to synthesise these inventions into an entirely new entertainment system based on recording and projecting of moving pictures. Cinema was not invented in one instance, but was an elusive goal for many entrepreneurs at the peak of the Victorian sensation culture and the domestication of electricity. The pioneers of cinema competed for technical standards during an intensive decade to bring a long era of infatuation with optical wonders and theatre into the 20th century. The progress of cinematic techniques was essentially a process of parallel development and small breakthroughs by visionary entrepreneurs situated both in the United States and in Europe, specialising in different fields of the engineering involved: chemical, optical, and mechanical, and of course electricity to power both the production and projection of films. Fifty years separates Louis Daguerre's metal plate photographs in 1839 and Eastman's production of celluloid roll film in 1889. The invention of the incandescent light bulb of 1870 was the result of fifty years of appliance development from the first successful experiments with electric power through electromagnetic induction by Michael Faraday and Joseph Henry in 1831. The stereoscope was first constructed in 1844 by Sir David Brewster (who had invented the *kaleidoscope* in 1815), a personal viewing device creating a depth illusion by separating the field of vision and showing slightly different images to each eye, merging the illusion into a single three-dimensional virtual image.[36] Fifty years later, in 1894, the first kinetoscope parlour opened as the result of Edison's efforts in moving image technique: wooden peep-show boxes where one person at a time could witness human action

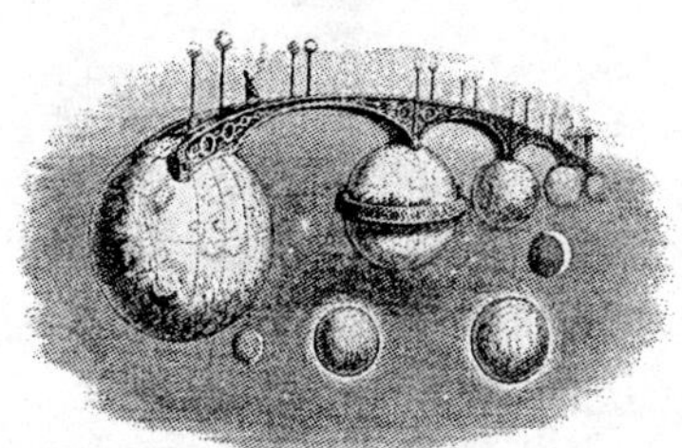

Grandville was a popular artistic contributor to French satirical magazines, like *Le Charivari* and *La Caricature*, in the mid-19th century. This illustration of a *flâneur* traversing the solar system on a cast-iron bridge, was published in 1844 in *Un autre monde*, satirize the hubris of human constructions, actualised by the building mania of metropolitan Paris at the time.

captured in short loops of less than twenty seconds (fig. 12 & 13). The kinetoscope came to be the first commercial adaptation of film technique, but it would not be the last.

Fig. 12 & 13

The development of the kinetoscope encountered many technical problems and delays. By the time the Black Maria was completed to meet the anticipated demand for film production in May 1893, only one functioning prototype had been assembled, despite all efforts to have a line of kinetoscopes ready for display at *The World's Columbian Exposition* in Chicago later that year. The first public demonstration of the prototype would instead take place at the *Brooklyn Institute of Arts and Sciences* on May 9, 1893.[37] The kinetoscope showed the first commercially produced film shot in the Black Maria, called "The Blacksmith Scene": an anachronistic piece where engineers and technicians from Edison's staff hammer an anvil and pass around a bottle of beer.[38] It is, however, difficult to establish a date for the first public demonstration of the kinetoscope. Gordon Hendricks argues in *The Edison Motion Picture Myth* that a demonstration of a crude prototype named *Kinetoscope No. 1*,[39] took place before a delegation of the *National Federation of Women's Clubs* invited to lunch at the Edison home Glenmont in West Orange already in 1891. According to

The Orange Chronicle of May 23, 1891, the group was guided around the laboratory by Edison himself, and in several papers the following week the public was informed that the ladies had experienced the marvels of the kinetoscope. They had seen "... through an aperture in a pine box standing on the floor, the picture of a man. It bowed and smiled, and took off its hat naturally and gracefully..."[40] (fig. 14) Hendricks addresses the problem of legal detours and shortcuts, as well as ante-dating for patent registrations, and the media-awareness cultivated in the competitive Edison enterprise, meaning that some of the accounts of his technical achievements might be manipulated in order to protect his patents.

Fig. 14

The viewing cabinet was at this time the only existing prototype, and the film inside showed Dickson in his shirt sleeves, with a vest and tie, tipping his hat. The same device that recorded the film would be transformed into a projector by changing the photographic lens to a projecting lens, while the filmstrip was developed and replaced into the machine. In fact, a device called the *telephonoscope* was cartooned already in 1878, more than ten years before work started on the kinetoscope: a wide-screen projection with synchronised sound, filling the wall of the living room (fig. 15). In 1891, a *New York Sun* reporter expressed his conviction that a "television-telephoto-photographic device" would soon develop from the germ of the kinetoscope into a device capable of accurate rendition of an entire opera with synchronised sound, "by means of a calcium light, the effect is reproduced, life-size on a white curtain."[41]

Fig. 15

Not until April 1, 1894, the first line of commissioned kinetoscopes were finished, at which time Edison branded his motion-picture business *The Edison Manufacturing Company.*[42] Ten of these machines were placed at the *Holland Brothers' Kinetoscope Parlour* on Broadway, New York City, which opened on April 14, 1894, as the first public viewing location.[43]

The idea of an entertainment system integrating sound and vision was strong in Edison from the outset of the kinetoscope project, in fact, the sound recording device of the phonograph, Edison's pet project, prompted the entire enterprise of filmmaking at West Orange. Rumours and visualisations of the *kinetophone* as the "next big thing" were spread in 1895, when Edison's manufacturing company suffered badly from – not least – overseas competition, due to the failure to patent the kinetoscope internationally. The dream of merging the kinetoscope with the phonograph was not realised until 1913, when a new improved version of the kinetophone was introduced to the market (fig. 17). Its failure was partly due to the poor synchronisation quality, but mainly to the fact that the appliance was a container without content. No productions were tailormade for the kinetophone. Even if the equipment for sound recording is showing in the foreground of the Black Maria interior rendering (fig. 2), the only surviving film material when it was put to use is the short "Dickson Experimental

Sound Film", recorded in 1894, where two men dance to Dickson who is playing the violin in front of the phonograph horn (fig. 16).[44]

Fig. 16

The prospect of fitting the phonograph with images suggests that *sound* would be its basic function, with visual stimulation added: a priority that would not become normative in the second industrial revolution, already with its focus on *vision*. Perhaps the simple beauty of the emanating principle of sound was more appealing to Edison, a force of travelling waves concentrically spreading from its source. Images crave directed attention – just like the camera, we need to orient ourselves as "viewfinders" toward their projection.[45] Sound spreads like ripples on a pond, surrounding the listener, modulating the acoustic space as it brings natural depth perception to the sense modality of hearing. When Marshall McLuhan connects the visual culture to individualism and the silent consumption and production of text that separates the individual from society, and an auditive culture to the collective, extraneous and tactile sphere of information, Edison's passion for the phonograph was of a very different social character than the, to him, less excitable stream of images that would conquer industrial media culture.[46] Instead of pursuing a predominantly auditive media, aided by images, the progress would focus on moving images, much later accompanied by music or screenside narration, and finally, thirty years after the invention of film, complemented with synchronised sound such as dialogue, sound effects and source music, marking the shift from the *silent* to the *talkies* in film production.[47] The spatial principle of the visual technique isolated the subject in front of the camera, then isolated the viewer in front of the kinetoscope, all instances reproducing the principles of the "private eye" and its environmental enclosure.

Fig. 17

A Dark Room

In the world of inventions, the Black Maria was far more sophisticated than its appearance. It was a workshop for mechanical transmission of matter into virtual existence, a time machine. The architectural principle of the Black Maria studio is actually an extension of the camera space into architecture. Like a camera house, the skylight window functions like a shutter to let in light needed for the exposure. With its dependence on sunlight, the Black Maria is related to the camera obscura, which Jonathan Crary identifies as a device impelling an ascetic withdrawal from the world, into the dark room, dividing the visible world into an exterior and an interior.[48] Crary also identifies the individuation at stake in the camera obscura: "it necessarily defines an observer as isolated, enclosed, and autonomous within its dark confines."[49] The Black Maria was one of the first architectural spaces to be captured into moving images, still its sole purpose was to shelter the equipment, workers and performers required in the recording process, providing an anonymous and neutral backdrop for the action. This revolving building belongs to the first stage of a process that compresses space and time into a point of radiance: a spatial point of creation and production of the virtual space of film.

The influence of Edison in the development of film is disputed, perhaps most notably in *The Edison Motion Picture Myth* where Gordon Hendricks pays a belated tribute to Dickson as the real inventor in Edison's motion-picture enterprise.[50] Edison was aware of the role of publicity in the process of invention, and above all he knew that in invention business there is no "second place": antedated and missing documents in the archives concerning the kinematographic process suggest that the records have been manipulated in order to put Edison ahead in patent registration as the pioneer of many steps in the cinematic technique development. Memory is a recording and so is film. The fate of the Black Maria is the result of a line of events, beginning with Dickson leaving West Orange in 1895 to co-found *The American Mutoscope Company*, for which he built a pivoting studio similar to the Black Maria to house the *mutograph*, on a Broadway rooftop in New York.[51] Edison would succumb to the projection idea with his engagement in the *vitascope* project 1896, in collaboration with the production company *Raff & Gammon*. This is a complicated history and Edison's personal role in the history of cinematography is once again disputed by some sources, and in others confirmed.[52] In 1896, the Black Maria studio was deemed inadequate to meet the needs of the vitascope project, partly because of its distance from the New York theatre district and entertainment establishments.[53] Seven years later, the Black Maria had fallen into disrepair. It was the same year, 1903, when the first plotted American film success premiered:

"The Great Train Robbery", produced and photographed by Edwin Porter for *The Edison Manufacturing Company*, met the audience in November.[54] It was a commercial and artistic achievement that would be unmatched until the breakthrough of D. W. Griffiths, the first American screen director of plotted feature films. The decline of the Black Maria coincides with the rise of the plotted feature films. It was dismantled in 1903. A replica, faithful in size and shape, was built in 1954 on the former laboratory grounds, now administered as the *Edison National Historic Site* (fig. 33 & 34). Edison's interests in film production and technology were already in 1895 out-sourced to an array of contractors, distributors and production companies. Film producers on both sides of the Atlantic improved artistic form and content, not to forget the progressive Russian and Indian filmmakers. At the turn of the century, Edison was surpassed by passionate investors such as the Lumière brothers, who understood the visual narrative possibilities of the new media. "The Wizard of Menlo Park" did not truly work his magic on cinema. Edison left the film industry in 1918.

An Internal Perspective of Mobility and Technology

The physical example of the Black Maria studio building illustrates the shift in photographic technology from static to moving images, which means adding temporality to the medium, but also a shift of perspective in this area of production. With the Black Maria, the film camera was internalised in a building instead of located in an outdoor experimental field. The shift to an internal production of images also affected the perspective of the subject and its mobility. Where the action in front of Muybridge's and Marey's cameras was predominantly of a horizontally passing motion of an animal or person (fig. 18), the kinetograph captured the continuous but statically placed motion of the subject directly in front of it (fig. 19). Even with respect to the fact that Marey's images were chronophotographs, still images displaying the composed motion at different points of its trajectory, there is a distinct idea of continuity in space and the temporal displacement within that space. The paradox of this perspective and mobility lies in the fact that, with the technological shift from still image to moving images, the investigation of subjects in *passing* ceases and an exploration of an animate subject in a *static* position begins. Dickson, who composed the shots of the invited subjects in the earliest Black Maria productions, together with his assistant and camera-operator William Heise, framed the subject as for a still photograph, in a half-body pose or a full figure, and let the motion take place on that spot, in one depth of focus and, in the earliest films, never violating this magical spot by having people enter or exit from the screen.[55] The temporal achievement (the action) was recorded in the anonymous spatial "void" – the interior stage of the Black Maria, that would not disclose any information about the constitution of the environment where the actor was captured by the camera. Looking at Eugene Sandow, "the world's strongest man", beautifully lit and well-built, there is no information in the image that would help us to perceive any depth, size or extension of the space the footage was captured in.

The French satirist Albert Robida illustrated the extension of human life into space in his futuristic picture of the Parisian sky traversed by flying rides and webs of communication wiring. The urban airspace is represented as a room for busy communications, both information and passenger traffic. The atmosphere is characterized as a carrier of information. This "three-dimensional" congestion of the city space also implies a density of time as an effect of intense communication.

The anonymous and versatile character of space is the essence of the interior of the film studio. The studio space serves the production of virtual spaces, scenes (re-)created within it, hosting temporary productions, staged by different people and populated by temporary characters. Speaking with Benjamin, the reproduction of a work of art lacks the presence in time and space, but in the case of film – a copy of

Fig. 18

time and space itself – the presence at the point of production is obliterated and completely useless.[56] There are no "real-time" spectators of film, only the people involved in the production, in front of and behind the camera. In fact, before cutting and editing, the plot of the production might be impossible to follow. No spectator can profit from or is rewarded by presence in time and space of the production of film. The Black Maria symbolises the virtual point of creation, a unique form dissipated in the anonymous black box interior. This studio is able to re-orient itself according to time (daylight) in order to make it possible to record the moment. The Black Maria is a remarkable example of versatile architecture serving the production of virtual space: by changing or maintaining its location by the aid of rotation, the building is able to bring time out of the "time-space" equation, keeping light conditions at a constant, enabling the recording of an event taking place inside.

In the previous chapter, the movement from exterior to interior was pursued, following authors like Huysmans,

Goncourt and de Maistre exploring the possibilities of the domestic interior as, and in, a narrative medium. In the early days of film production, Edison and Dickson chose to take the camera inside to document simple body actions, while

Fig.19

other film pioneers opted for the everyday urban scenery of unstaged events such as crowds and traffic. This suggests a relocation similar to the writers-in-residence (Huysmans and Goncourt) whose novels are concerned with the refuge from outside reality to the constructed privacy of the interior, still without any attempts to present a narrative content. Drawing on the prison wagon analogy of the Black Maria studio building, new technology could either liberate or imprison the spectator – albeit as a refined form of enclosure in motion. The narrative examples in the first chapter feature the art of travelling in inertia, where the subject in isolation is filtering the perception of the world through sensory-augmenting artifice in a complex relation to both mobility and technology as liberating in their voluntary imprisonment. In relation to the issue of mobility in the domestic interiors of the narrators in Huysmans' *A Rebours* and in Goncourt's *La Maison d'un artiste*, the mind's capacity of immersion in memory, in contemplation of an object (art, craft, literature), suggests an intellectual compensation for the spatial isolation. The expansion of the mind is limitless in time and space, provided that the physical space serves and facilitates this kind of immersive virtual activity. The fixed position in space and time of the interior is overridden by the mobility of the mind. The mediated artificial interior of Baron des Esseintes in Huysmans is a celebration of technological innovation and sophisticated machinery. Still it becomes a prison to its habitant, as the space is designed to serve the mind and gratify the senses, not to attend to basic human needs. The Baron is divided into a dreaming mind and a decaying body as a result of the artificial manipulations of his environment and the addictive mind journeys that make the return to physical space more and more unbearable. Huysmans' account of the Baron actualises issues of technology as substitute, and as both cause and effect, of his isolation. In the commodified existence of des Esseintes, technology offers freedom and liberation, while the technical modernity of the urban world, kept at distance by his artificial domestic environment, is uncontrollable and threatening. New technology tends to be, to the same degree, empowering and enslaving, creating fears and hopes attached to the artifice that enters our lives. The virtual worlds of Huysmans, as well as the projected virtuality of the film screen, create a double inhabitant and a double spectator. The media experience offers liberation and imprisonment, as does technology itself. Des Esseintes indulges in the artifice of his mediated environment. Huysmans' rhetoric against nature is an intended provocation in an era of considerable changes of the urban environment of Paris and the intensive media development of the second industrial revolution.

In the cultural context of the 1880s, a crisis in the individual could be discerned as perceptual, social and cultural changes accompanied technology and mobility. I have argued in the previous chapter that the critical effect of the late 19th century media on the individual could be characterised as a doubling of the self. The split subject as a product of an increasingly mediated environment is a doppelgänger, representing both desire and repulsion. Desire materialises as technology and the engineer becomes a modern hero, while technology counts new phobics for every step of the same scale of progress. Illusory perspective and illusion of mobility are aspects of both the split subject and the mediated architecture of the late 19th century. Bergson develops, in his philosophy of the mind, a theory about the doubling of consciousness taking place in the self in the process of memory and perception. Bergson imagines a scene where one self "conscious of its liberty, erects itself into an independent spectator of a scene which the other seems to be playing in a mechanical way."[57] The two distinct selves are described in this scenario, where the selves alternate between two states of impressions; "we act and yet are acted".[58] The free spectator observing "the other automatically playing his part" is a duplication "of the mind between perception which is only perception, and perception duplicated in memory."[59] The two parts constitute an independent subject, governed by the workings of the mind.

Industrial progress takes its toll on the urban atmosphere. In 1884, John Ruskin published an essay, "The Storm-Cloud of the 19th Century", a critique of industrial urbanism and its consequences, based on research into meteorological changes and observations of increasing pollution. Ruskin was concerned with the "plague-wind", a "wind of darkness", that "blows indifferently from all". His ominous reading of the London sky concludes with the words "whether you can affect the signs of the sky or not, you can affect the signs of the times."

The spectator situation in relation to the kinetoscope and its live image contents, was "consistent with the individualised, peephole nature of the viewing experience".[60] In correspondence to the locations and apparatus constructed for cinematic entertainment, the new medium also created its audience. In the pre-mature era of cinema, different types of projection were tried before the spectator came to rest in the dark salon facing an illuminated screen, a peculiar hybrid situation of social activity (sharing the experience as a community) and passive consumption. The prevailing format for film projection space was to place the audience in a "black box", partaking in a constant retrieval of information, attention fixed at the illusive three-dimensionality of the screen as a "white cube": a space tailormade for the representation of images.

Fig. 20

A Closed Loop

The kinetoscope was designed for the compound machinery to feed a gelatine film loop to be observed by a single person peering from the outside, through an enlarging lens mounted in the eye-piece, into what looks more like a packing case, a piece of storage furniture or a pulpit (fig. 13). The social dimension of the kinetoscope was largely eliminated, creating a feedback loop between the viewer and the perpetual filmstrip like an animated still shot. Like Benjamin's lonely "reader of a novel", the spectator of the kinetoscope becomes isolated in this vantage point of perception.[61] The closed loop of the kinetoscope filmstrip reminds us of the domestic architecture created by Huysmans' Baron des Esseintes, whose isolation serves an inner imagery, furnished with machinery to maintain the illusion. Whatever architectural environment the kinetoscope is placed in, it is obliterated by the isolated experience of viewing, similar to the closed circuit between the reader and the novel. Yet, the plot that would absorb the spectator was not applied to the first films made. Inside the kinetoscope, the footage had no beginning, no middle and certainly no ending, just a simple animated scene from human life, looped to serve the spectator who could enter and exit at any point of the action.

To Benjamin, film is a medium that has created a new mode of perception. While other critics express their contempt for the passivity of the spectators, exposed *en masse* to a medium that does not lend itself to contemplation in the same way as a work of art such as a painting, Benjamin brings these worries into perspective: "Clearly, this is at bottom the same ancient lament that the masses seek distraction whereas art demands concentration from the spectator."[62] The opposing perceptive modes of concentration and distraction position the spectator in a different relationship to the perceived object: art may have the power to absorb an individual spectator, while architecture is an example of a work of art that is being absorbed by the mass of spectators. Benjamin places film in a position between the experience of art and that of architecture: "reception in a state of distraction".[63] The audience follows the plot of the film, mediated by a stream of art as succeeding images, none of which may be contemplated as an isolated frame, absorbing the space on the screen in an act of collective perception. Film is art minus concentration and architecture minus touch. A distractive visual space remains, of which the desire of immersion is governed by the story and the images that serve it. Dickson's viewing apparatus was designed for individual contemplation, the spectator looking into a black box that eliminates the surrounding architecture and creates a closed circuit of perceived reality – a virtual space – without a plot.

Fig. 21 & 22

Keeping it Reel

Scientific studies propelled progress in the early days of moving images – the study of the mobility of animals and humans in Muybridge's and Marey's work were not directly intended for an audience. They did not pursue the cinematic technique for the purpose of commercial success but with scientific intentions to visualise the most basic ”unseen” human behaviour of walking, jumping, lifting, in short, interacting with obstacles and objects in various forms. Cinema had to expand into a commercial use beyond scientific applications in order to attract manufacturers and turn the technique into a modern industry. Edison's investments in proto-cinematic technique became the incentive for industrialists like the Lumière brothers, taking the inventor's interest as a guarantee of success. In less than five years from the first demonstration of the kinetoscope, film business was a reality that had nearly lost its initiator along the way. Edison was, despite his commercial intuition, mistaken in his conviction of the peep-show principle of moving images. Louis and Auguste Lumière placed their bet on the projection to a large audience, perhaps inspired by the former glory of Parisian dioramas and later optical illusion shows, gathering an audience without excluding the character of a social event. Although the first live image shows attracted media attention, the film industry did not break through to the larger audiences as entertainment media until the mid-nineties, more precisely around Christmas in 1895, when the Lumière brothers presented their live image show at *Volpier's Grand Café*. Their *cinématographe* début with a paying audience took place in the basement floor of the *Grand Café*, called the *Salon Indien*, on December 28, 1895. It instantaneously obliterated the kinetoscope. A ticket price of one franc included ten films of just over a minute. The audience enjoyed the capture of scenes from the bourgeois family life of Lumière: Madame Lumière fishing from the pond in "La pêche aux poissons rouges", a gardener's work in "Le jardinier", the family eating in "Le repas" – but also geographic locations like the celebrated realistic view of the sea in "La mer" and the frightening perspective shot of "Arrivée du train en gare de La Ciotat". The first films by the Lumière brothers showed urban exterior scenes such as a train stopping at a station, a horse carriage in the street, or a crowd of people. Lumières' audience were sitting in a café, a social environment that made the film a collective experience, although the room was dark and the attention was directed towards a screen. As the film medium found its form, the screen started to communicate directly with the audience. Rather than trying to direct the attention toward a host or a presenter, the screen itself gave the information and directions needed to create and control the experience.

In 1897 the first fully dedicated cinema hall was built in Paris.[64] Even if some films had the character and theme of "animated family albums", the most popular reels were simple urban scenes – a boulevard on a Sunday or workers leaving the factory, like the Lumières' first film ever to be shown, "Sortie des Usines Lumière à Lyon-Montplaisir", which premiered on March 22, 1895 at a special viewing at the *Societé d'Encouragement à l'Industrie Nationale* in Paris.[65] The urban crowd was caught in a perception attraction of collectively watching ordinary people moving about in the same city. The cinema salon was a darkened room where an audience could engage in the self-reflection of watching urban scenes, in a substrate loop of individuals absorbed in the individuation process. The filmed crowd of the street was the mirror of the spectating crowd of the salon. The character of these "crowd films" would have inserted mixed feelings of joy of recognition and a sense of perpetual surveillance in the spectator, and maybe a thrilling feeling of immortality or its opposite: a sense of invisibility and fusion with the crowd. The possibility of being or becoming part of the representation stood in stark contrast to the plotted stories that lay ahead in the development of film: scripts that would claim the narrative efforts of a screen-writer and convincing actors to perform the plot. The crowd shots were documentary urban views, filmed with a static camera as the only immobile subject in the film environment. There is no narrative content or storyline ambitions in films like "Sortie des Usines Panhard & Levassor" by Léon Gaumont or Méliès' "Le Boulevard des Italiens". Films like "Chez un barbier", "Les plongeurs" and "Un menusier à son établi" still remained popular in 1897, featuring plain leisure activities without any significance or ambitions of actuality. These titles did not attract their audience by placing celebrities or performers in leading roles – they were simply plotless everyday scenes where ordinary people did ordinary things, like leaving their workplace in the afternoon.[66]

Black Maria as Scene – Through the Peephole

The first copyrighted film recorded by the kinetograph features Fred Ott, a member of Edison's staff, in the "Edison Kinetoscopic Record of a Sneeze", registered as No 2887z, on January 7, 1894 (fig. 23).[67] The earlier mentioned filmstrip where Dickson greets film history by lifting his hat was captured before the sneeze but was not dated and copyrighted (fig. 14). Curiously enough, a journalist claims to have seen as well as *heard* Ott sneezing, which is more likely to be an example of synæsthetic experience (where one sense modality trigger a reaction in another sense), since there is no account of a synchronised phonographic recording of the sneeze. A succession of acts suitable for the ten-second format followed, including a man smoking a pipe, horse-shoeing, a barbershop scene, a tooth extraction performed by the dentist Dr. Colton, Professor Welton's boxing cats (fig. 24) and "The Widow Jones Kiss", featuring the actors May Irwin and John Rice performing a scene from a musical comedy (fig. 25), which became the most popular film of 1896 and got a full-page illustrated review, "The Anatomy of a Kiss", in *The Sunday World.*[68]

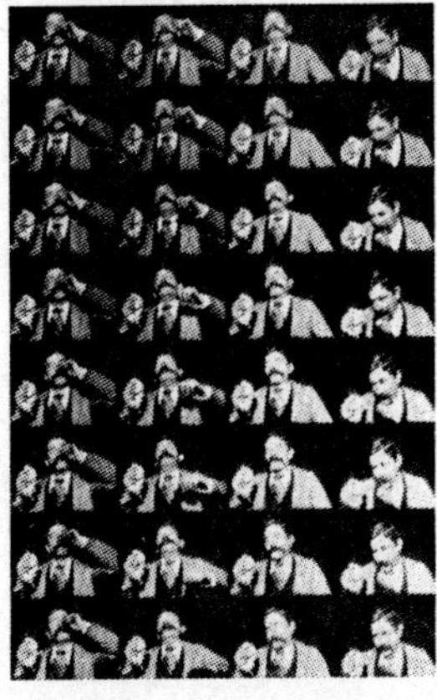

Fig. 23

The short duration of the filmstrip fitted for the kinetoscope naturally contributed to the limited possibilities of presenting a plot. A single person performing the basic motion pattern of a sneeze or smoking a pipe was an instantly recognisable and unmistakingly human action. Two people kissing or hammering completed the twenty seconds available. No acting was required, just the animation of the body as centre of action.

Fig. 24

As kinetoscope film production progressed, professional performers added to the sense of uniqueness of the films, a step from the indiscriminate choice of "actors" in the direction of cinematic iconography created by the motion picture industry half a century later. Thanks to Edison's status and the high expectations for his new invention, a line-up of invited vaudeville acts, having already proved themselves in front of live audiences, visited the Black Maria in the mid-nineties. The crossfeeding between the existing entertainment industry and the new medium was established from the beginning. Performance actors, athletes and celebrities arrived to perform in the Black Maria studio interior, at first for free, like Sandow who flexed his famous muscles in front of Dickson's camera simply for the honour of assisting Edison in his media project (fig. 19). In the search for thrilling outdoor scenes, the kinetograph was brought to the amusement park at Coney Island to record the thrill ride in the film "Shooting the Chutes".[69]

Fig. 25

The female subjects were mainly represented in several more or less exotic and artistic dance acts. Among the kinetographed ladies were Annabelle Moore who performed her "Butterfly dance", a woman called Carmencita in an exotic flamenco number (fig. 26), the modern dance pioneer high-kicking Ruth St. Denis and Madame Bertholdi, a famous contortionist. "Little sure-shot" Annie Oakley, the star from *Buffalo Bill's Wild West Show*, performed shooting stunts in the Black Maria, which had to be repaired with some extra tar paper after the bullets had penetrated its cladding (fig. 27).

Fig. 26

The aforementioned films were produced from around 1893 to 1896, and limited to the duration of kinetoscope reel – less than twenty seconds. The Black Maria also housed boxing games, like "The Leonard-Cushing Fight" in June 1894 (fig. 28) and the six-round match named "Corbett and Courtney Before the Kinetograph" in September 1894.[70] The stage area of the Black Maria was smaller than a normal boxing ring, and the rounds were shorter than usual, but the films were very popular. In order to satisfactorily capture the prizefights, the duration of the films were pushed to the limit of the capacity of the kinetoscope. In order to extend the film duration, the kinetoscope was adjusted for longer filmstrips, and by reducing the amount of frames per second down to thirty, which is more than adequate for the human eye to perceive as steady motion.[71] In the kinetoscope parlour, however, the boxing-game audience had to move from one kinetoscope to another to see the entire game (fig. 21 & 22).

The boxing games inside the Black Maria were held in front of a live studio audience, just a few people but visible in the background focusing on the match, so that the kinetoscope viewer would be virtually positioned on the opposite side of the ring.

Fig. 27

The formatting "language" and narrative sculpting method for cinematic time and space – cutting and editing – was not applied in the pre-mature cinema. Around a decade later, when cinema had been established as a collective distraction (in Benjamin's terms), George Méliès was among the first to explore the full narrative potential of film. Image depth did not exist in effect until the narrative element prompted a set. Still the very first sets imitated the theatre stage, with a limited depth of view, restricted by a backdrop against which the action was set, possibly with elements such as window or door as attributes and part of the action. Before a cinematic language was invented, the elements of the scene were limited to the performers and their attributes, that is, objects directly involved in the action. The backdrop was simply the obscure interior of the Black Maria. Like the motion studies performed by the scientifically oriented Muybridge and Marey, the background was a "black box", as neutral as possible to the sunlit actors.

Fig. 28

The short duration of the films and the plotless action created a non-narrative display of mere human appearance, an intimate situation where the viewer was situated in front of the action. The kiss and the sneeze, for example, represented the acting figures in half-body, cut from the waist up, as if seen across a tabletop (fig. 23 & 25). The aperture/view was reflected in the viewer's situation of the kinetoscope "peep show": the static camera position only allowed one view, reducing the perspective to the kind of view you would get through "a hole in the wall": no tracking shots, no panning, no zooming. A curious detail in the discussion about the peephole perspective is that the very first films were circular because of the round lens aperture of the kinetograph prototype (fig. 29). Spectators were fascinated to see people disappearing outside the screen and then returning into the field of view; the discontinuity of appearance was puzzling when it appeared on film. The peephole situation added to, and repeated, the technological limitations of the camera: a static position (duplicated in the viewer), like a hole in the wall, through which the viewer observes something forbidden, while remaining unnoticed, outside the scene itself.

Fig. 29

The Captive Image and the Liberated Drawing

From the isolation of troublemakers in the original "Black Maria" police wagon to the first film studio, the notion of captivity is inherent in the terminology. The motion captured by the kinetograph was repeated as a concept for Edison's kinetoscope, in effect an enclosure of the image. The dual purpose of the closet was to hide the mechanism and to both lock up and expose the film. The containment is further accentuated by the isolated perspective of one person looking from the outside in through a peephole. Soon enough after the introduction of kinetoscope parlours, concerns about the moral impact of film were expressed, as generally happens to any new media. As a film industry was spawned, voices were raised regarding the morality of showing illegal prize-fights and daring lady dancers.

Edison was also critizised by his own collaborators who urged him to reconsider the idea of image projection, as "the motion picture was demanding to be liberated from the little black box."[72] Edison's resistance to the idea of the projection screen is documented. The kinetoscopes had proven to bring in good business, as expected, and in the interest of commerce, Edison explicitly rejected the "screen machine": "it will spoil everything".[73] Despite the fact that experimentation on projection took place in the laboratories of European film pioneers, Edison insisted on the single serving "pay and play" units. In his opinion, an estimated number of ten screens in the United States would suffice to fill the market for moving images, and a global market would be saturated by fifty screens.[74] In a more abstract sense, the moving image was held captive. Due to Edison's protective control of his patent holdings, other American film experimenters emigrated to the west coast to avoid the patent legislation, and laid the foundations of Hollywood as a nexus of cinema production. Despite these references to the captured image and the financial drives that accompany innovation, the main motivating force of cinematographic development would be the creative freedom of exploring the possibilities of the new media.

Fig. 30

The above strip is taken from the 36-second-long kinetograph film "Three Acrobats" from 1899, where the comic performers use a fake brick wall for acrobatic stunts (fig. 30). The wall has four cleverly hinged hidden openings used for the choreography of negotiating a fictive exterior and interior, and a painted backdrop picturing townhouses. While the clowns play with the set design building, the film illustrates the confused ontology of the Black Maria film studio. The Black Maria problematised the concept of exterior and interior with its numerous openings, hatches and doors in the walls and roof. In its interior, outdoor sets were often constructed, adding to the ambiguous character of inside and outside. These set décors created for the kinetoscope films mirrored the visual setting of a theatre stage: a functional or illusory backdrop — designed to be perceived from the point of view of a theatre audience. The static camera faced the stage like the immobilised spectator of a theatre play. With an infinite number of insides and outsides assembled together in a purpose-built interior, the Black Maria reflects the idea of Baron des Esseintes' domestic contrivances. By the aid of an artificially enhanced environment and a work of art, space is subject to the transitional mind of the Baron, who may experience vivid memories and illusions of any environment, exterior or interior, linked with the fine threads of dream logic.

The door-slamming comedy act of the "Three Acrobats" plays upon the dissolved solidity of the brick wall, triggering a sequence of arbitrary openings and closings, hidden and exposed, the whole confused array spiced with excessive comic violence as the only elements of cause and effect in the act. In "Three Acrobats", the camera is static, and the top-lit stage depth is minimised and flat, reduced to what could be described as a "pavement" shot: the camera position – the audience's point of view – is constructed as if seen from straight "across the street": the field of view is a "façade", extending indeterminately to the left and to the right, with a limited stage depth directly in front of it. From a narrative point of view, there is no plot building up to the acrobatic pursuit of butt-kicking and pan-smashing: the spectator is thrown into the action without beginning or end, in a way that would be appropriate to the closed loop of the kinetoscope filmstrip (fig. 31).

Fig. 31

Produced in Edison's studio in 1900, "The Enchanted Drawing" took the liberty of dissolving the limitations of spatial dimensions. The draughtsman is a magician who effortlessly creates two-dimensional objects and then liberates them from the flatness of the drawing. First he draws a character, the face of a man, then he adds a glass and a bottle in the upper corner of the paper. As the draughtsman removes the objects from the flipchart, and takes a drink of the wine, the drawn face changes from neutral to displeased, until he is treated to a gulp of wine poured into his painted mouth. The illustrated face is not satisfied until the props are restored to the drawing plane, together with a hat and a cigar. The illustrator creates both his supporting actor and the props, objects that passes from two- to three-dimensionality and back again. The film mixes real-time drawing sequences with stop-motion tricks, to create the illusion of self-generated reality. The interaction with the animated character and the arbitrary passage of objects "through the surface" suggest an early exercise in virtual reality creation, presenting the idea of both 3d-modelling and rapid prototyping.

The peculiarly weak three-dimensionality of "Three Acrobats", where the set décor mimics the theatre stage, is succeeded by the interactive "Enchanted Drawing". In both films, characters and objects pass through a suggested "screen": the brick wall or the drawing paper, but the first example is indicating depth by emphasising simple spatial positioning of outside or inside, in front of or behind, where the latter allow objects to pass between dimensions and even allow them to be consumed either as two- or as three-dimensional.

Fig. 32

Benjamin appointed film as the liberator of the material world and of the human mind alike. He argues that film has contributed to a "deepening of apperception" because of its impact on optical, and later acoustical, perception.[75] The experience of the viewer of moving images is based on changes of place and focus, as if travelling through the imagery: "Let us compare the screen on which a film unfolds with the canvas of a painting. The painting invites the spectator to contemplation; before it the spectator can abandon himself to his associations. Before the movie frame he cannot do so. No sooner has his eye grasped a scene than it is already changed. It cannot be arrested."[76]

The early kinetoscope films had the form of animated photographs, extended portraits or mirror images of trivial actions. The first performers were not actors, and even if they were, there was no plotted script to act out. In the pre-mature cinematic experimentation that took place in the Black Maria, the "non-actor" performing the "non-plot", like the sneezing man, is just a piece of the clockwork mechanism, like any other moving part of the machinery of the filming process. The filmed subject acted "not for an audience but for a mechanical contrivance" – the film camera.[77] The performance is generic and unmasked, stripped to the basic motion pattern of a direct action without plot and with no ambitions of illusory depth in the image composition itself. Benjamin argues that in film, in contrast to stage play, the greatest effect is achieved by denouncing dramatic acting. The unscripted immediacy of the subject in the films recorded in the Black Maria meets the spectator halfway in its unauthoritative form.

In the shift from stage to screen, the reciprocity of the performance is lost, as the audience is relocated in space and time from the actor in the space of the recording studio. This is one aspect of the fundamental splitting principle that governs film: "the reflected image has become separable, transportable."[78] The last stage of the production line of film (from recording to projection) is to deliver the images to the spectator, who perceives the act separated from "its presence in time and space, its unique existence at the place where it happens to be."[79] This separation in time is further complicated as film technique proceeds to cutting and editing, by which not only time but space and material reality become negotiable. The bending of space and time, using the montage as main instrument, is what makes film an art form in its own right. Film overrules architecture, for example in disobeying spatial continuity in a scene where someone jumps through a window and lands outside another. This juxtaposition of architectural space is possible thanks to montage technique, where an unsuspecting audience experience the flow of images oblivious of the artifice. Benjamin identifies the freedom of montage of space and time as the essence of the film medium. The audience will accept the final edited result of a film project in all its discontinuities of both time and space as long as the illusion is carefully handled and reassembled with respect to the rules of the montage.

Fig. 33

The Cinematographical Habits of the Mind

In Henri Bergson's philosophy, time and space are considered dynamic expressions of the human mind. In *L'Evolution créatrice*, Bergson used the film camera as a metaphor for the artifice of human perception that reveal a cinematographical character of intellectual knowledge. The "task" of the cinematic image is to reproduce the fluidity and variety of life. However, the photographs, aligned in a sequence, reproduce the mobile motif in an "attitude immobile", that is, in one still after the other.[80] The "cinematographical habits" of the mind is a way of coping with the constant movement and unceasing change of life. The intellect isolates and traces boundaries of both bodies and events, and thus struggles with the intuitive fluidity that is also a capacity of the human mind. The mechanistic construction of reality suffers from the same illusion as created by the film camera that presents frozen moments with the objective to represent true motion. Our intellect frames reality as snapshots of spatialised time in an effort to create a stable view where form can be discerned in the constant continuity and change that is reality. Using the Black Maria as an image to illustrate Bergson's critique, the studio location for production of illusory motion is a space capable of real *motion*, ruled by the motion of light in *time*: the second primacy of film. The revolving studio is an example of spatialised time, in the function of adjustment to daylight, programmed to serve the production of images as a machine-building.[81] This particular animated building could be regarded as a manifestation of Bergson's *durée*, not fixed in time but capable of continuous motion in space.

A division of time into work and leisure emerged during the 19th century. Amusement parks became not only social scenes but also mechanised playgrounds, a pandemonium of constructions for speed and frenzy. The divertissements were in a form that was rather similar to those industrial environments from which they sought to offer distraction; with the noise, the smell, and the steel, this machine park reminded one of the conditions on the factory floor in more than one sense.

In order to create the illusion of motion, there has to be motion somewhere in the process, if not in the apparatus used for recording and/or projection. The projector working on the sequence of immobile images recorded by the film camera, is the animator of a succession of rests, which is not equivalent to a real movement. The analogy of the mind as "a machine operating on a multitude of images" complicates the understanding of the fluid nature of true reality in Bergson's argument. The mind's efforts to create form from a relentlessly mobile reality prevail over the immediacy of experience, which is why Bergson reminds us that "there is no form, since form is immobile and the reality is movement. What is real is the continual *change* of form: form is only a snapshot view of a transition."[82] The loop of perpetual recommencement in Bergson's critique may be found in the viewing apparatus of the kinetoscope, where a loop of images is reeled in front of the viewer.

The illusion becomes more "complete" and satisfying as the medium of film develops technologically and artistically into a narrative image in colour with sound, working within the experience frame of images. Bergson was concerned, not with the artistic quality or suspended disbelief or even projection quality, but with the problem of extracting mobility from still images, however smoothly aligned and replayed. Although the mechanistic principle is more or less the same today in terms of celluloid film, the digital tools and techniques indicate a silent revolution in film that would interest Bergson with respect to the possibilities of extensions to and manipulations of perception. With contemporary digital technique and multiple camera set-up, special effects development has reached a stage beyond Bergson's horizon of technical limitations. By use of the so-called "bullet time" technique, a term coined for the digital visualisation used in the film "Matrix" from 1999, film is capable of creating a paradox of "static" view in motion: for example a frozen moment of a suspended glass as it shatters on the ground while the camera moves around it.[83] Bergson let film represent the illusion of mobility, now it is capable of representing the illusion of immobility.

Fig. 34

"Our taverns and our metropolitan streets, our offices and furnished rooms, our railroad stations and our factories appeared to have us locked up hopelessly. Then came the film and burst this prison-world asunder by the dynamite of the tenth of a second, so that now, in the midst of its far-flung ruins and debris, we calmly and adventurously go travelling."[84]

In fragments of the wide-spanning essay construction *Paris: Capital of the 19th Century*, Benjamin identifies the "end of the chapter of the interior" with the introduction of props into film.[85] The interior becomes fictionalised to the point of obliteration, at which point it enters the space of fiction. The loss of individual significance of the domestic interior (its central function of casing, moulded from the inhabitant) coincides with the first decades of the 20th century when film environment becomes a deeper and more detailed illusion. In a separate fragment of *Paris: Capital of the 19th Century*, he attributes permeation as the main principle of film, and of the new architecture as well as for colportage.[86] Benjamin's interest and understanding of film inspired him to suggest the idea of animating the map of Paris, a chronological succession of changes that spans the whole 19th century in half an hour, with the reservation that the *flâneur* is already involved in that kind of activity.[87] In comparison with the perspective of the aforementioned Edison film "Three Acrobats", the pavement view of the flâneur would be, one must assume, the opposite to the static camera position "across the street", but a subjective point of view, a steady rail track shot by an experienced film photographer assisted by a skilled focus puller. If the flâneur only could record his motion through the urban scenery, it would be an example of the reader becoming writer, a development related to availability of media due to an "increasing extension of the press" that Benjamin discusses in the *Work of Art in the Age of Mechanical Reproduction,* blurring the distinction between author and public.[88] Benjamin attributed a large part of the liberation of authorship to the film industry, where changes came about in a decade, achieving the same "transitions that in literature took centuries".[89]

In conclusion, the observations of the kinetoscope viewer in relation to the subjects of the kinetoscope films, is a mirrored position, as in a reflection or a dialogue. The isolated pose and the "inert travelling" of the kinetoscope spectator remind us of the secluded residential arrangements of the narrated interiors of the fictive character des Esseintes and the narrative personae of Goncourt and de Maistre. The domestic environments enable virtual travelling (in time) from a static position in space, while maintaining individual isolation. The static camera and the peephole view allowed for a layer of animation in front of static observers, first before the recording device of the camera, then before the experiencing spectator. The Black Maria provides a neutral backdrop; a non-experiential, transitory instance of time and space. The building itself illustrates a paradoxical reversal of an animated building hosting a static camera. The Black Maria studio is located at the intersection between the static point of recorded origin and the dynamic distributed representation, a mediator between singular place and multiplied time. This chapter has shifted focus from the object to its workings: from the production site to the consumption space of moving images, to the plotless form of these. The development of the spaces and products and their modes of viewing in pre-mature cinema has been discussed through the issues of perspective, mobility and technology involved in the process.

Film as a medium has been described as architecture of time and illusion of mobility. The film medium offers a joyful narrative experience, extended in real time, in the same way as novel-reading is bringing us close to the featured characters and inducing us to be immersed in its virtuality. From the first sensational moving images available for public view, more than fifteen years would pass before the film medium was capable of telling a story. The 20th century has since been a schooling period for both filmmakers and their audience, to the point of obliterating the traditionally opposite roles of creator and spectator. Film often represents a multiple authorship: a director who realises a story from a writer's manuscript, aided by a crew of specialised artificers. The contemporary era of affordable image production technology implies a merging of the roles of producer and consumer into a single narrator using digital technology for the production of moving images. The game player's virtual existence is in most games represented by an image, controlled and animated through a continuous camera view, possible to adjust with respect to motion and perspective. The traditional, collective art form of filmmaking reminds us of the co-operative organisation of research that governed Edison's laboratory. Finally, this non-authorial paradigm marks the accidental architecture of the Black Maria, governed by the architectural principle of extending the camera space into architecture.

3

Shelf life

–*The Primer of Virtuality*

Spaces in Perpetual Becoming

At the turn of the last century, we were as preoccupied with dreams of our digital networks and virtual reality as a digitally mediated experience, as the 19th century fin-de-siècle audiences were infatuated with the prospects of the wireless telegraph, telephone communications and cinematography. And to the same degree, regardless of a century of separation, the technologies incite changes in our perception of spatiality, materiality and the relations and information circulating within them. By revisiting the spatialities of the 19th century, and by applying a view of the virtual created in the same period of time, we may reverse our view of virtuality to a point before the technological efforts that have made "virtual" synonymous with "cyberspace" or immersive digital environments. Within its technologically mediated extensions, virtual reality offers a choice, not just of temporal and spatial environment, but also a choice of embodiment and mode of subjectivity, and the type of interactions and simulations to sustain the personalised architecture. We remain within the same realm of senses, facing a larger capacity for simulation in the digital world. Instead of thinking of virtuality as a concept realisable or even realised by technology, we benefit from the fact that virtuality is what makes technology possible, being a precondition of the space of emergence of the new; the not yet realised, thought, cooked or assembled in the real world. We may have to adjust ourselves to a new psychology of inhabitation and to a new internal perception of our bodies in digital simulations, unaided by a storyline or a prescribed temporality.

Madame Tussaud's wax cabinet in London (established in 1835), and the *Musée Grévin* in Paris (established in 1882), are spaces *furnished* with famous fictive and real characters. The celebrity is a product of 19th century media technologies that generated a demand for exposure, sensations and novelties. The anachronistically arranged display of doppelgängers mixes time, character and space in a dreamlike environment that defies linearity.

The studies conducted in the previous chapters show how these kinds of investigations into virtualities have been undertaken in the form of the novel and the film at the end of the 19th century. Huysmans, Goncourt and de Maistre explore the virtual within their own domestic spaces, in a transitional act of recording and informing real space into the form of the novel, communicating the psychology of inhabitation that they investigate. The Black Maria film studio was a building constructed as a camera and also equipped with a camera for the capturing of the human body in action against a black background. The recorded action, isolated in a looped timeframe, was replayed for a single spectator peeping into a kinetoscope, equalising the object and the space in a virtual state of isolation and duration. The distance between the isolated writer-in-residence and the perpetually sneezing man in the kinetoscope may seem unbridgeable, but the distance is closed by the virtuality at play within the frames of the novel and the film. The field of play, as perceived by the reader and the spectator, is a space in a state of perpetual becoming. The same difficulty we find in constructing the temporal becoming of hens and eggs is experienced when trying to work out whether it is the real or the narrative that in the writers-in-residence is the "true" point of spatial generation.

The writers-in-residence wish to preserve their space, not as it is, but in how it becomes. The *excitoir* as space is a process, it is space in service of its production, like the Black Maria being one of the world's first filmed interiors, of which no image persists other than the darkness behind the actors. The studio building behaves like a camera in order to serve the camera in its interior. The same darkness, against which an isolated body is captured on film, becomes the darkness of an isolated viewer, captured by the film. The perceived space is statically in flux, as a vehicle for immobility, as it is represented without prescribing a procedural line that summons our belief in cause and effect. The interpreter of the novel and the film is left to her own devices concerning temporality and organisation, experiencing the frame of action without any promise of reaching the end or perceiving space in a state of finitude. The consumer of the plotless narrative experiences duration, and all potential spatialities that are contained within the unrealised moment of closure.

The Test of Time

The departure point for this chapter is a discussion of the form of plotlessness in literature and film within the late 19th century. This chapter provides a theoretical approach to explore the examples from the previous chapters. As we are leaving the developmental trajectory of the writers-in-residence and the Black Maria, this chapter attempts to recapture the previous chapters in terms of the nature of the virtuality created within the examples, which enters theoretical arguments by the French philosopher Henri Bergson (1859–1941), made at the same time of development as the studied examples. Bergson's theory on virtuality brings us back to the pre-digital media landscape of the late 19th century, contemporary to Huysmans, Goncourt and Edison. In the study of virtual spaces of the 19th century in this thesis, Bergson represents a sort of "degree zero" terminology, since his theory on virtuality concerns the workings of the human mind rather than being descriptive of an environment formed and informed in a certain way, as is the case in digital virtual reality. By bringing back the concept of virtuality to the late Victorian society, the preconceptions and oblique strategies connected to computer-generated virtuality is obliterated.

This chapter extends the discussion of virtuality by exploring a crossbreed of architecture and narrative, introducing Neal Stephenson's novel *The Diamond Age*, first published in 1995. This novel describes the *Primer*, which is a reinvention of the book as a virtual space that draws its content from actual space, centers the plot around a designated reader and inserts characters and events from the reader's environment. The Primer takes the form of a synthesis of book and film, capable of producing plots by drawing them directly from the reader. Stephenson's fictive invention of the Primer emulates all existing media into the universal archaic form of the book, which is however constructed with advanced nanotechnology and uses live actors to augment the interactive reading experience. *The Diamond Age* is set in a post-digital and post-national future, after the nano-technological revolution, featuring a strictly stratified society where the privileged class of the neo-Victorians evade extreme urban conditions by secluding themselves in a community that upholds the virtues, morals and customs of the Victorian era. This novel relates to the examples of the writers-in-residence and the Black Maria by the projection of a neo-Victorian society beyond the present, into the fictive future, bridging the centurial distance from the point of its creation. From the perspective of the bonding between reader and book, the close interactive relationship between the Primer and its pupil reflects the creative connections and reflexive production discussed in the first chapter of the thesis. This final example points to the potential of actualisation of architectural space inherent in narrative space. It departs from the ability to operate on time and space, mediated by a plotless book or a film or a hybrid of these, as in the Primer, where the plot is nonexistent until the book finds its exclusive reader. The Primer will be discussed in relation to the examples from the previous chapters, and finally, it will be analysed from the perspective of the new type of narrativity it suggests, although still in the form of a book: the game.

The spectacle of the individual reached its most extreme expression in the freak show, showcasing Siamese twins, dwarfs or giants or other sensational physical curiosities or deformities, even if it rarely occured to the audience that the "bearded lady" was most likely a man in drag. The freaks were, contrary to what one might have expected, well respected moneymakers, marginalised but not necessarily victimised.

Applying a theory of virtuality to the examples in this thesis invokes an understanding of space exposed to the process of its own making. In *Architecture from the Outside*, Elisabeth Grosz, philosopher and interpreter of Bergson, suggests that "the virtual is the realm of productivity, of functioning otherwise than its plan or blueprint, functioning in excess of design and intention." She continues: "This is the spark of the new that the virtual has over the possible: the capacity for generating innovation through an unpredicted leap, the capacity of the actual to be more than itself, to become other than the way it has always functioned."[1] My ambition to call a new kind of spatiality into play, by questioning its organisational forms, relates to the title of this chapter. Shelf life is an expression for a "use-by-date", in this context alluding to the life of a book, while suggesting the question "does it stand the test of time?" It is not just the possible fate of books warming shelves that is implied here. The development of media and its modes of retrieval put all traditional means of organisation of space and time in line of the question. What is the shelf life of architecture as we know it, and how will the contemporary notion of virtual reality stand the test of time? The answer is pending to this opening, if not rhetorical, question. The chapter pursues the discussion of plotlessness into the multiform and social character of the game as an instigator and merger of various forms of media. The game as extension of the self into experimental fields of interaction, strategy and communication, with all its openings on complex matters like codes, rules, models and patterns, has a lot of shelf life in it, but then again, the shelf is not the intended playing field. As the game expands to the making of worlds, bringing people from around the world into virtual action in these, and as it acquires strong cultural identification and since it has already exceeded the figures of the global film industry in turnover, the game might be the most important medium for both architectural and narrative expression.

The Virtual Residing in the Real

The philosophy involved with virtuality relates to many fields, especially to a long tradition of metaphysics and phenomenology, which feed into the "creation of worlds", complemented by studies in a wide range of research areas from narratology to neurology. An initial distinction needs to be made between the meaning of virtuality and virtual reality, as *virtuality* will be the outset for this discussion and *virtual reality*, in the contemporary cultural discourse, denotes a mediated application, often synonymous with cyberspace. There are nearly as many definitions and expectations on virtual reality as there are creators or potential fields of use, and the development of theories concerning virtual reality lies ahead of practice. The field where virtual reality is most consistently applied as a spatio-temporal "world creation" is in computer gaming, where the combination of digital networks and a graphic and/or narrative interactive techniques provides a platform for interaction in a virtual world. Virtual reality, according to the dictionary explanation, is an environment "generated by computer software, with which a user can interact realistically as by using a helmet containing a screen, gloves fitted with sensors, etc." The quality of being *virtual*, in the sense of "possessed of certain physical virtues or capacities, effective in respect of inherent natural qualities or powers", is today less used than the computer-related definition of virtual as "not physically existing as such but made by software to appear to do so from the point of view of the program or the user."[2] The virtuality in Huysmans, Goncourt and de Maistre is not generated by computer software, but still matches the requirements of digital virtuality: an immersive and interactive space, existing for and oriented around one user only. Furthermore, their physical spaces possess the capacity to *generate* (external) reality as a function of their (internal) stream of consciousness, which matches Bergson's description of virtuality as the ontological modality of duration. Bergson's virtuality is located somewhere between a spatio-temporal immersive construction of a parallel reality, and an agency of creation, inherent in the

The escape acts of Harry Houdini could not have been more symbolic of his time, as everyday urban life had by then become a struggle for living space. His performances were dramatised as double suspense: his own struggle for release was reproduced in the spectators, their attention fettered to the act before them, until that moment when Houdini broke free from his chains, and the audience in turn then being released from their own suspense. Well aware of his uniqueness as a performer, Houdini patented some of his acts.

mind. This expanded sense of virtuality as a generative quality of both internal and external space, brings us further towards an understanding of its creative potential than the dictionary definition of an environment that only appears to exist from a vantage point of view.

Elisabeth Grosz exposes the difficulties involved in explaining what the virtual is: "One cannot of course directly specify what a virtual is, for insof ar as it is, insofar as it exists, it exists as actual. In the process of actualisation, the virtual annuls itself as such in order to re-emerge as an actual that thereby produces its own virtualities. At best one can specify what the virtual may produce, what effects or differences it may generate."[3] Virtuality is already residing in the real, which makes the term virtual reality a tautology. Instead of prevailing in a concept of virtual reality fixated by wired contraptions, Bergson allows us to enter another end of the media spectrum, into a development of a spatio-temporal realm governed by intuition and imagination, where a book might as well represent the apex of technological sophistication. The reason for bypassing a computer-generated definition of virtuality is to explore the nature of the narrative virtual space brought forward in the examples of the previous chapters, where virtuality is a mode of production of space, rather than a competing space in itself. The virtuality present in the examples from literature and film is one that is not limited to technology but inherent in a process of forming and actualising space, as transformation and augmentation, of the real; in short, the capacity of making a difference.

A 19th Century Theory of Virtuality

From the year 1900, as professor in philosophy at the *Collège de France*, Henri Bergson represented what would be called the "new philosophy".[4] He was awarded the Nobel price in literature in 1927, for a line of important works, among which we find his ideas about virtuality developed in, for example, *Matter and Memory* (1896), *Time and Free Will* (1889), *Creative Evolution* (1907) where he discusses the virtual as a process of self-differentiation of life, and in his short *Introduction to Metaphysics* published in 1903. As one of the first philosophers to speak about virtual reality, related to but independent of the sense given to the term today (computer-generated, digital virtual reality), Bergson is read here as a philosopher of the virtual contemporary to the architectural fictions under investigation. This discussion will be structured along some of the key terms in his philosophy, starting with his concepts of time and space, followed by the aspects of the mind that experiences them, that is, memory, perception, intuition and imagination.

The discussion in this thesis has expanded from the novel via the film medium to the game as environments synthesising time and space. These media – the novel, the film and their potential convergence into, for example, the game – provide us with alternative uses of (narrative) time and (architectural) space as organisation and control of (plotless) fiction. The virtual spaces created and/or controlled by the authors, spectators and users exemplified in the previous chapters may not be defined as virtual in the technological sense, but virtual in the sense of a mode of experience and production of the kind of dimensions explored in imagination, in memory, and in dreams.

Bergson's virtuality is linked to his theory of time and space, and to the modes of retrieval of time and space; perception and memory, aided by imagination and intuition. Time in Bergson is the endless becoming (other than itself) where space denotes the relations between entities in the flow of time. Two types of time coexist and are mutually dependent, the actual (present) and the virtual (past). Bergson places the self in this dynamic flow of reality, the *durée* or durational time, a continually giving (unfolding) reality, a "work-in-progress". The present is the intersecting point of our perception and action: the site of duration. The terms Bergson employs to describe reality are all aspects of fluctuations in time and space: reality is subject to flow, duration and motion. The mind, by aid of intuition and memory, makes it possible to "tap" onto the flow of reality, to sample positions within it as well as recall actions. These features of the mind are in direct connection to – and corresponding forces with – duration (reality). Memory functions like a grappling hook that pulls you into the future by translating perceptions into experiences. Duration as a temporal flow contains potential times, various possibilities of actualisation accessible to creative thought, in other words, a virtual multiplicity. In duration, every moment passes through the whole of its virtual past, which links up to a coexistence of the past in the present. This would explain Bergsonian virtuality as a parallel, and not alternative reality. The virtual and the real is a non-oppositional pair, since the virtual is what is contained – but not actualised – in the flow of the real. The opposite of the virtual is thus the actual, which cancels virtuality in the moment of its actualisation. The virtual is the multiplicity of parallel options, a layer of possibilities of changing reality. Reality is the actualised state of matter, the coming into form of all potential forms.

A man tries to alight from the omnibus in the era of the "*crinolinomanie*": an effort worthy of Houdini himself. Through the dictates of fashion, women are paradoxically occupating public space at the expense of male territory. The limited motion scheme of the women, clad in steel-frame hoop skirts, ultimately also impacted on the mobility of the men.

At the core of Bergson's critique of the metaphysical tradition is the general neglect of the constant becoming (*devenir*) of things. Space is the environment of the actual, of the materialised, a place of possible division of itself and of matter within.

The concept of *durée* is in Bergson embraced as a continuous giving and becoming. Duration is the multiplicity of succession and differentiation that keeps together the different tendencies and modalities of the mind. The durational consciousness is both identical and alterable, meaning it is both a keeper of its identity and an altering force of itself. The conscious mind is keeping together the past while anticipating the future. As the sum of our history, the mind and its actions are rooted in the past. Consciousness develops in a flow of events that cannot be foreseen, in such a way that not even the artist painting a portrait knows the final result of his efforts. Intuition and memory constitute the self's experience of itself. The writer-in-residence makes use of this insight in his isolation, as his agenda is to gain unmediated access to his inner imagination, and ensure the direct access of the self to the self.

Virtuality as a Host Dimension

In my licentiate thesis *The Dying Dreamer – Architecture of Parallel Realities*, Huysmans' *A Rebours* was analysed from the perspective of contemporary notions of virtual reality, suggesting that the fictional space presented in the novel is a proto-digital virtuality.[5] The virtual world created and used by the Baron is identified by "a new kind of existence: the integration of the body in an immersive virtuality, a dreamer-friendly interface packed with soft- and hardware to relieve everyday spleen in any century."[6] His domestic space has numerous functions in common with the computer-user-interaction and the implications for the body in cyberspace. Furthermore, Huysmans' narrative structure for the novel is congenial with navigational and organisational methods applied in digital networks. The narrative form is akin to the reading we are accustomed to in digital format, hypertext, where reading of one text allows detours, sidetracks, archive visits, catalogue posts and a multitude of possibilities that are present at once, making choice an operational aspect of a writing/reading system which begins to dissolve the concept of one linear plot. A set of environmental characteristics in des Esseintes' interior reveal similarities in both design and function to some expected qualities of a digital virtual reality. The residence itself could be regarded as a memory archive or a hard-drive into which the Baron inserts different software to operate on the data stored in the mansion. His environment will assist him in the time travelling and mind-altering activities, often of synæsthetic character.

For a growing proportion of the population, life in the 19th century was divided into work and play, separated in time and space, creating a double life that was to culminate in holiday celebrations with its mixture of high and low culture, decadence and sea breeze, elegance and vulgarity, prudeness and exhibitionism, ballrooms and freakshows, afternoon teas and recreational drugs. High society had lead the way to seaside resorts as Blackpool, Southend and Brighton, where the first generations of holidaymakers strolled along the *West Pier*, a steel construction designed by the engineer Eugenius Birch in 1866.

Among the identified virtual features of the space is the Baron's way of interacting with objects, in the same way that a computer-user might click on *icons*, the effort- and timeless mode of bodiless travelling reminiscent of the *virtual displacement* enabled by computer games and of the Internet. Besides the navigational functions embedded in certain objects, the rooms are fitted to trigger the imagination of this one particular user, who has invested his æsthetic codes in the *user-specific* domestic interior with the extended function of virtual transportation into fantastic dimensions. Des Esseintes ultimately experiences that a complete replacement of physical reality with a virtual existence of the self results in disembodiment. Computer interaction as we know it, despite efforts to integrate body motion sensors and various immersive equipment, is still based on the perception modes that is best supported by digital systems; sight and sound, combined with mechanical control devices such as a mouse or joystick.

With a predominantly visual and auditive perceptual form of interaction, the body is, in Huysmans and in de Maistre, a burdensome matter, a simple beast carrying the sophisticated mind machinery. De Maistre goes so far in his dichotomy of body and mind as to refer to the body as the beast, "la bête", grounded in physical space. As Bergson puts it, "the body is only a place of meeting and transfer, where stimulations received result in movement accomplished".[7] The freedom of the mind, on the other hand, is exercised by journeys in both time and space, dissolving the organisation of both aspects of reality while applying a Bergsonian approach of duration. To Bergson, the body is just an image in another system of images: the material world. Regarding the material world, including the body, "interiority and exteriority are only relations among images", matter is thus an aggregate of images.[8] Although the domestic situation is important to the writers-in-residence, the body "has the power to choose and decide a step of action among several that are materially possible. The objects surrounding a body, therefore, reflect its possible action upon them. It is for this reason that it is capable of *virtual* action."[9] Virtual reality unites the general characterisation of an environment or image "possessed of certain physical virtues or capacities, effective in respect of inherent natural qualities or powers", and Bergson's virtuality as the ontological modality of duration as (external) reality and as (internal) stream of consciousness.

Perception and Memory

According to Bergson, time and space are fundamentally asymmetrical and heterogeneous, with respect to the fact that time has direction. The implication of this is that we can move freely in space and not in time. Memory, "a synthesis of past and present with a view to the future",[10] is different from perception, it is virtual.[11] Perception is what we use to create models and abstractions, it is a "measure of our virtual action upon things".[12] Memory and perception constitute experience. Memory is what makes the past accessible. Perception operates on actuality, and "indicates the possible action of our body on others"[13]. Bergson has also approached an understanding of synæsthesia, the conjoined perceptive mode so favoured by des Esseintes, as illustrated by his synæsthetic invention, the "mouth organ", the instrument that composes drinks, implying an audio-gustatory convergence. With the example of the scale of musical tones, where generally a high note gives the impression of a higher location in space, synæsthetic perception is something that occupies both interiority and exteriority in perception and space.

The idea of recreational seaside resorts, following a few rules, still govern leisure life today: something for everybody, providing for all genders, ages and preferences with a mix of shopping, restaurants, thrills and sensations in the form of daredevil divers, femmes fatales and burlesque singers, as well as flower gardens, aquariums and string quartets. Children were treated to junk food, carousels, donkey rides and rental paddling boats. The only difference from modern-day holiday resorts are the actual bathing routines, where in the former times bathing was preferably in the form of being safely inside a swimming wagon driving through the water.

The chapter *The Dying Dreamer – Looking into Huysmans' Virtual Worlds* of my licentiate thesis identifies three temporal modes in *A Rebours*. The Baron shifts, with the *present* as "base camp", to either *revived* space – recollections from memory – or *evoked* space where he transfers himself into the imaginary world of a painting or a text or simply a scent, losing himself in the possibilities of that scenario.[14] The relocations expand the space of the novel, and at the same time emphasises the (self-chosen) limitations of his existence. Translated into Bergsonian time modalities, a shift of perspective takes place, without losing the multitude of temporal states of the mind. The present state is arrived at from memory, which means it is accessed from the past and not reversely, retrieved from the future. The present is directed simultaneously ahead and back in time, it is not dividing two kinds of time modes but joining them. This is what happens in the three temporal modes in *A Rebours*: present time joining the virtualities of memory and imagination. Recollection of a memory is a process of gradual calling into perception: first we become conscious of the act of retrieval. When the memory region is found, we try to pull the object into focus, making adjustment as if holding a camera. The recollection remains virtual until focus is achieved, when the memory passes from virtual to actual. Once the recollection becomes distinct and coloured, it tends to imitate perception, but still its roots are in the virtuality of the past.

Baron Haussmann was responsible for one of the most radical urban renewal projects in modern times: the fifteen-year long reconstruction of the city of Paris, known as the Haussmannisation era. He was assigned the prefecture of the Seine in 1853, a position that licensed him, on direct orders from the Emperor, to realise the dreams of the state, at the loss of complexity in certain parts of Paris, and in the interest of organising and controlling the remainding parts.

As the Baron quite consciously engages in experiences outside of the immediacy of his physical present, he claims to occupy all temporality of time and all spatiality of space, that is, virtuality. He displays an understanding of the Bergsonian notion of duration and location as specific points, only when plotted by movement and action. His domestic space is not merely a container for himself and his objects, but the point of actualisation of itself, a passage from one state of space and time to another. He is exercising his memory to access the virtual past, and he is training his imagination to overcome the specificity of space, as when his intentions to take a trip to London is over-shadowed by the impressions he gets while trying to get there: filling all his senses, the virtual London trip proves far superior to any "real travelling" – as his mind was already set for a space there was no need to seek it out on location or experience it in the geographically correct position. The validity of the mind-travelling experience could be explained in the words of Bergson: "But we must not confound the data of the senses, which perceive the movement, with the artifice of the mind, which recomposes it. The senses, left to themselves, present to us the real movement, between two halts, as a solid and undivided whole. The division is the work of our imagination, of which indeed the office is to fix the moving images of our ordinary experience, like the instantaneous flash which illuminates a stormy landscape by night."[15]

In Bergson, time is neither linear nor cyclical, but multiplied and complex, and space is more of a material accessory to events and changes taking place within itself. His theory represents all the diversion and multiplicity that the plot aspires to organise: time and space do not behave in a plotted way, but the plot is used to transform the heterogeneous, serial, indeterminate, interrelated space and time into a singular line of successive events in neutral space. The writer who seeks to organise space, but not time, does not achieve a plot. The result is instead the experience of casting oneself into spatiality, "to become spatialised with all of space".[16] The process of the writers-in-residence, who are operating on space by the acts of memory, perception and imagination, is a process of individualisation of space, as Grosz describes it: "In opening up space to time, space becomes amenable to transformation and refiguring; it becomes particular, individualised."[17]

Intuition and Imagination

Bergson is an advocate of intuition and imagination as important sources of absolute knowledge. He even suggests intuition as a new style of philosophical thinking, modelled after duration. In order to illustrate the concept of absolute knowledge, where the meaning of "absolute" has more to do with intuitive understanding (from within) than with completeness (a state which would only be observable from a point outside the object), he uses the example of a fictive character in a novel whose experiences are shared by a reader.[18] The novel character is brought to life by an author. Actions and words pass through the fictive figure. If there were a possibility for the reader to merge with the character, only for a moment, there would be no sequence or distance to organise the knowledge about the character. There would be an absolute knowledge only available to an unmediated situation where the observer merges with the observed. Any form of representation or semiology positions the observer outside the observed, according to Bergson, which is why history, description and analysis keeps us outside absolute knowledge, from a relative viewpoint where perspective and positioning are defining the observed. As long as we rely on symbols and history, the unique remains out of reach, since the observed is judged by general assumptions on likeness and associations. The outside position can never disclose the essence of the thing, on the contrary: from the exterior position, analysis is the mode of operation, essentially a process of

Thomas A. Edison's *General Electric Company* was responsible for the first electric streetlights installed in 1882 in Paris, Berlin, New York and London. Thanks to outdoor gaslighting and later the electric streetlight, workers could do double shifts, as shown in this picture of nocturnal road work in Paris 1877, in the dawn of the 24-hour city.

reducing the observed to familiar concepts and arrange them into symbols. Merged with the thing, knowledge comes as an instant sympathy with this internalisation. It is by use of imagination that one may transfer oneself to this inner dimension, where no further positioning and no more symbols are needed for intuitive understanding, or what Bergson calls sympathy, with the observed. Thus intuition is opposed to analysis as a mode of understanding of reality.[19]

Bergson complements the example of our relation to the novel character with the viewer's position vis-à-vis a photographic image. We experience the picture from a mediated position in terms of a particular viewpoint causing a loss of (three-dimensional) information. The same incompleteness and entropy of nuance is experienced by a reader of a translation of a poem, or a translation between any semiologic systems.[20] Analysis is a translation to symbols, and a symbol is a reduction. Walter Benjamin discusses the notion of originality and dissipation of meaning in the age of mechanical reproduction using the same examples as Bergson – the photograph and the translation – in texts like "The Task of the Translator" and "The Work of Art in the Age of Mechanical Reproduction".[21] The 20th century begins with the philosophical questions of the implications of the new forms of representation, concerning the broken entirety of the environment (the photographic image is a record but also a loss of information), and the distance produced by deviation from the original (as in the translated poem). A general loss of control of representations occurs, as we get more instruments to create them and a more diverse field of experiencing representations, of which cinema is only one. The multitude of cultural expressions and their modes of dissipation provide an image of reality as a faceted and circumscribed existence instead of one authoritative discourse.

Bergson claims that intuition, the sympathy with which one enters "the thing", is the only way of ensuing absolute knowledge, in contrast to analysis that reduces the thing to already known elements, not the unique and inexpressible, but what is common to the thing and things related.[22] Analysis works with symbols in a positivist scientific model. Intuition gives us the ability to merge with reality (synonymous with constant change), and imagination and memory allow us to navigate the continuous motion of all existence. Only a mind capable of memorising images can create coherence from the succession of images that is duration. With all the difficulties to gain knowledge of, and not least to transfer, reality from within, through intuition and not through analysis, there is one instance where we gather knowledge from within: our own personality, the duration of the self.

A Double Room

Looking at the literary interiors created by the writers-in-residence – Huysmans, Goncourt and De Maistre – it seems that the domestic interior served a double purpose; the isolation required for immersion in *imagination* and a transparency sustaining *intuition*, the mental view with the perspective of being on the inside looking out. The architecture of seclusion has to allow some sort of passage or controlled exchange to avoid cannibalistic tendencies of the mind. Baron des Esseintes' cyber-hermitage, as soon as it reaches a level of perfection and the latest hyperæsthetic experiment has exhausted his interest, numbs him into hibernation mode: "He had to live on himself, to feed on his own substance, like those animals that lie torpid in a hole all winter. Solitude had acted on his brain like a narcotic, first exciting and stimulating him, then inducing a languor haunted by vague reveries, vitiating his plans, nullifying his intentions, leading a whole cavalcade of dreams to which he passively submitted, without even trying to get away."[23] The interior could be seen as a domestic aspect of the mind itself: a tamed set of familiarity of representations.

In one of his prose poems, Charles Baudelaire precedes both Huysmans and Goncourt with the theme of a multiplied domestic sphere. In *La Chambre double*, a man dwells in the sanctuary of his domestic interior, "une chambre paradisiaque", when he is brutally disrupted from his floating dream world and forced to return by a fierce knock on the door.[24] The situation shows both the vulnerability and the efficiency of the illusion. Within this doubling of space, the doubling of self takes place as in the critical division of body and mind of the Baron, in the consciously declared double existence as thinker and "beast" (bête) in de Maistre, as well as in Goncourt's position with one foot in the 18th century with his collections and in his writings, and the other in modern Paris and his contemporary literary discourse. Their virtual creations bring about a division of the indivisible – the individual – into a dual being which enables a passage or a transformation between forms of existence. This idea of a multiplicity and projection of the self into virtuality is equivalent to the avatar in digital virtual creation as a figure representing the player in a computer game.[25]

The late 19th century media culture was changing, with the growing market for daily newspapers and journals. The amount and regularity of the press made news both more global and more local. With the daily newspaper and its mechanisms of commercialisation of the narrative, the amount of information available to any single reader was radically increased. The picture above illustrates the headline "Horse Smashed Cable Car Window" in *The New York World* in 1897.

Huysmans the inventor, Goncourt the collector, and de Maistre the prisoner, extend physical space into multiple existences. The narrative form is one mode of existence, within which several layers are contained; virtual modes of revived, evoked and present space, mind journeys, art and literary criticism, inventory lists and catalogue-like passages. The novel characters are all "travelling light" by means of their objects, artwork, books and interior decoration. However, it is not the plot driving the narrative along these trails. The mode of travelling is reflecting the condition of the reader. The mind creates or interiorises the narrative space, an experience that is reproduced in the reader's double existence; time is spent simultaneously in the space generated by the book and in the physical space occupied by the reader. Their virtual creations are based on an understanding of the immersive qualities of imagination and intuition, aided by an acute sensory perception that allow space to emerge by means of excitement of any sensory modality or combination of senses. In his perfumery laboratory, des Esseintes directs a journey exalted by scents – he moves across a meadow, through a field and into a city until the journey culminates in a sulphurous degenerated industrial landscape – in an environment mediated by olfactory sensations, displayed directly to the mind as images.[26] To Bergson, the *image* is "a certain existence which is more than that which the idealist calls a *representation*, but less than that which the realist calls a *thing*".[27] The image is neither interior (mental), nor exterior to the mind. What then of physical environment as image? Following that matter is "an aggregate of images", the domestic interior would be inhabitable as both thing and representation.

Bergson opposes himself to the division of subject and object: "The mistake of ordinary dualism is that it starts from the spatial point of view: it puts, on the one hand, matter with its modifications, in space: on the other hand, it places unextended sensations in consciousness. Hence the impossibility of understanding how the spirit acts upon the body or the body upon spirit."[28] In contrast to "ordinary dualism", the concepts of duration and virtuality in Bergson aim at bringing together psychology and metaphysics, "where subject and object coincide".[29] Matter, in the shape of duration, in effect, a succession of moments – and memory, the continuous product of perception – correspond to the basic essence of the novels studied here. Durational space is the field of play for perception and memory, where the writers-in-residence, protected by their isolation, experience the freedom of virtual creation: in the words of Bergson: "Thus, between brute matter and the mind most capable of reflection there are all possible intensities of memory or, what comes to the same thing, all the degrees of freedom."[30] The interaction between matter and mind, and the possibilities of different positioning of the subject in the imagery of space and memory, are what Huysmans and Goncourt describe, in their strict reduction to man and space, isolated but with access to the wide gap of virtual freedom between the traditional binary oppositions such as body and mind, space and time, interior and exterior reality.

Bookbonding

"'Open it', he said.
'How?'
Harv leaned toward her, caught the upper-right corner under his finger, and flipped it. The whole lid of the thing bent upward around a hinge on the left side, pulling a flutter of cream-coloured leaves after it."[31]

In *The Diamond Age*, a book has found its reader, a four-year old girl. Although she is not the intended owner of this unique volume, she fits the description of a young female that the book is programmed to bond with. This is not an ordinary book. Neal Stephenson has envisaged the future of the book as an object, which on the first encounter with its reader recognises and activates its database to respond to all events and persons in relation to this particular person, in this case the young Nell, who has just "met" *The Young Lady's Illustrated Primer*.

The Primer is one of the main characters of *The Diamond Age*: a book, or rather an interactive device, created for the private education of a girl in the uppermost classes of a neo-Victorian society, though by theft gotten into the hands of a child at the bottom of the highly stratified society. The Primer has been programmed to bond with a four-year-old girl, a description that fits with Nell, although the exclusive volume was intended for a far more privileged child. The incredibly costly Primer project was commissioned by Lord Finkle-McGraw, as a gift for his granddaughter, with the intention of stimulating independent thinking and self-confidence, even to inspire some subversive ideas, as a complement to the traditional neo-Victorian upbringing and schooling that lie ahead of her. The duke is wise enough to understand that the highly segregated culture created in the wake of the collapse of the nation-states, where urban society has been divided into strata of enclaves, cannot withstand the reality outside its gates and rely on internal order and the ties that bind through Victorian discipline and protocol.

The *Statue of Liberty* was constructed by Gustave Eiffel and the sculptor Frederic-Auguste Bartholdi in Paris, from where she was shipped to New York in 1884. Although she is globally recognised as a symbol of liberty, most people are, however, unaware of the architectural freedom of form of its interior. This photograph, taken from below, inside the copper toga, provides a view of the demanding formless geometry that is comparable to the most advanced organically-shaped architectural projects of today.

There is no writer in the traditional sense involved in the making of the Primer. The closest resemblance to authorship might be assigned to John Percival Hackworth, an artifex (nano-technological programmer) of the company *Bespoke* – "a design rather than a production house" – and the architect of the Primer.[32] One of the plotlines of Stephenson's novel pursues the events of Hackworth's life after having compiled an illegal copy of the Primer for his own daughter, the copy that gets stolen and ends up in the hands of Nell. Yet another copy needs to be manufactured to compensate Hackworth's loss, whereby the storyline of *The Diamond Age* follows the development of the three Primers and their readers: Nell, Hackworth's daughter Fiona and the intended unique copy of Lord Finkle-McGraw's granddaughter. The dense plot of *The Diamond Age* builds upon the rectification of the intensions of the Primer project's initiator: a "unique copy" is not just a contradiction in terms, it is a violation of the principle of the book as a viral object.

The Primer could have been designed as a computer or shaped like a console or game box. Instead it has the archaic form and character of a book, with pages stacked and bound together to a familiar handheld device. Stephenson describes a book with all the characteristics of a fully developed virtual space, which can take the proportions of an opera or a cabinet, formatted in a media that treats text as architecture. With its ability to adapt to and grow with its reader, the Primer constructs a dynamic and continuous time-space, guiding the user through real and virtual environments for training and development, aided by "ractors", physical performers transmitted into the plot as a hybrid reader and actor. The plot reflects the development of the user herself, merging the role of author and reader into an interactive entity. By recording the environment of its assigned reader, the Primer will at any moment of reading incorporate the chart of the physical and psychological environment and reversely, use that chart to perform a dynamic mapping from its narrative database onto the reader's particular terrain.[33] We might apply *plot* for both a process of collecting data (plotting), and its result in the form of the storyline. First, the book plots a dynamic copy of the

A river-bend away from the *Statue of Liberty*, Lamarcus Thompson's *Switchback Railroad*, the "world's first rollercoaster", was constructed in 1884 at Coney Island. For ten cents a ride, it offered the sensation of mind-boggling speed and tremendous racket, experienced from a wooden wagon running along a double track.

architectural environment and position of the reader in space and time. Second, following the plotting of the space of the reader, the virtual plan collected from the mapping of her situation in the physical environment forms the organisation of a narrative plot: a storyline. Henceforth, having bonded with its reader, the Primer will always position the narrative in the absolute presence of the reader, using the actual space as a set and making its characters present within the narrative, for incorporation with the plot.

The nano-technological society described in *The Diamond Age* has developed from the ruins of our computer networks designed to meet the demands for privacy and security of a national monetary and political system. The cable television system that relied on passive consumers of entertainment was abandoned along with any structure designed for one-to-one connections, such as the telephone system. The infinite possibilities of a post-commodity world enters the world of *The Diamond Age* in the account of the matter compiler or MC: an almost alchemical production unit present in every household regardless of standard and in public spaces, a microwave-oven-like device that creates objects, garments, substances, household items, even furniture and synthetic food, from a diamond molecule structure which is a form of currency in itself.[34] The plot of *The Diamond Age* evolves from the matter-compiling society based on "feed" to a world recreated from "the seed", suggesting the same evolution for the financial system that the media system already had gone through, where humanity rebounds by committing to organic-mysticist holism.[35] The plot thus culminates with a return to the root sense of virtuality, *virtus*, or the virile force of life whose mode of actualisation is coded into the gene or the seed.[36] The convergence of all plotlines involves an embodied convergence of *techne* and *logos*, a merging of the roles of the hacker and the actor into an intuitive demiurge and creator of a new world order.

In the company of the Primer, Nell will move through all the steps on the hierarchy of needs, from security to self-fulfilment.[37] She escapes the brute environment of the Leased Territories to find sanctuary outside the urban density.[38] Nell is a so-called thete, a citizen of the Leased Territories that surround the gated communities where the higher social classes reside. As in contemporary large cities, the level of pollution decides the geographic separation of lower and higher classes: the leased territories are polluted with a fine dust smog of "toner", decaying nano-mites that have been working the airspace for different purposes, such as surveillance and recording. The neo-Victorian city *Source Victoria* in the New Atlantis clave is placed on the hills above the toner clouds.[39] Climbing the echelons of society after escaping from her abusive domicile, Nell finds a temporary home with a family of craftsmen in the residential clave called Dovetail, where she can safely withdraw into the narrative worlds of the Primer. The artisan population of Dovetail is appreciated by the "Vickys", the residents of the neo-Victorian society, who are the privileged customers of hand-made commodities. Her acutely acquired survival skills are in this new setting substituted for a rapid development of her intellectual abilities. Her brilliance will soon be discovered in her new harmonious environment and earn her an accommodated internship at a girl school academy in New Atlantis.[40]

The Ractor and the Wreader

The narrative of *The Diamond Age* contains the "meta-narrative" of the Primer. The story created for Nell by the Primer includes her alter ego Princess Nell, recurring as episodes set in a different typeface to distinguish it from the core text of *The Diamond Age*. Stephenson uses chapter titles in a Victorian novel style: a short disclosure of the direction of the narrative, for example: *"Hackworth departs from Dr. X's laboratory; further ruminations; poem from Finkle-McGraw; encounter with ruffians.*"[41] The alternating sections of core text and inserted episodes from the Primer follow the reader throughout the novel, until a point of convergence of the two plotlines occurs.

The text is the main narrative element of the Primer, to which is added animated illustrations and graphics. Stephenson's fictive invention of the Primer is a vision of a book that has done away with both author and plot, laying bare the power structure of the book as a cultural item: the author decides the plot and the reader is driven along the lines toward a closure, which is also in the hands of the narrator. *The Diamond Age* is not a plotless narrative, on the contrary, Stephenson creates a complex map of parallel and intersecting plotlines, subplots and connections that begin to disclose a creative world order revolution at the horizon. The Primer device, on the other hand, is plotless in a very accurate sense of the term, since it has no narrative content until it has a reader. The plot is generated by and from the reader and her immediate environment, which means that the role of the author is replaced by an artificial space-sensitive plot compiler. The outline or basic stuff of the story exists in the Primer in the form of a database of universal ideas mapped onto local cultures, mythological characters, folklore, symbols, religious elements, all in all "a catalogue of the collective unconscious."[42] Drawing from the archive of folktale and mythology, the necessary props and characters are employed for the narrative

It would require a further 75 years for an invention of Paul Nipkow, patented in 1884, to become a household appliance: an electromechanical viewing machine, capable of producing images of visible objects at a distance, in short, a television. Similar televisual machines were developed after Nipkow's, many of them as two-way communication devices, functioning like a videophone. However, since the beginnings of broadcasting and, subsequently, the ubiquitous media of television, television has come to symbolise the relationship between a commercial sender and a passive receiver.

immersion, for example the trickster figure who has different names and shapes but is universal in its function; the Raven, the Coyote, *Loke* in Nordic mythology, the Sumerian *Enki*, the Greek *Hermes* and *Prometheus* are all instantiations of the hero character of the *hacker* in Stephenson's mythology.[43] Hackworth, the programmer of the Primer, describes its responsive process of synthesizing the reader's physical space with the bank of universal imagination. Having found its designated reader "…thenceforth it will see all events and persons in relation to that girl, using her as a datum from which to chart a physical terrain, as it were. Maintenance of that terrain is one of the book's primary processes. Whenever the child uses the book, then, it will perform a sort of dynamic mapping from the database onto her particular terrain."[44] Nell is represented by her alter ego "princess Nell" in the plot derived from her physical existence by the Primer, which also reflects her mental and physical states in order to help her. If Nell is sad or hungry, "princess Nell" displays the same symptoms and guides the physical Nell in the direction of improving her condition.

The stories that the Primer generates for the education and solace of Nell are, to their form, archaic storybook tales. Nell's sinister existence and neglected childhood is transformed into a tale where the residential block turns into a dark castle and her restricted life space surrounded by urban wilderness is an island. This artificial distance to physical space generates a narrative model, a familiar environment but with a sense of "other-worldliness" added to meet the young reader's need of both excitement and security. Princess Nell, the young girl's alter ego, escapes from the Dark Castle – the residential block where she grew up, and on her way she has to fight pirates and trolls – dangerous and harmful people. The stuffed animals she carries with her are scanned into the stories as companions and take on different roles to meet Nell's needs: Peter and Dinosaur teach her survival skills, Duck has more compassionate qualities to teach her empathy and ethics, and Purple will offer intellectual and emotional guidance for the teenaged Nell. The ractive Primer is plotless in the sense of being programmed to create any plot from the information gathered from the reader and her environment. The term *ractive* is constructed from re-active reading and acting built into the media device, linked to the services of a *ractor*. Nell's Primer is connected to the ractor Miranda (cunningly named after the naïf in Shakespeare's *The Tempest*), whose body is fitted with a sensor grid that scans her actions and facial expressions for mapping onto characters active in the narrative. The Primer mediates her actions through the tale figures, and compress and filter Miranda's voice into different personalities. Miranda is working for a high-profile ractive company, where she gets the more advanced racting assignments by virtue of the quality of her dermal grid of implants that is plotting her body into action in the interactive mediatron productions. An assigned ractor is the most sophisticated type of interaction: a real person doing the character impersonations that – in a less advanced medium than the Primer – might as well be animated by simple software robots. The interactive relationship between Nell and Miranda (who is anonymously hidden by the characters she embodies) starts with an intensive session mediated by the Primer: "Because the way that the ractive was hooked up, she didn't

In 1884, the *Greenwich Meridian* was accepted worldwide as the zero meridian for global time (GMT). Before the introduction of GMT, the several time zones and local systems that existed complicated transportation and communication. Synchronised time was crucial for international railway traffic and broadcast services. The longitudinal timelines, intersected by the physical network of railway lines, enabled controlled transfers in time and space, and formed a pattern that is still used today as a term for our most recent and perhaps most important media device: the internet.

get direct feedback from her counterpart on the other end. She assumed it was a little girl. But she couldn't hear the girl's voice. Miranda was presented with screens of text to be read, and she read them. But she could tell that this process of probing and focusing was being directed by the girl. /.../ Before she signed off on it [the ractive session], she checked the little box labelled MARK HERE IF YOU WOULD LIKE A CONTINUING RELATIONSHIP WITH THIS CONTRACT. The relationship box, they called it, and it only came up with higher-quality ractives, where continuity was important."[45]

The increasing frequence and facilitation of transport and communication set the population of the world in motion and increased the exchange of narratives on all levels, from colonialism to the migration of people from the perifery to the central nodes. With the greater mobility of workers, large cities became destinations, towards which smaller cities were merely stations along the railway. This increasing mobility had a direct impact on people's lives, not least on the street level.

Once Nell has mastered reading, the Primer advances to unvoiced text, but before then, it functions as a screen where the ractor Miranda brings life to the characters of Nell's own story. The *ractor*, combining the roles of reader and actor, is matched by a neologism from Marie-Laure Ryan in *Narrative as Virtual Reality* to illustrate "the accession of the reader to the role of the writer": the *wreader*.[46] This term is used to denote the new role of the interactor within a hypertextual environment. Still, the reader, as co-creator of a hypertext, has more of the character of selector of trails and paths through the hypertext. These merged roles illustrate the detachment from the physical body, or rather the integration of the body with the body of the text.

When the ractor Miranda signs in for the job at the ractive company, she is trusted with a secret of the business of simpler ractives. The ractor does not enjoy full freedom for the sake of satisfaction of the customer/viewer: "Computer decides where you go, when. Our dirty little secret: This isn't really ractive, it's just a plot tree – but it's good enough for our clientele because all the leaves of the tree – the ends of the branches, you understand – are exactly the same, namely what the payer wants, you follow?"[47] The cynical return to "passive" form is due to the fact that the clientele, given a choice, display very predictable preferences. Fiction films still exist, in the same way that we enjoy black and white or silent films in cinematographic societies. Evolution of moving pictures is in the nanotechnologcial era divided into sophisticated entertainment systems that are inhabited in new ways, and a ubiquitous type of recording that takes place nearly everywhere by cinestats, as a security camera system called sky-eye. Aerostats of infinitesimal size would congregate to record for example criminal activities, then summon another type of nano-device with the purpose of tagging the victim and the suspects as part of the crime investigation.[48] Nanotechnology enables every type of surface to display animations; wrapping paper, boxes, clothes etc, so film is transgressive to package and pattern design. The media entertainment central of *The Diamond Age* future, the mediatron, still shows 20th century "passives" (as opposed to the "ractives") for the less interactive audience, and for the cult value of non-interactive projected films.[49] In the Primer, the medium of the book and the medium of film merge into an interactive story, generated by the reader and her environment.

The Book as an Anachronistic Artefact

In a science fiction novel like *The Diamond Age*, the artefact of the book stands out as anachronistic element. The archaic and anachronistic qualities of the book are evident in the setting of a nanotechnological society capable of producing even animated wrapping-paper. The magic and symbolic value of the book as an object are enforced and finally lead up to the information revolution and a global new order where the women raised by Primers will have the key roles. However sophisticated the Primer is technologically, it retains the form of a book, although it has more in common with a computer game. Apart from the fact that it is æsthetically in accordance with the neo-Victorian culture, the book has qualities that ensure its survival, even in a nanotechnological future. Marshall McLuhan argues that the book-printing process was revolutionary not just in terms of multiplicity of information – by an increasing number of available copies – but of mobility; the accessibility of the book where- and whenever.[50] The quantity of books was as important as the quality of portability of the book. The Primer, designed as a book, does not require any external equipment, since nano-scaled technology supplies the device with power. Being a book, the Primer does not attempt to "disembody" its reader, in the way that a digital interactive interface would separate body and mind, instead it incorporates the existing environment into the narrative by appropriation of the immersive qualities in it: spatial, temporal and emotional.[51] Katherine Hayles reminds us that "embodiment is always instantiated, local, and specific".[52] Instead of violating the local and specific body, the Primer merges the time and space of the reader with a virtual narrative aided by creative agencies embedded in the object (sensors and plot compilers)

Between 1860 and 1900, a new type of environment was established in Paris: *les grands magasins*, or *magasins des nouveautés*. The department store borrowed the cast iron structure and glass atrium from the architecture of train stations, like *Les Grands Magasins du Bon Marché*, built in 1872. The *grand escalier* was modeled from the opera, a large staircase where customers would pass to see and be seen, functioning as a kind of vertical catwalk, orientating view and gallery at the same time.

and the ractor (a generic acting body giving a personal performance). Interaction takes place on both sides of the "page". The merged media of book and film into the multimediated reading of the Primer, is immersive in the same way that any novel could be, but also agencied in the reader's space, offering an interactive setting that mirrors the reader's own physical space. The book retains its respectability and aura of privacy in the nanotechnological future of *The Diamond Age*. The book and its serene mode of interaction is socially accepted and fully internalised as an image of civilisation. Reading is an activity that is encouraged and a book is most often considered harmless, particularly in the hands of a child. The commodity of the book became an important signifier of status in Victorian society, with its interest in collections and museums. The book in particular had a prominent role in the bourgeois domestic interior, with its symbol value for an educated class with inherent self-confidence issues.[53] Along the lines of the æsthetic and traditional values of the neo-Victorians, the Primer is designed and featured as a book.

Stephenson's novel describes a future society that not only socially, but also materially, seems like a regression to Victorian society. This particular anachronism is pertinent to the genre called "steampunk" or "steamclash", a subgenre of speculative fiction that returns to the visions of Jules Verne and his likes, sometimes called "clockwork punk".[54] The "punk" of the genre name is a pun on cyberpunk, but instead of, or alongside with, the convergence of digital media with the body, steampunk fantasizes the Victorian era technology – steam engines, clockwork automata, the difference engine – crafted and utopian machinery resounding so well with the desire of converging the beauty of craft and the peak of technology; artificial intelligence rendered in brass and teak, so to speak. It is however not simply the tantalising æsthetics of Victorianism that serves the plot in *The Diamond Age*, it also points at the class and gender differences of 19th century society, against which the subversive roles of the girls (who aided by their Primers start a humanist revolution) are created. The Victorian era bears resemblance to contemporary society with respect to the (actual and perceived) advancements in technology and the existential problems accompanying the extension of perception and information processing (speed and performance in the development of media, transport, entertainment, appliances etc), which is why it is so smoothly adaptable to science fiction literature. The strict social codes of Victorian life are revealed in *The Diamond Age* as one manifestation of a society governed by the principle of control. Protocol stands not only for the etiquette that governs human interaction, it also denotes the set of rules governing the exchange of data in for example a communication system.

The Victorian period valued crafted detail and materiality, as an effect of the changes in consumer culture during the era.[55] The modes of production evolved from manufacturing of unique objects to industrial mass production of commodities, offering the consumer a choice between the status of novelty and the status of handicraft. The artisan qualities fused with technology in steampunk fiction may be a response to the failure of creating desirable products and media devices for the contemporary consumer market, although this favouring of craft and craftsmanship is displaced to an era of industrialised production of commodities. Authentic steampunk has the ambition to liberate the machine from efficiency and advocate for a design by desire and dreams. The Victorian "mass-produced" object balances on the boundary between man and machine, as a perfect reflection of the society with its feet in the countryside and its head in the city. There is no conflict in the combination of Victorian design and nanotechnology, simply because the technology has evolved beyond visibility, whereby the AI and processing power is inserted into an object that has all the characteristics of, say, a fountain pen, but with the processing power and storage capacity of a hefty computer thanks to its design and physiognomy on a sub-molecular level. This scale naturally obliterates many arguments of form and function in terms of taste and decides that the "ground zero" of neo-Victorian product design is the 19th century æsthetic code, to the extent that a person-sized vehicle is given the shape of a metal horse, a "chevaline" saddled up for ultra-speed negotiation of the intra-clave causeway.[56]

The great department stores, such as the *Grands Magasins du Louvre* (1860), *Le Printemps* (1874), *Bon Marché* (1872), and Coin de Rue (1860), had many functions beyond commercial trading. They became important social and cultural scenes, with the ambition of educating its customers, mostly female, in modern lifestyles. The stores doubled as concert halls and as exhibition spaces, and included lecture halls and function rooms where language and music were taught. Women could safely spend time in this public space, while the men spent their time playing cards or reading in the store's library or smoking rooms.

Nanotechnology takes place in a scale where laws that govern matter visible to the eye behave differently. Artificial creation on nano-level is mimicking nature and its structure of materials with desirable qualities, for example a synthetic mother-of-pearl that combines a perfect equilibrium of elasticity and shock resistance, which has proven useful for military purposes.[57] The structural principle in nano-scale reminds us of the design principle of Aristotelian physics: the act of imitation of nature is in nanotechnology taken to its atomic limits, the closest imitation possible of nature's perfection. Scientists studying nano-particles have to unlearn the control and governing principles that characterise engineering. Solutions that are evident in visible scale do not apply at nano-level, where electrons are small enough to escape from a system governed by rigid mechanics. Organic structures contain their own conditions for propagation, and use soft protein programming to create a low-entropy system with harmoniously compatible components. A chair, or an entire home, may be woven into shape by nano-particles instructed by a minimum of governing code. Finally after a global process of deconditioning in terms of both production and consumption, we could quite possibly witness, as Stephenson suggests, after the diamond age revolution, a chair grow from a seed. Stephenson, as a utopian writer, imagines a post-commodity era, working with the laws of nature instead of against them, ideally replacing the old economy with the great equalizer of renewable sources of energy. The Victorian era of mass production and mass distribution of media marked the beginning of immaterial economy based on ideas (intellectual and copyright industries), and a proliferation of services in relation to product development, for example advertising and marketing. The progression from a digitally networked global economy to a suggestion of a more organic organisation is a step in the direction of the most basic form of virtuality, and at the same time the most potent: in the power, *virtus*, is the force to actualise itself, its potential, *virtualis*.[58] Both virility and potency designating male power originate in this etymology. The presence of the oak in the acorn, as Aristotle would have argued, is an image of virtuality as something in possession of the force to develop into actual existence.

From Page to Stage

The sites for the media investigated in the previous chapters of this thesis have been found in the late 19th century, at seminal points of development in literature and cinema. The writers-in-residence Huysmans and Goncourt had retired, in disdain of the city and the undifferentiated mass consumer culture, to the domestic interior where a generative loop of architectural space and narrative would generate "catalogue narratives" or "inventory novels" and inspire further æsthetic experimentation.[59] The interior world of space informing text and vice versa is a closed world, designed from imagination and intuition, customised for their creators' highly individualistic tastes. The authors show little interest in developing a plot; the character's interaction with the setting is exceptionally favoured in this narrative form. The inhabitants of the interiors narrated in *A Rebours* and *La Maison d'un artiste* share a perspective of being on the inside looking out. Their architecture admits no origins or models, aspiring to be as unique and independent as possible. Although they indulge in antiques, art and literature, it is the personal selection and staging of the object that counts.

The world's first indoor film studio, the Black Maria, is a parallel example of arbitrary architecture, with the designated purpose of experimentation in moving images. The functional principles of the media generated the form of the building, and vice versa. The designer, William K. L. Dickson, was not claiming any architectural ambitions when he constructed the building like a camera: light, mobile and phototropic, bearing more resemblance to the police wagon it was nicknamed after than a regular building or, for that matter, any other purpose-built film studio ever since. The films produced in the Black Maria were displayed in the kinetoscope, a wooden cabinet allowing a single viewer at the time, looking

The 19th century department stores became centres for cultural education, marketing the *shopping experience* as much as the commodity. Our present-day lifestyle consumerism is modelled on this first generation of shoppers, in the sense that we still think in terms of novelty value and seasonal changes and that we are subject to the same mixed feelings towards the shopping experience as the female consumer of the 1880s: conquest and guilt, punishment and reward, need and excess.

from the outside in, sealed off from the surroundings while looking into "another world", only to find the kinetoscope films showing almost a mirror image of the spectator: a person in front of an apparatus. The very sensation of the emerging film medium was of course the prospect of witnessing "animated photographs", in other words, made possible by a sequenced mobility of images placed in a mechanically driven loop before a lens and a light.

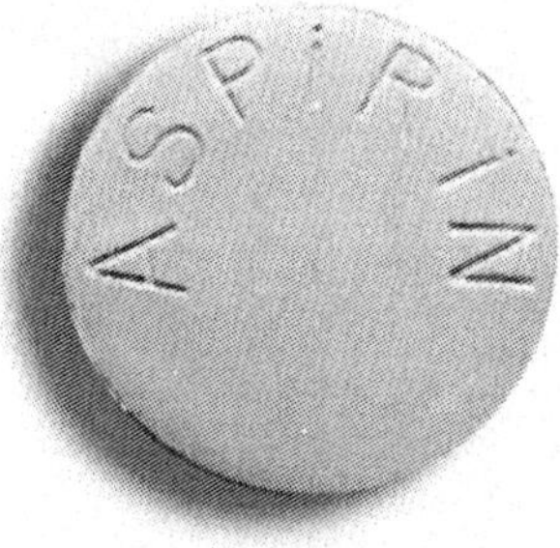

The drive of technological development of media has been towards immersive qualities, by involving, engaging and amplifying all the senses involved in experience. With regard to progress towards combined audio-visual media, visual techniques have been ahead of sound recording. Edison's phonograph experiments suffered from the limitations imposed by the applied storage media: wax-rolls. It was first in 1899 that sound was recorded on magnetic wire. Aspirin was invented the same year.

The body is the centre of perception, mobile in physical space and equipped with a mind that habitually wander into virtual non-physical space, a quality celebrated by the writers-in-residence. The body may also be instrumented by means of technology, from the simple extension of the senses by interaction with media to more critical physical manipulations of cybernetic design, like the dermal grid of Stephenson's ractor. The Baron in *A Rebours* distinguishes himself as the most enthusiastic disciple of all things artificial, due to his agenda to reverse all things natural, including the metabolism of the human body. Goncourt, in turn, reminisces about the artificial manners and affected society of the 18th century, from which he collects fetishes like a mug formed after the breast of Marie Antoinette. The proto-cinematic technique was endowed with bodies, people and animals – from Eadweard Muybridge's motion studies of horses and women descending staircases, to the chrono-photographic gun of Etienne-Jules Marey to "shoot" birds with – a line of experiments culminating in the individual cult of the film star, once the film medium got "plotted" and the generic bodies had used up their roles in the pre-mature non-narrative films. The Black Maria housed productions starring cats and boxers in a varieté-kind-of-ambition level that in time would include more famous stage acts, attracted by the good name of Edison. Many concerns have been expressed regarding the "duplication of the real by means of technology"[60]: the split subject has its own manifestation in fiction; the doppelgänger as a gestalt in literature and film is an uncanny paradox: both the self and the other, illustrating a process of individuation that has gone out of control, a violation of boundaries of the self in space and time.

Katherine Hayles argues in *How We Became Posthuman* that "when narrative functionalities change, a new kind of reader is produced by the text", reflecting the argument of Jonathan Crary in relation to how optical devices form a new type of observer.[61] Functionality in this sense is the constitution of the interface: virtual reality equipment that allows the reader to negotiate the narrative space. Hayles challenges the "metanarrative about the transformation of the human into a disembodied posthuman", by calling up the resistance of the narrative to disembodiment: "With its chronological thrust, polymorphous digressions, located actions, and personified agents, narrative is a more embodied form of discourse than is analytically driven systems theory."[62] Technological determinism is suspended by the fact that "human being is first of all embodied being".[63] This is the lesson of des Esseintes, whose disembodied existence in imaginary worlds suspended by his architectural arrangements had to be aborted in the end. His methods of immersion were imperfect, paradoxically, for being too perfected. By replacing his physical existence with an æsthetic existence, the illusion became increasingly materialised and convincing, to the point where artifice had reached a critical moment, resulting in a conflict with the physical body. His ambition to reverse nature by the aid of architecture – an expression of the will to control the environment – is fuelled by the desire to lose control. This is a conflict that leads to a situation of conflicting dreams and designs, of clashes in virtuality and reality. Stephenson's "ractor" and Ryan's "wreader" are both embodiments of the threshold condition between actor/writer and the writer/reader. These agencies cooperate in the production of the narrative environment, although both the existence of the ractor and the environment are rendered as virtualities, there is human intuition and imagination at work in both the producing and the consuming end of the interactive system of the Primer.

The new roles of the ractors and wreaders, suggested in *The Diamond Age*, are the performative figures in a system of representational forms expanded from the writer-reader-relationship. Digital virtual reality is an environment that generally leaves the physical body at the keyboard, in fact no matter how sophisticated immersive technology equipment you have access to, the body remains, in the words of de Maistre, "the beast that is joined to our souls". Of the writers-in-residence in the first chapter, he is the author among the three with the most articulated account of the split subject. The disembodiment of the reader (perhaps the re-embodiment is appropriate for the emotional duplication of the Primer's reader) is reflected in the kinetoscope films produced by Edison in the early 1890s. Cabined in the kinetoscope was an anonymous man sneezing, in another strip another man was tipping his hat, in a peculiarly suspended plot. The internalised screen showed a kissing couple, as if you would have been sitting opposite them in a train.

Pre-mature cinema was filled with "anybodies", a generic display of motion of the body of one, two or a crowd, as in the popular scenes of workers leaving the factory, or a family strolling in the park. The body on the screen was an anonymous character recorded by a developing disembodying medium, which would soon develop a cult of the individual that would surpass any previous media; the movie star, a singularity comparable to the spectacular individualism of des Esseintes. An interesting turn of this concept of singularised celebrity individuals on the film screen is found in *The Diamond Age*, where interactive media called mediatron productions filter a generic actor into a specific role character, without bringing the features of the actor onto the stage, just the motion pattern of the body and the face, and the responsive acting ability. The virtual reality entertainment could thus reproduce any movie star from the era of the "passives" into action by mapping his or her features onto the ractor. The celebrity becomes reproducible, and the singularity of the celebrity is annulled in the virtual ractive system.

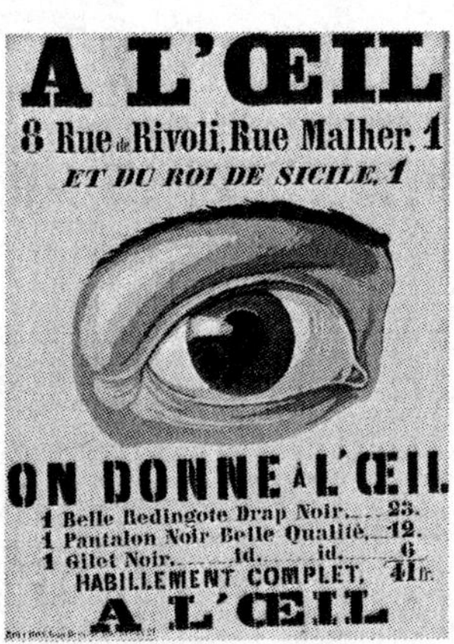

By the 1880s photography had become both a profession and a popular hobby. Photography replaced graphic techniques previously used in the press (engravings, etchings, mezzotints etc). While media embraced this new exactitude of representation, the magic of the photograph remained intact. Postmortem photographs picturing the dead, dressed and poised as sleepers, occurred during this era. At her death, Queen Victoria had a collection of more than a hundred thousand photographs.

Just like the ractors are name- and faceless embodiments of the story characters, fully rendered to the spectator, the environment of the film studio functions like a generic backdrop, an anonymous and versatile space, like the blackened interior of the Black Maria. The neutral backdrop obliterates the actual space of the actor; the darkness surrounding the action might as well be the darkness of the interior of the cabinet in front of which the kinetoscope spectator is situated.

Walter Benjamin argued that "the characteristics of the film lie not only in the manner in which man presents himself to mechanical equipment but also in the manner in which, by means of his apparatus, man can represent his environment."[64] Visual media, developing from the prevailing æsthetics of the film media towards interactive forms of media, obliterates the specific environment in which a specific actor performs. At this stage of development, we return to the neutrality of the stage and the anonymity of the actor, in order to create a versatile architecture for interactive narrativity. The environment is in visual production interchangeable and eliminated, for example by the simple use of a "green screen" used for digital separation of live action in front of the camera from the background. In the same way, Stephenson describes the technology that eliminates the individual form of the actor in the function of the ractor, whose only function is to embody the story.

The *Eiffel Tower* was the crowning event of the *Exposition universelle* in Paris, 1889. Gustave Eiffel had an office installed on the top floor of the tower, to which he invited Edison to a meeting. Their encounter has been immortalised in the form of waxworks placed in the office. The engineer and the inventor were literally "on top of the world," designing the structural frame and dictating the media of the new city.

Nineteenth century Victorian technology causes a crisis in the individual in relation to the mediated environment. A new kind of reader and spectator of these mediated environments has been traced: the split subject who experiences conflicting desire and repulsion towards the mediating artifice, at once imprisoned and liberated by technology. The experience is both private and public, singular and shared, but first and foremost, disembodied. Benjamin's identification of the unique existence (experience) being substituted by a plurality of copies is conflicted with an isolated experience mode, maintained by the design of the kinetoscope which here symbolises the conflict of the shift towards a collective media experience. The desire for mastery at play in the pioneering era of cinema stretched beyond the mere development of a new technique for direct representation of motion, after the first utilitarian applications in the service of science (by Muybridge and Marey), the marketable implementation was the next step in the process. After the novelty value had worn off the new media, the question of content was actualised. In a very brief moment of history, film was just (plotless) moving images, in this momentary lapse of authorship, the kinetoscope pictures were merely mirroring man in his most trivial postures. The commodity (the recorded film strip) is the temporal entrapment of an actor (the recording of an instant in time). The viewing situation repeats the entrapment in the kinetoscope cabinet with a peeping hole. This pay-per-view media format would lose ground to the collective projection screen format launched by the Lumière brothers in the mid-1890s. A century later, the profits of the game industry have exceeded those of the film industry, and Edison himself has entered the virtual world as the main character of a computer game based on his deeds as an inventor of new media and technology.

An Ecology of Virtuality

Walter Benjamin describes reading fiction as an act of passionate consumption in isolation: "A man listening to a story is in the company of the storyteller; even a man reading one shares this companionship. The reader of a novel, however, is isolated, more so than any other reader. /…/ In this solitude of his, the reader of a novel seizes upon his material more jealously than anyone else. He is ready to make it completely his own, to devour it, as it were."[65] The intimate relation between reader and book reminds us of Baron des Esseintes in Huysmans' *A Rebours*, who is capable of inhabiting all conceivable layers of fiction. Huysmans' novel is partly a book about reading books. Among the unique artefacts of des Esseintes' collection is the specially designed and bound editions of his favourite books:

in resonance with the contents, the volumes are composed of specific materials, customised graphic design and ornamentation, with carefully chosen colours and exclusive textures to encase the manuscript and customise the item. The books take on tactile, sensuous, almost erotic status, bound in individual fashion to make justice to the content. Des Esseintes takes the exterior of the book, the item itself, as seriously as he appreciates the immaterial qualities of its narrative contents. The virtual "inside" is mirrored by a correspondingly physically appealing exterior of the object. The two readers featured in *A Rebours* and *The Diamond Age* share an intimate relationship with their narrative environments, the Baron who comes to life through his books, and Nell, whose reading brings the Primer to life.

Huysmans' *A Rebours* stands out as an avant-garde chronicle of artificial consumption and creation in restless anticipation of more sophisticated design technology. Huysmans' twist on the concept of artifice is so satirically exaggerated in the novel, that the artificial creations become perfectly convincing in their unconventional æstheticism. At the height of æsthetic creation in *A Rebours*, des Esseintes engages in the design of a hothouse, where selected specimens of real plants are displayed for their unnatural looks, a kind of horror chamber of nature's most improbable creations, featuring perverse organic shapes where textures and colours resemble metal and skin. The Baron, looking through his fish tank window where the water may be coloured according to taste, with mechanical crabs (real fish are perishable), is a consumer beyond the commodity level: he is a creator attempting to organise a new nature, albeit in reversal of the "old" one: an interior instead of an exterior nature. The Baron designs for his own mind, to promote the processes of intuition and imagination, creating an ecology of virtuality in the interior of his own home.

The use of artifice, technology, and architecture is justified by the general idea of good order and meaning. There is a presupposition that architecture really is capable of formulating a purpose and suggests a design that serves the purpose. The process of design implies an external purpose. The suggestion of an internal purpose of design implies virtuality, that is, an innate possibility of actualisation, a potential form in and by itself. Looking at the form of virtuality in narrative media, whether actualised by whatever digital or artificial means we master at the moment, or fictitious, like the description of the Primer in *The Diamond Age*, there is the dream of both control, order and design applied to the virtual, and the desire to obliterate the agency of the machine and enter into a realm of imagination and intuition. The aim is to create a medium that responds to our need for experience and to stretch the ability to experience further, which means our sensory realm would expand. Benjamin observes the development of new forms of communication as a function of the isolation of the reader from direct experience, while the story maintains a form that preserves experience: "Historically, the various modes of communication have competed with one another. The replacement of the older narration by information, of information by sensation, reflects the increasing atrophy of experience. In turn, there is a contrast between all these forms and the story, which is one of the oldest forms of

While the steel skeleton of the *Eiffel Tower* projected into the Paris sky, a protest petition was organised in an attempt to prevent the disfiguration of the Paris skyline, signed by, among others, Maupassant, Emile Zola, and Edmond de Goncourt. In his *Journal*, the latter referred to the previous exposition in Paris (1867) as a "grand monstre de choses." His opinion of the monstrous appearance of the tower was perhaps not too far-fetched: Frankenstein's monster and the *Eiffel Tower* have the principle of the transparency of construction in common: no secret is made of the ingenuity of the engineering behind it, the bolts and joints are visible.

communication. It is not the object of the story to convey a happening per se, which is the purpose of information; rather, it embeds it in the life of the storyteller in order to pass it on as experience to those listening."[66] The Primer responds to the desire of an immersive form of media with an intact narrative agency. Its power and workings are in the fictitious form described as nano-technological, a form of artificial creation that has only just begun to develop in our time, at this moment with only a few applications ready for the market. Its nearly infinite potential lies in the ability to affect and merge with organic matter, not least inside the physical body.

The 19th century was fascinated by the power of the artefact: technical inventions, commodities, arts and appliances were displayed in universal expositions, celebrating industrial progress and marketing national identity. The successful Paris exposition of 1889 raised the expectations of the *World's Columbian Exposition in Chicago* in 1893, commemorating the discovery of the New World. An entire city in white was constructed to host the fair, where the artificial citizen of tomorrow, the robot *Boilerplate* could be seen mixing with the hordes of visitors.

As medical research has just begun to explore the potential of nanotechnology, the fields of communication theory and the entertainment industry have yet to be reinvented from a nanotechnological perspective. The idea of self-organisation and autonomy is presupposed in nanotechnology, since the scale is out of reach for regular control mechanisms. The workings of the nanodevices, their function, proliferation and decay are coded into the parts from the outset: they obey the rules of the programmer, while operating independently to fulfil their purpose within the system. The Primer device has similarities to the electronic media we use and recognise, borrowing its form from the book and functioning like a high-end computer, albeit with functions beyond our technical achievements so far. The way it constructs its narrative, deriving it from the reader and the reader's environment, is a variant of procedural authorship created by electronic media, as Janet Murray explains it: "Procedural authorship means writing the rules by which the texts appear as well as writing the texts themselves. It means writing the rules for the interactor's involvement, that is, the conditions under which things will happen in response to the participant's actions. It means establishing the properties of the objects and potential objects in the virtual world and the formulas for how they will relate to one another. The procedural author creates not just a set of scenes but a world of narrative possibilities."[67] With its references to rules and scripted behaviour within a set environment, the text begins to assimilate what in our time may be the most progressive narrative form: the game.

The Game – Adrift in Intuition

In narrative, the plot has the function of organiser of space and time. In our examples of the "plotless" novel and film, temporal and spatial order is weakened for the benefit of a "soft order", exploring the possibilities of virtual existence using intuition and imagination. The sites of the page and the stage have developed virtual qualities in the example of the Primer in Stephenson's novel *The Diamond Age*. The Primer's synthesis of narrative and responsivity to time and space into a site has the character of a game. A game of any kind is a versatile form of immersive organisation, a space for activity governed by a set of rules, capable of generating a new narrative every time. Its main feature is autogenerative plotting, drawing the elements for the story from the mental and physical situation of the reader in real time. The model for interaction with the Primer is based on difficulty levels, although embedded with great sophistication into the adaptive learning curve. The soft organisation of the game allows for architectural simulation where the player operates in an investigational and navigational mode. The Primer combines the propositions that cultural expressions often choose between rather than combine: the "sit down and I'll tell you a story" and the "stand up and we'll play a game".[68] With its sophisticated form, the Primer offers to its reader an architectural presence that has "the exterior clarity of a film and the interiority of a novel."[69] As a virtual object it is not a passive container, but an active generator of narrative space and time, like a game.

The *demi-monde* (literally, "half-world") was the term for a prostitute, a commodity for wealthy men of the bourgeoisie. There was a separation of bourgeois life in the 19th century into a public and a private sphere, as well as a division of life into male and female spheres. The term *demi-monde* suggests a positioning between these worlds, as a female in the public social sphere whose trade was the satisfaction of private desire. The more sinful sexuality became in the domestic environment, the more of a commodity it became in wider society.

A game is a type of media that deviates from the rules of linear narrativity, while maintaining much of the idea of plotting: a game is often constructed as a progressive struggle towards closure, in interaction with other participants who dynamically change the outcome, and where the outline of the environment is perpetually expanding. The procedural time and the expanding space are particularly assets of online role-playing games, like MMORPGs, MOOs and MUDs,[70] that have become players' "second home" on the Internet for years. These are not just games, but entire societies of considerable size: the subscription-based massively multiplayer online role-playing game (MMORPG), *Worlds of Warcraft* has a worldwide customer population of more than 3.5 million: a global population of players the size of Sydney.[71]

The virtual world is created and sustained by its interactors as readers, writers, spectators, actors, players and programmers, often in combined roles, who are engaged in the game and generate its form and content. This type of game does not offer closure in the sense of "reaching the end", it is a continuous and persistent virtual reality limited only by the desire and creativity of its players. Murray reminds us that hypertextual narratives may refuse closure: the richness in bifurcations and variations of the hypertext forces the reader to decide when to end the story, which is "closure as exhaustion, not as completion." The electronic closure, as in a computer game in the form of a puzzle or a quest, "occurs when a work's structure, though not its plot, is understood."[72] As in the plotless novel or in the perpetually looped kinetoscope film, a reader or spectator may enter at any page or stage, without loss of temporal understanding.

In an electronic game, technology circumscribes the possibility of action. You can only perform actions that the programmer has allowed for, meaning that in an adventure game that has a "goal", the solution of the task is built into the spatial environment of the game. The connected spaces would have to contain elements that lead towards conclusion: an object, instrument or the clues necessary for the pursuit and navigation towards higher levels and the final closure of the game. A hall with four closed doors is designed to offer the player either the possibility of opening all of them without effort, or refuse that possibility until a sequence of particular actions allow for their opening. The task of the designer/programmer is thus to ensure that there is a way to pass through the entire game in its narrative time and space, even if dead ends may exist. The architecture of the game needs to be designed with respect to the temporal succession of certain actions and movements, where one or some paths may lead astray and others may lead ahead. Murray expresses surprise in finding "the losing endings of the game /.../ much more satisfying than the winning ending."[73] It is the losing endings that keep the player within the space and time of the game. The space holds the key to the dissolvement of the plot, and the player is engaged in finding the right spaces in the right sequential order.

The book as a device is essentially designed for interaction with one person, in the sense of one reader at a time, even though the text might be read to an audience. This single serving unit may be compared with Edison's kinetoscope, where only one spectator at a time could view the film inside the cabinet. The kinetoscopes were collected in a salon called the *Kinetoscope Parlour*, where the cabinets were arranged in rows, not unlike the *Game Parlour* or amusement arcades, to use an even more anachronistic term. Arcade games are most often designed for interaction with one or two players, as opponents or as a team against the machine. With the increasing computer use (affordability and availability) and the possibilities of online gaming, the arcade games develop towards more socially attractive player activities like the dance game or direct body interaction with the game, like Sony's *iToy*, that could potentially attract an audience.[74] A variety of game stages emerge, where the game could be enjoyed by both player and audience. The fate of the single-serving arcade games could be shared by the decay of the arcades in Paris, described by Walter Benjamin as architectural relics of 19th century society and culture and its actors, exemplified by the flâneur and the gambler, among others. Benjamin argues that the phantasmagorical experiences that the flâneur seeks in space, correspond to the phantasms that the gambler seeks in time.[75] The game transforms time to a drug, and reinterprets space as part of the game: the flâneur

The word individual literally means an indivisible unity. Fin-de-siècle man was subject to multiplication, being photographed, recorded, filmed; captured in more ways than was ever possible before. The narratives on the theme of duplicated beings, or doppelgängers (alter egos, multiple personalities, double natures) were popular in this era, for example in Robert Louis Stevenson's 1886 novel *The Strange Case of Dr. Jekyll and Mr. Hyde*, and Oscar Wilde's *Picture of Dorian Gray*, from 1890.

transforms the arcades into a game parlour or casino, in which everyone becomes a gambler and where fate guides the experiences.[76] Benjamin's discourse of game in the *Arcades Project* regards hazard games, yet he communicates the player's relation to time and the intuition with which he operates on space. The player is a consumer, even a destroyer of time,[77] yet the passion for games is the noblest of all passions, since it incorporates all other passions.[78] The player's most important asset is intuition, the ability to react in a pre-perceptual way on signs.[79] Reading, Benjamin claims, is the highest manifestation of the gift of presence of mind.[80] The player's relation to time is a desire for duration, the constant drift in intuition.

Beginning of a New Life on and off the Shelf

Losing the plot – the plan, the site, the scheme – means a loss of the control instrument in narrative or a loss of the fundaments of architecture. The domestic space featured in the writers-in-residence, the accidental architecture of the Black Maria studio and the nondescript early kinetoscope films are examples of architecture without architects. These architectural (virtual or physical) environments prove to be, in turn, generative of a multitude of virtual spaces; imaginary travels, memory excursions, films with dancers and boxers, daydreams. They are plotless in the sense that they are not created from a scheme or plan, but from imagination and intuition. In the sense of sitelessness, the examples are virtual creations anchored in physical space by collected items, or non-static or multiplied in physical space.

Contemporary digital media culture is constructed by a "higher form" of plotting, not in an artistic sense necessarily, but on another semantic level: the programming code, the protocol that govern information and communication systems. There is no narrative value in reading a code, except maybe for a programmer familiar with the programming language in question, instead the user value is in the executional power of the code, on the level of implementation. Beyond authorship as we know it in narrative and architecture, there is another mythological character: the *hacker*, a threat to any system, and a Prometheus-figure in science fiction and cyberpunk literature. Having access and the ability to interfere with the code, the hacker is a reader and writer of *organisation*, rather than of text. It is the order of a system that reveals itself to the hacker. An environment built with instructions is attacked by contradictory orders. A skilled hacker is a locksmith and a burglar merged into one: the embodied promise that any closed system has openings.

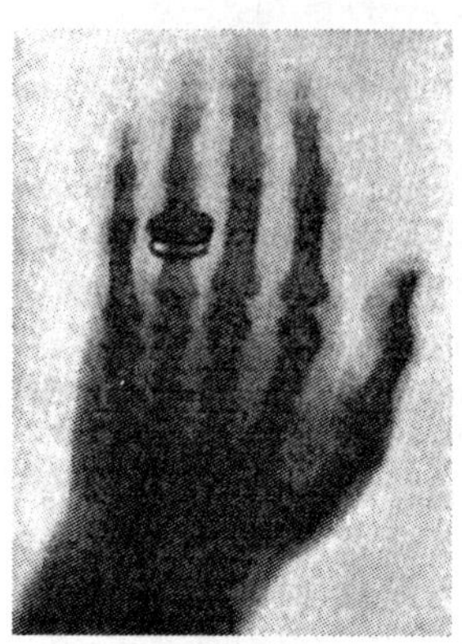

While conducting experiments in light phenomena and electrical emissions in various media, Wilhelm Conrad Rœntgen discovered the x-ray, which would take the marvels of photography a step further. This image is considered to be the first x-ray picture: a *radiograph* of Rœntgen's wife's hand. She commented on the event with the words: "I have witnessed my own death." The sensational *Rœntgen picture* technique came not only to be applied in science but also in the context of the spectacle, as people were still unaware of the risks involved in exposure to x-rays.

From the perspective of the objects brought forward as examples in this thesis, that all have a place in the prehistory of how we understand virtuality today, we are still in the developmental phase of "faithful" reproduction of space, governed by familiar principles of organisation: a mimetic, photo-realistic, simulated environment is created virtually as a copy of our space, instead of liberating ourselves from any of the obvious constraints that we experience in physical space. We do not yet possess the tools for a new thinking of space, but persist in our habits of negotiating problems of transport, of simultaneity, of communication, of gravity and so on, bringing those problems into virtual space where we aspire to feel at home among our restrictions. The examples in this thesis help us to study the mental labour of rethinking space in a virtual situation, and to watch that shift take place, the point where we realise that we are free, at least to represent a new reality, to fulfil our desires. Paradoxically, habit has a power over desire, as we tend to desire what we have always desired, uncritically. The Baron challenges himself into redesigning his pattern of desire: to create new sensations, not persist in the same desires but find new ones, by means of space and technology. His work of art was to remap the pattern of his own pleasures. The same goes for our ambition to project our wildest imagination onto technologies of virtuality, yet we are caught in a habitual thinking of space. It takes a real concentrated artistry to revisit the possibilities of virtual space. The examples aim at shifting the level of the modern concept of virtual reality and how that concept might have evolved technologically had we been more attentive to remapping desires. We are in that sense still in the "stone age" of virtual experience, since we have no competence to ask the right questions yet on how that space might be designed to meet desires we do not yet have. Baron des Esseintes exposed the necessary creativity to rethink space from the bottom up, in order to be able to ask new questions of what space can do for you.

At the turn of the 20th century, the powers of visual media had penetrated the flesh, as x-rays rendered the interior of the body visible. Sigmund Freud introduced psychoanalysis in 1896, providing the tools for penetrating the human mind. Access to the interior of the psyche was made possible through the interpretation of dreams - the motion pictures of the unconscious, narrated to the analyst, whose role might be characterised as that of some kind of inverted film scripting or directing. The hidden and the unconscious were made scientifically accessible. Both the body and the mind suddenly had an inside and an outside.

Among the dictionary entries for "plot", many refer directly to the practice of architecture: the site, the plan, the scheme, the diagram, the sketch, the outline, a purpose, a design, in all senses an expression of the power of observing and recording data: the idea of trying to foresee the outcome of something, visualisation, keeping an eye on, staking out the boundaries for, preparing the ground for, telling things apart, scaling, achieving change, preserving static, differentiate, classify and discriminate; all agencies for maintaining control and power in a dynamic and changing reality. In *How We Became Posthuman*, Katherine Hayles argues that "conscious agency has never been 'in control'."[81] Control is an illusion, and with that illusion comes the notion of autonomy of the self. If we would be able to set aside the "desire for mastery" and the "imperialist project of subduing nature", we would be able to deal with complex environments in a "natural" virtual way, where "embodiment replaces a body seen as a support system for the mind".[82]

Against this backdrop, we should be losing the plot. This poses a challenge for the architect and the author alike, whose methods and tools aspire to govern space and time, and to all of us as consumers of means of organisation. Assuming that there is some shelf life left in both architecture and narrative, the loss of the plot would not dissolve their respective structures, but open up for design powerful enough to bring life even to the bookshelf itself. After all, the aim of the plot is to lead the narrative towards a closure, which means – however satisfying for the reader, and however satisfying for the author having brought the reader this far – closing the book.

Epilogue

Notes from the Excitoir

The Excitoir – Space as Process

The neologism *excitoir* draws from the French *escritoire*, a small desk used for correspondence, and the quality of something that is *excitatory*. The *excitor* is that which excites or instigates, adding to the combination the property of exciting, stimulating, energising, provoking or calling into activity.[1] In our days, the escritoire denotes a slender bureau or secretary to store stationery and documents, yet it has furnished salons since the eighteenth century.[2] The escritoire was designed in both male and female versions, suggesting that this was regarded as a highly personal commodity. Some early escritoires were portable, even minimised into pocket size, with the size and shape of a laptop computer, providing the convenience of written communication wherever one would be stationed. Stretching the term to activity on a cellular level, we find the *excitatory neuron*, able to communicate through the synaptic biochemical process by which an electric signal, called an action potential, causes a release of neurotransmitters to either fire (discharge), that is to generate action in other neurons if it is an excitatory neuron, or prevent firing, as does the inhibitory neuron.[3] This neurological process is the root of our production of experience, originating in the fields of virtual action or action potential. The sense of excitoir might finally comprehend the audible component of *exit* – a passage leading out or forth, the departure of the player from the stage – reminding us of the function of the writer's domestic space as departure point for the mind travels and for dreaming.

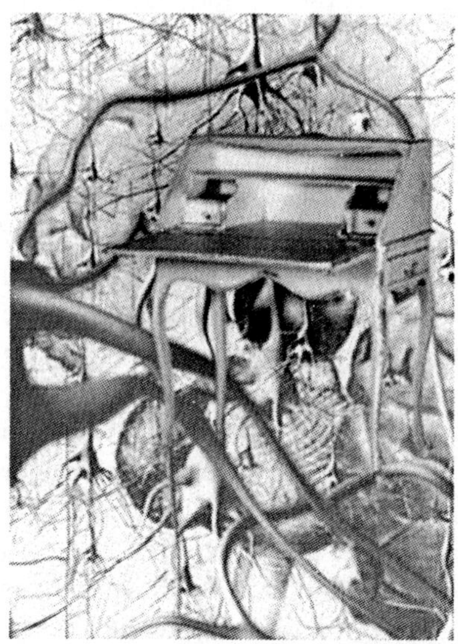

Fig. 1

Putting Experience to the Test

The purpose of expanding the neologism of the *excitoir* by looking at its semantic components is to indicate an expanded function of space and architecture. The first chapter of this thesis suggests the term *excitoir* to denote the function of the domestic spaces of the writers-in-residence as an excitant or stimulant of narrative production.[4] The chapter focuses on the mutual spatial creation of dweller and text, with the ambition to analyse the interrelated influence of fictive and real space, under influence of both writer and reader. Space becomes an operational part of a writing method that depends on the exchange of impulses between literary and architectural creation. The space created by the writers-in-residence is a vehicle for immobility, a means of expanding the boundaries of the mind in the process of internal travelling. They invite us into a durational *experience* of space governed by memory, perception, intuition and imagination.[5] The experience of this space is liberated from the procedural imperative of the plot.

The second chapter presents Edison's Black Maria, a studio building nicknamed after a police wagon. Its unprecedented architecture had more in common with the apparatus it was built to contain, as it was designed from the functional principles of a camera, and its exterior form of a vehicle was enforced by its actual revolving mobility. The architecture was purely contingent upon an opportunity to capture images. The examples of the writers-in-residence and the Black Maria have in common the very tight association between the organisation of space and what the space is meant to produce.

The third chapter introduction of Stephenson's Primer finally suggests an infinite number of readings drawn from the environment and mind of the reader herself. The Primer, being a reinvention of narrative media, adapts itself to the level of experience of its reader, merging all available media forms from text to motion pictures into layers of interaction in time and space, all contained between the covers of the archaic form of the book. Its narrative design follows the mind of the reader in a way that resembles the thought process itself, capable of reflecting the detours, shortcuts, retakes, outlines, in-depth-explorations, halts, ideas, zoomings, framings, whims and fancies, in short, responding to the immediacy and shifting perspective and organic mobility of the mind. The nanotechnological narrative device of Stephenson's Primer takes on the character of a multimedial game, bringing together the virtual qualities of the 19th century novels featured in the first chapter, and the adaptive time-laboratory of the Black Maria in the second chapter, into a powerful interactive plot engine. The Primer is, similar to the writers-in-residence, feeding on (information from) physical space, for the creation of a virtual narrative environment. The difference lies in the autonomy of the device, since the book is writing itself, it synthesizes environment and reader into a reflective narrative. The grand plot of *The Diamond Age* anticipates a convergence of the human mind, the earth and the body, with the pervasive global information systems, into a holistic understanding of the interrelations of all living systems. The key to this information revolution is the internalization of data modeled as a simulation of the brain and its capacity of imagination, in short, to enable the mind "to interface with the universe of data in a more intuitive way."[6] The narrative models of Huysmans' *A Rebours* and Goncourt's *La Maison d'un Artiste* correspond to this dream of an intuitive environment, one that responds to the needs of the mind, where space seems to relate intuitively to the dweller.

Katherine Hayles finds in *How we Became Posthuman* that "those organisms that survive will tend to be the ones whose internal structures are good metaphors for the complexities without."[7] If we might stretch her comment from the design of organisms to comprise forms of media, we find that complexity has less to do with the degree of technological implementation of the media than with the compatibility of the media and the human mind. Our present level of media technology often circumscribes, rather than expands, the possibilities of action, it outlines and delineates – plots – the field of operations. The form of the book is strangely persistent, as Hayles establishes: "When I open a book, it almost always works, and it can maintain backward compatibility for hundreds of years."[8] The book, even before being upgraded to the form of the fictional Primer, offers immersive experience, accessible at any time, at any speed, and nearly anywhere, in return for attention. In the Primer, the reader becomes a selector immersed in the most advanced hypertext imaginable: one that includes your physical reality. Selection, organisation and navigation of the narrative time and space become operational parts of the reading in this virtual environment, that gradually develop the quality of a game.

The examples in all three chapters expand the concepts of architecture and narrative *as* and *in* process, without attempting to control the temporal flow. The building, whether in material or narrative form, is contingent upon the opportunity to create experiences. The organisation of space does not strive towards closure, as does the plot, but serves the process of creation by its internal and external dynamics, even by technically facilitating changes in perspective and mobility. In different ways, the examples increase the bandwidth of architecture, and this communication channel increases at the expense of control. In our examples, this is reflected by the lack of plot in the novels and by the absence of an architect for the building. Consequently, there is something of the object at stake while the virtual possibilities of the object expand.

In the exemplified literary works, the material world is an archive of experience that, excited by memory and perception (our access modes to the virtual), presents itself to consciousness, and thus opens for self-actualisation. Walter Benjamin investigates the transfer of experience in poetic narrative form in his essay "On some Motifs in Baudelaire", where he finds that the modern reader is increasingly "unable to assimilate the data of the world around him by way of experience."[9] A novel like Proust's *A la recherche du temps perdu* may be regarded as "an attempt to produce experience synthetically".[10] The synthetic experience is present in Baron des Esseintes' space, which is created "Against Nature"[11], according to its ideal of self-containment, without a plot.[12] Benjamin approaches the mode of calling space into consciousness by an "excitatory process" (remembrance), where memory actualises consciousness, thus reaching a closure. This process reflects the way the virtual ceases to be virtual in the moment of its actualisation. This mindplay is drawn full circle in the excitoir, where excitated states of actualisation in text and space, merge the consciousness and memory of the creator or writer with the matter of space.[13] Benjamin finds in Henri Bergson's *Matter and Memory* a theory of the nature of experience that depends on the structure of memory and commends Bergson for achieving a theory of experience which takes into consideration that "experience is indeed a matter of tradition, in collective existence as well as in private life."[14] Benjamin finds that a growing inventory of dispersed matter and disparate chunks of information does not make for experience, instead the multitude of objects around us is shielded off by consciousness that works like a "screen against stimuli."[15] The "protective eye" keeps the urban media consumer from involvement, as does the mode of transferring information within this urban context. The intention of media is, in Benjamin's words, essentially "to isolate what happens from the realm in which it could affect the experience of the reader".[16] The chain of diminution of experience leads from narration to information, and finally sensation as the substitute for the chance play of time and space that memory and imagination awaken into consciousness from the world around us. Benjamin suggests a reversed perspective of the object itself: "To perceive the aura of an object we look at means to invest it with the ability to look at us in return". Benjamin outlines an image of a responsivity between man and matter that resembles a social relationship.[17] This is the office of the writers-in-residence, where the excitoir is the response of space to the unprotected gaze of the dweller. Similarly, with respect to the mode of perception in operation when looking into the kinetoscope, the gaze – undirected by the plot – is responded: "the person we look at, or who feels he is being looked at, looks at us in turn".[18]

Henri Bergson formulated his theories on the tendencies of the mind and virtuality in the turn-of-the-century context contemporary to the authors and creators in the examples of this thesis. Memory, in Bergson, is what translates perception into experience, "the necessary field of our activity".[19] This fundamental act of creation, a process of mediation, urges the actual from the virtual. The excitoir is an ideal field of action for the creative processes of narrativity and design. Its continuous becomings makes it an excitator of virtual architecture. Bergson finds the virtual in duration, the dynamic flow of consciousness, in which perception and memory operate to form experience. Creativity and action lifts the virtual into actuality from duration, a passage from the possible to the real. Bergson famously associated the thought process with the cinematographic procession of images. Bergson discusses perception by using "images" as a term for perceptions, i.e. incoming information about the "universe". Among these images, the body is the most privileged image, occupying the centre of the interlayered imagery where "interiority and exteriority are only relations among images".[20] The centre of our experience, the body, is a place of passage of sense stimuli in the process of experiencing the world, and the threshold of creative action: "Itself an image, the body cannot store up images, since it forms a part of the images, and this is why it is a chimerical enterprise to seek to localise past or even present perceptions in the brain: they are not in it; it is the brain that is in them. But this special image which persists in the midst of the others, and which I call my body, constitutes at every moment /.../ a section of the universal becoming."[21] With a quote from Bergson's *Matter and Memory* on how we build knowledge from this passage of images that we call the body, we might approach an understanding of the moment of true experience – "the immediate contact of the mind with its object".[22] Bergson describes "certain habits of thinking" and perceiving that need to be challenged in order to lead us to a turn of experience: "Such is, in truth, the ordinary course of philosophic thought. We start from what we take to be experience, we attempt various possible arrangements of the fragments which apparently compose it, and when at last we feel bound to acknowledge the fragility of every edifice that we have built, we end up by giving up all effort to build. But there is a last enterprise that might be undertaken. It would be to seek experience at its source, or rather above that decisive *turn* where, taking a bias in the direction of our utility, it becomes properly *human* experience."[23]

The decisive turn towards source experience that Bergson resorts to after the fragile edifice of empiricism has crumbled, too conscious of its own principle, leads to the two narrative illustrations in the next section. The two stories indicate the precise moment where human experience operate on external and internal images, where our knowledge of things appear to "no longer be relative to the fundamental structure of the mind, but only to its superficial and acquired habits".[24] The narrative illustrations feature representatives of two different perspectives of the same object, in two situations that converge at an ingenious collapse of communication that open up to a source experience. These are two stories about form and content, projection and imagination, external and internal images, and each story splits a presupposed representational mode into a play of virtual states of existence at a level of direct experience.

Fig. 2

Illustration one: The White Screen

This story came to me the way stories do, a long time ago, without careful annotation and without proper references, so it will be handed down to you with its anecdotal character intact. The story about the anthropologist living among the tribesmen of a very remote part of the world, isolated on an island or in a deep jungle, could possibly have taken place around the beginning of the 20th century. This anthropologist had spent some time with an uncivilised tribe, and had come to be accepted as a worthy member of their community. He had earned their respect by taking part in work and rituals, all the while recording and documenting their life with his film camera. After several years, he re-established contact with the civilised world and had his film rolls developed and delivered back to the village together with some basic viewing equipment. The time for his departure was approaching, but first, he wanted to show the tribesmen some of the footage taken over the years. One evening, he set up a simple cinema in a clearance. He had arranged for some seating place in front of a projection screen, and the hand-cranked projector was equipped with special lenses to concentrate the fire from a torch into a strong enough projector light. The tribe gathers in the clearance, and with the patience of a representative of a technologically "higher culture", the anthropologist carefully explains that what the audience was about to experience was not witchcraft or sorcery, nor were souls snatched from the bodies of those documented on the film, it was just sequenced images captured by light flowing into the camera, the box he had been carrying around in front of him, remember? As the first frames of the film lit up the screen and the black and white shadows danced in front of the audience, there were some upset voices at first, then more of them, then people leaving their seats to examine the screen on both sides. The spectators were touching the screen, running their fingers along its edges and around the corners of it. The filmmaker urged people to return to their seats and settle down, explaining once more that everyone's souls were in their right places and no one was damned by the shadows. At this point, a spokesman for the audience replied gently that they understood perfectly well how the camera worked, capturing light and creating images, which was perfectly fine and in order. What then, inquired the puzzled spokesman for the civilised world, what was so upsetting about this viewing event? The tribesman gestured at the screen: This! The colour! The form! With corners sharp as spearheads! The object of their distress was the symmetrical and severe square, unseen in this natural environment, never before experienced by a native of this tribe, since nature rarely produces perfect rectangles in any overwhelming scale and geometrical accuracy, let alone illuminates them to stand out and dominate the field of vision as this preposterous white screen.

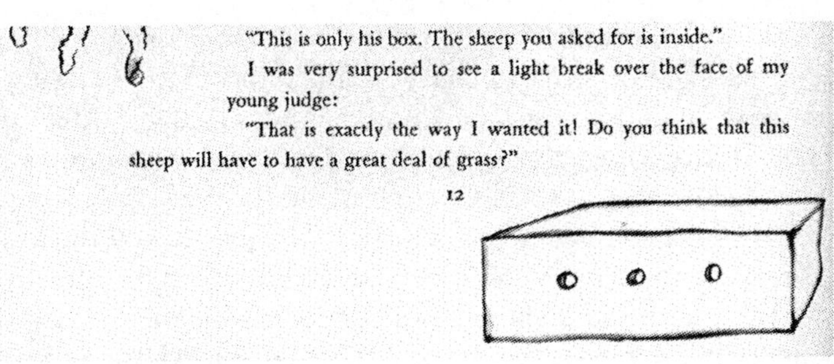

"This is only his box. The sheep you asked for is inside."

I was very surprised to see a light break over the face of my young judge:

"That is exactly the way I wanted it! Do you think that this sheep will have to have a great deal of grass?"

12

Fig. 3

Illustration two: The Black Box

In the middle of the desert, an aviator repairs his aircraft after an emergency landing. Coming out of nowhere, a young boy approaches the pilot with a request. The encounter begins with the little prince asking the pilot to make a particular drawing, and the above box is the result of this scene from Antoine St Exupéry's *Le Petit Prince*.[25] The sketching task is simple: a sheep for the prince to bring back to his home planet for the purpose of keeping baobab sprouts short, since these seeds would threaten to devour the small globe entirely, were they to obtain full size. Despite the aviator's efforts, the first sheep is rejected for its sickly appearance, the second for being a ram, and the third for being too old. At this point the aviator draws a rectangular box with three breathing holes for the sheep asleep inside. Having disregarded three efforts of representations of a suitable sheep, the prince immediately embraces the idea of the box with the desired content.

Debriefing the Illustrations

These two narrative illustrations set up a suggestive example of information exchange, that share the fact that communication takes place beside itself, on a level of direct experience, and that this exchange reveals the presence of a virtual level of information, outside of the conventions of media, or the chosen method of representation, where both sides of the communication situation have to adjust to a momentary loss of control and adopt a new understanding of the situation. The anthropologist's expectation of a possible turmoil was met, yet he was completely unprepared for the actual reason for the reaction he had anticipated. The prince and the aviator, in a moment of complete agreement, abandon the realistic rendering of a sheep for a super-realistic one; a virtual sheep that bypasses the drawing skills of the aviator and surpasses the expectations of the prince.

The task in both examples was the transmission of an image. In the process of transmission, the images undergo a virtual shift, actualising themselves as the media of the message, the bearer without the load, the container without its contents, the projected without the image. This is only a failure of the media if one expected that the external imagery would be in total control over the internal imagery. The tribesmen were not as interested in the film as in the absolute geometry of the illuminated projection screen. The prince was not interested in any of the sheep drawn at his request, but happy with the indirect representation created by the brief comment that it lies sleeping in the box. There is no reason to explain the reaction by appealing to the innocence of the receiver of the image, it is rather the innocence of the sender, who retrieves his authority by believing that he is in control, and by relying on the supposition of an innocent receiver. The illustrations show what Hayles describes as a misunderstanding of the nature of experience from the point of view of authority: "In the posthuman view, by contrast, conscious agency has never been 'in control'. In fact, the very illusion of control bespeaks a fundamental ignorance about the nature of the emergent processes through which consciousness, the organism, and the environment are constituted."[26]

The problems of container and content, the projected and the perceived, the extended and the unextended within these illustrations are all related to the processes of architecture and the authority assigned to the role of the architect to create experience. The epilogue seeks to formulate a desire to increase the bandwidth of architecture, an operation that implies a loss of control. On what level of agency do we invest experience in architecture? Should architects become better at drawing boxes or perfect the ability of telling stories about its contents?

The White Screen Problem

In the first illustration, the "pay-off" is the reversal of expectation that turmoil was caused by a shocking encounter with modern technology. This presupposition is not too far-fetched – after all, the urban audience did indeed panic when the Lumière brothers' train rolled towards the film camera, so one would expect a shocked audience of natives being shown a film picturing themselves.[27] After a short schooling period with the new media, people were habitual moviegoers as far as the perceptual sensation, the next step would be to add a story to the flow of images, at which point the raw experience of moving images was replaced by the expectation of an entertaining and exciting plot. The white screen illustration suggests instead that commotion was caused by the static contrivance of the screen, an object assumed to be the backdrop of action, a component part of the machinery serving the illusion. The story serves here to indicate a blind spot in our relation to media as a plot-bearer, and its various technologies and forms. The entire 20th century has passed by on a screen. The screen is the birthplace of, and the backdrop for, the modern icon, the film star, the hero and the goddess. In the realm of fine arts, the black box wittingly denotes an opposition to the traditional gallery environment of the "neutral" white cube; a space mainly for display of new electronic media, often presented on a white screen within the black box, or in monitors distributed around the darkness. The screen is a two-dimensional framing of a projection, the backdrop form on which a story will take place. However, when distracting the audience from the show, the white screen unintentionally becomes the focus of interest in an environment with no previous experience of visual media, but with an understanding for the concept of narrative storytelling. The drawn box holds the promise of just the right visualisation and even animation of the desired content, giving it a soul and an autonomous existence, thus it is just the right gift to a subject who is accomplished in visual conceptualisation and who just need to be told the right story to accompany the image.

The Black Box Problem

In the second illustration, the box fulfils its purpose as container for the desired object because it is accompanied by a story. An agreement is met between the prince and the aviator, based on the versatility of the mode of representation. Opening the box to verify its contents is not an option once the mental evaluation is made. The magic power of the drawing is inherent in the story, since the two parts never question the prospect of bringing back a two-dimensional sketch on a piece of paper to protect the Prince's home planet from the growth power of large trees. The box is a three-dimensional container that depends on the narrative declaration of its contents, and the prince is a receptive and trustful consumer of the story. The narrative compensates for the deficits of its visual representation.

The black box was during the second world war a Royal Air Force slang expression for the navigational instrument in a plane that enables fighter pilots to see in the dark and through clouds, a magic contrivance that renders visible to a human eye what without the technology would be invisible, a god's view over the world.[28] Later on in flight history, the black box would become synonymous with "flight recorder", the indestructible black box in a plane that automatically records functions in the aircraft, information that may be consulted to retrace a string of events prior to an airline crash. Once retrieved among the debris, it becomes the remaining and impartial witness, holding the "plot" that describes the disaster. In cybernetics and computer logics, the black box is a term for "systems whose internal mechanisms are not fully open to inspection".[29] The suggested description of the Little Prince's box as a "black box" borrows from the definition of its most familiar application, the protected recording unit of the flight recorder, and its scripted equivalent in a software code. In programming, the black box denotes "a device or system or object when it is viewed primarily in terms of its input and output characteristics."[30] It could be a testing procedure, functioning like a "digital flight recorder", or a program where the inner workings are hidden from the user. Black box theory is a term used in mathematics and philosophy in various senses, one of which is the black box theory of consciousness which handles the impossibility of working out the workings of the human brain from a simplistic pattern of input and output.[31] Following the medieval use of the word "black box" for coffin, the mysterious qualities are intact, denoting the contents of the box as any processes beyond our event horizon.[32] Death, in Benjamin, "is the sanction of everything that the storyteller can tell."[33] The black box denotes absolute closure, the final container of the story. All these black box connotations and meanings serve here to illustrate the suspended communication breakdown, evaded by the virtual meaning embedded in a box, whose contents may be scripted, but not accessed. The prince and the pilot agree on a story, which is the code of the sketched black box, programming its function but not accessed other than in memory (the mental image of a sheep), aided by intuition and imagination.

For Emptiness to Fill

The black box, inaccessible until an acute point of actualisation, and the white screen, a vertical tabula rasa, are receptors of any story and also spaces within themselves. As points of access, or sites for actualisation of a story, we may through these images achieve an understanding of virtuality of the medium itself, in its yet to be actualised state, before the story or after the crash. The white screen and the black box are semantically charged spaces for the free play of imagination, a brief journey into virtuality through the illuminated and the obscured, the projected and the hidden. Film began as looking into a black box, one by one, and later, with a full audience looking into the framed space of the illuminated screen, the individual experience became collective. The black box and the white cube aspire to be empty vessels, pure containers for the duration of experience of an art work such as the reflection of a human subject, projected in full on an illuminated screen, or peered at through a hole in a black box. These origins of these forms of media retrieval can be traced to Plato and beyond, but they reached a status of sites for production and consumption during the last century. To progress from these experience forms into actualisation of immersive media lies in the future, according to Margaret Morse who claims that "it is left to genres of cyberculture to develop the full implications of the impression of being immersed inside a virtual world – what amounts to appearing to enter inside the box and the screen."[34]

With respect to the nature of the experience, there is a peculiar resemblance between the camera obscura, a dark room (literally) through which passes an image of external reality through a small aperture and reflects on the opposite wall, and the Platonian dark cave where prisoners are absorbed by the only reality they are aware of: the shadows dancing on the walls, though these are phantasms of the true imagery of reality outside the cave.[35] The cave allegory from *The Republic* is used to illustrate the separation from reason by the dim process of perception, as Plato develops the story in a succeeding interpretation, a model borrowed for this section beginning with the stories of the White Screen and the Black Box, of which the interpretation has reached its conclusion.

Fig. 4

Storytelling and Storyselling

Architecture and literature have already been identified as agencies of *plot*. The plot (and its absence) is the key term that assembles the discussion about the *domestic interior* and the *novel*. Within these environments, as sites for spatial creation, architecture comes into existence both as text and image, in representation as well as in the form of *virtual reality*. Virtuality is manifested explicitly in the texts in the form of immobile *mind travelling*, narrated as a *travelogue* within the novel, and other methods of escapism into alternative realities by means of various forms of *artifice* (collections of artwork, books, objects), narrated in a *catalogue* form. The virtual is a function of the parallel production of text and space, manifested in the minds of the fictive character, the author and the reader. The interplay between the individual and the private space requires isolation from society, in the case of Huysmans and Goncourt, from the urban Paris of the 1880s marked by the inception of *mass consumption* and its related *media culture*. In Huysmans and Goncourt, architectural space becomes the framework that holds narrative variations on time and space, such as for example daydreams, memories, reflections and, to a large degree; cultural critique. The authors in this study sought to separate themselves from popular culture and its commodities. Their distance is manifested in their literary theme of "elite consumption" and a hyperæsthetic relation to the objects in their possession, that often intend to intensify the separate individual *experience* by displacing the protagonists to the virtual realities triggered by the object of interaction.[36] While popular fin-de-siècle culture was determined by a mass mode of consumption, the reading experience in essence remained a personal, silent activity: an individual mode of consumption. The process of literary creation in Huysmans and Goncourt is particularly influenced by the idea of a private space, both reflecting on the domestic staging of the novel, and how this space is reflected in the reader's mind.

From the point of view of contemporary consumer culture, where commercial producers continually target the "individual experience", mass consumption takes the *form* of elite consumption. Consumption becomes an act of selection, of discriminating between objects, of making personal choices to delineate the self, which brings us back to the sense of "plotting" as an act of demarcation. The ability to categorize and order becomes equally critical in media culture. A large part of the enterprise of media is the recording process: the preservation and storage of culture. The accumulation of information in material and virtual archives demands higher precision of the questions asked. The test of time in storekeeping is called shelf life: the length of time that a commodity may be stored without becoming unfit for use or consumption. By a broad definition, shelf life is the period of time during which something remains popular, and in this sense it can be regarded as an instantiation of time in a media and consumer culture. The collector of the 19th century has developed into a correspondent character in our time: the selector. Contemporary culture could be seen as a "DJ culture", where selection has developed into an artform in itself. The multiple choice culture generates performers like, for instance, the discjockey selecting and mixing a music session, the stylist selecting designer clothes for a fashion shoot or the curator selecting artworks for an exhibition. Hypertext is its narrative form: reading as an act of selection. This mode of consumption may be perceived as both demanding and liberating for the reader and the consumer. Within the architecture of narrative media, the reader may both choose and lose her narrative way.

The Internet as a forum has fuelled the development of "plotting" for everything from grand conspiracy theories to personal accounts of everyday life in the form of the blog (weblog), an open diary available for online readers.[37] The desire and need for plot is symptomatic of our time, and as such, it has developed its own currency rate. With the popular novel, a new area of narrative consumption was introduced, distributed along with the intensified consumer situation in all urban culture. The artifice of the plot was refined by Dickens, exaggerated to the detective novel, and boldly redefined by Flaubert, until towards the turn of the century, the plot was seen by Freud as the operative analytical tool in psychoanalysis. The plot allows us to construct a whole, with its ability to create connections and relations. Considering the emphasis on narrative unity and progression in Aristotle, managed, reinforced and widely spread as formula in the novel of the progress-oriented 19th century, and in the same spirit incorporated with the 20th century market economy in the form of commercials and branding, the structure of the plot has become the matrix for individual life: striving towards *closure* with an emphasis on (individual) *action* and consumption and creation of (social) *events*. The individual in Western society is (still) preoccupied with creating the story of the self (the great bourgeois ambition), following the formula of the plot: the pursuit of a career, the desire to impact on other people's lives or in the environment, to make a difference, leave a footprint, strive for public acclaim, get recognition as an individual in a growing collective, in short, to "realise" oneself means to progress from the virtual realm of *possibility* to the physical realm of *action*.

The narrative element has in our days become intimately involved with the commodity. Using the plot to demarcate, outline, enclose and exclude values in regards to a product, the story has developed as the main instrument of branding, a branch of marketing involved with creation and maintenance of a brand identity on the global market. Commercial storytelling has become a patent solution in the marketing industry. Business actors formulate what story they want to sell or tell along with their product, with the purpose of creating a sustainable contextualisation of the commodity, investing credibility and defining a particular branded experience in conjunction with the product or service provided. Scriptwriters for the film industry have developed an extreme speciality of oral performance since the pressure to perform a perfect sales pitch is, if possible, even more condensed than for any salesman of any other product, for here the plot is the product. In the world of story trading, the writer or script agent is given the time of an elevator ride between two floors to present the commodity of the story – plot and setting, characters and casting idea, from beginning to end. The judgement skill to spot a selling plot is just as perfected in the immensely powerful storybuyer. To its character, the plot already exists in a system of exchange with a self-powered ability to spread, and perhaps most importantly, as Peter Brooks points out in *Reading for the Plot – Design and Intention in Narrative*, to be recognisable regardless of what media is used for retransmission.[38] According to Brooks, narrative design creates individual and collective meaning in fiction, philosophy, science, and most importantly perhaps, in history, with subcategories as archaeology, historiography, mythology, anthropology, any evolutionary theory, where the pattern of understanding places us in a position of tracing a coherent story from a vantage point of view towards an origin or a degree zero.

During the 19th century, narrative production increased significantly: the novel, the news and not least in science with the interest in processes of production of origins, genealogy, evolution and progress.[39] The development of a passive group of consumers of narratives from the late 19th century turning into the 20th century, is in the era of the Internet balanced by an increasing amount of text and media producers. A variety of "plot engines" can be found on the internet, also called "narrative software" or simply, "writing machines". These automated story-generators are most often designed for use in role-playing games. The "GM" or game master who is responsible for outlining the plot, its setting and characters, could simply fill in a form with lists of friends and foes, locations, assets among other plot elements that would be part of the narrated environment compiled by the plot engine.[40] Even if some narrative software aspires to direct any hopeful novelist towards an international best-selling product, the plot engine is more suitable for game construction, since games embrace the realm of possibilities within narrative in an instrumental way. The plot is contained in its most expanded senses in the game – the plan, charts, navigational issues, conflicts – in short the outline or demarcation of the "field" of action and interaction. There are games clearly intended for closure, games intended for perpetual and parallel existence, and games entirely executed in narrative or spatial form, and many more kinds that combine these experiential structures. The cultural development of the game as an artform is still pending, yet this would be a potent extension of the electronic arts scene, since, as McLuhan points out, "art, like games, is a translator of experience. What we have already felt or seen in one situation we are suddenly given in a new kind of material. Games, likewise, shift familiar experience into new forms, giving the bleak and bleary side of things sudden luminosity."[41]

The global forum of the Internet enables readers to become writers, consumers to take on the role of critics, and allows the individual or local story to exist side by side with more powerful actors. This development should be aligned with Jean-François Lyotard's assertion of the fall of the grand metanarratives as an effect of the postmodern condition.[42] These universal tales of human evolution, plotted as stories with a beginning, middle and end, are found in classic texts and in scientific accounts of truth. His critical theory concerns the increased incredulity towards the overarching stories that ordered modernity in terms of successive and progressive historical accounts. In an experienced situation of little or no power, conspiracy theories thrive as an attempt to make sense of the world, an attempt to wrestle order out of chaos. This type of plotting spreads and regenerates by subscribers to the theories, and adversaries who confirm it by finding it worthy of questioning, since affirmations and denials serve the exchange of plots in equal measures. It is in the nature of conspiracy theories to grow into large thought constructions of interrelated indices and circumstances, and the Internet provides a fertile ground.

From Cabal to Cabbage Patch

Apart from signifying the string of incidents that are the basic material for a story, the plot spans definitions from the slightest impact on a surface, such as a spot, to the small patch of land, and further upscaled to the ground or city plan, across to the graphic methods involved in architecture and navigation – the plan, chart, scheme or diagram – to the malicious plan – the conspiracy or cabal – suggesting secret or criminal prearrangements. Moreover, a plot is not just the aforementioned nouns, but also the activity of plotting: making plans, constructing the story, the drawing of graphs, to form or take part in a plot. This "instrument of authority" has been the concern of this thesis, mainly in its sense as a control instrument for the spatio-temporal design of a storyline, and mainly studied through the effects of its absence.[43] Its function as a regulator of space and time into a causal chain of events is identified by Friedrich Kittler to constitute the influential force of reality to which traditional arts subtend: being "subject to the conditions of an external reality that they imitate: 'space, time, causality'."[44] Jennifer Bloomer describes a more dynamic powerplay where the plot may serve as well as challenge conventions: "Besides being architectonic constructions, plots, like architecture, are both singular and non-singular, both submissive to paradigms and deviant from established models, both in conformity with tradition and in rebellion against paradigms from the tradition."[45]

New media forms transform their spatial and temporal context, as Kittler argues along the lines of McLuhan in their studies of media culture. By selecting the objects of study from the media culture of the late 19th century, permeated by their contemporary discourse network and movement of ideas, the thesis has assumed a position where concepts of virtuality can be studied from a pre-digital position in media history. This shift of perspective has not been made in order to write a new history of virtuality in media (in which case the study should have to address history from the first sign of human communication), but to enter a point in history when certain creative actions take place that shift the power and control of narrative.

The attempt to read plot through media involves certain historical relationships, that in the examples of this thesis stretches from Xavier de Maistre's virtual travels, described in a late eighteenth century novel, to the core study of plotless creation during the last two decades of the 19th century, in the form of a reinvention of the novel and the invention of moving images, and the extension of this historical era into the anachronistic neo-Victorian setting in *The Diamond Age,* where Stephenson introduces the Primer, a new media device that incorporates not only all previous media forms into the plot, but also the reader and her environment. This object of analysis is written in 1995, but reaches back to the 19th century fin-de-siècle, from which we are separated by a century of wirelessness, networking, and convergence of old and new media. This historical process, however, has not obliterated the book, which has proven to be a sustainable media form among the numerous production and consumption forms that have expanded the narrative world. The sustainable structure of the narrative form of the book has been compared to the power of built reality as a bearer of meaning. With the words "this will kill that", Victor Hugo declared the superiority of the printed word to convey meaning to modern man, at the expense of the ability to decode the building such as the cathedral, lamenting the fact that the novel will take its place as a semantic container and monument of human life.[46]

The media culture between 1880 and 1900 expanded not only by geographic and social diffusion, but also by engaging multiple sense modalities, thus becoming more demanding in terms of attention – simply put, during this era the amount of space occupied by media in people's lives increased dramatically. This is the backdrop to the writers-in-residence, who respond to this media culture by withdrawing into æsthetic isolation and a necessitated return to the non-causal narrative without beginning or end, as an alternative construction of reality. This is the era when Edison realised his ambition to "do for the eye what the phonograph does for the ear",[47] which means separating the perception of space and time from the space and time of its production: the original field seen by the kinetograph or heard by the phonograph. Where the writers-in-residence engaged in elite consumption, Edison aimed at a mass market: his projects focused on the development of marketable goods for a broad audience and inventions that instantly became indispensable to households and work-places worldwide.

The virtualities in these examples consist in the transposed experience, via media, delaying and reproducing perception to the eyes of the spectator and to the ears of the audience. As media inventions move into the market, an entire mode of perception comes along with the product, as McLuhan expresses it: "The business of the writer or the film-maker is to transfer the reader or viewer from one world, his *own*, to another, the world created by typography and film."[48] The contemporary conception of a digital media transposal of virtuality needs to be challenged because the current discussions of this are fetishising the technological novelty, which erases the experience found in the pre-digital narrative environments where vibrant alternative realities challenge perception in the most archaic as well as in the most incunabular forms of media.

INTRODUCTION

1 Plot v.1: *The Oxford English Dictionary*. 2nd ed. 1989. OED Online. Oxford University Press. 8 Oct. 2005. <http://dictionary.oed.com/cgi/entry/50181741>

2 First Chapter: Paper presented at the *Society of Architectural Historians' Annual Meeting*, Providence, Rhode Island, April 2004 in session chaired by Barbara Penner & Charles Rice: Interiorities. Published paper: Malin Zimm. "Writers-in-residence – Goncourt and Huysmans at Home without a Plot". *The Journal of Architecture*, vol. 9, nr 3: 2004, Routledge Taylor & Francis group, pp. 305–314. Second Chapter: Paper presented at the *CongressCATH: The Ethics and Politics of Virtuality and Indexicality*, Bradford, June 2005.

3 Bartlett School of Architecture 1997–1999: Diploma studies, unit 15, tutor Nick Clear. Pre-diploma theoretical dissertation: *The Autistic Architect* (1998) tutor: Dr Jonathan Hill. Diploma technical dissertation: *The Synæsthetic Mediator* (1999) tutor: Dr Rachel Armstrong. Graduation: BA hons, Bartlett School of Architecture, University College of London, 1999 and KTH School of Architecture, Royal Institute of Technology, 1999, supervisor Dr Katja Grillner.

4 Malin Zimm. "The Synæsthetic Mediator", in Roy Ascott (Ed.). *Transmodalities: Art, Technology, Consciousness- mind@large*. Bristol, UK: Intellect Books 2000, pp. 123–128. See also: Malin Zimm. "En Synestetisk Mediator", *Offentliga Rum*, Årg. 3, nr 2: 2000, Artik Publishing, pp. 50–55. Malin Zimm. "En Synestetisk Mediator", 00-*tal*, nr 1: 2000, pp. 138–145.

5 Jonathan Crary. *Techniques of the Observer: On Vision and Modernity in the Nineteenth Century* (1992). Cambridge, Massachusetts & London, England: MIT Press 1999.

6 Second Industrial Revolution: *Wikipedia: The Free Encyclopedia*. 8 Oct. 2005. <http://en.wikipedia.org/wiki/Second_industrial_revolution>

7 Aristotle (384–322 BC). *Poetics*. London: Penguin Classics 1996, ch. 4.4, p. 12.

8 Aristotle, 1996, ch. 5.1–5.5, pp.13–17.

9 Aristotle, 1996, ch. 10.1, p. 38.

10 Aristotle, 1996, ch. 5.3, p. 15.

11 Aristotle, 1996, ch. 5.4, p. 15.

12 Peter Brooks. *Reading for the Plot – Design and Intention in Narrative*. Oxford: Clarendon Press 1984, pp. 3–36.

13 Brooks, 1984, p. 6.

14 See for example: Vladimir Propp. *Morphology of the Folk Tale* (1928). University of Texas Press 1968. M.M. Bakhtin. *The Dialogic Imagination: Four Essays by M.M. Bakhtin* (Caryl Emerson & Michael Holquist, Trans.). University of Texas Press 1981.
Claude Lévi-Strauss. *Structural Anthropology*. Basic Books 1963 (A collection of essays outlining his program for structuralism).

15 Herman Hesse. *Glass Bead Game (Magister Ludi)* (1943). New York: Henry Holt & Company 1990, pp. 18–19.

16 Sheherazade: The heroine of *The Thousand and One Nights* who saved her life by spending the nights telling the Sultan Shahryar stories that kept him in a thrill of anticipation. In the end the king, who previously married and killed a new spouse every day, makes Sheherazade his queen. (Sir Richard Burton's *Book of The Thousand Nights and a Night* 1885–88 has become the best-known English translation of this work of uncertain Middle Asian origins). *Tales from the Thousand and One Nights* (N. J. Dawood, Trans.). London: Penguin Classics 1973.

17 Friedrich A. Kittler. *Gramophone, Film, Typewriter* (1986). Stanford, California: Stanford University Press 1999, p. xii.

18 Friedrich A. Kittler. *Discourse networks* 1800/1900 (1985). Stanford, California: Stanford University Press 1990, p. xiii.

19 Friedrich A. Kittler. *Maskinskrifter – Essäer om medier och litteratur.* Gråbo: Bokförlaget Anthropos 2003, pp. 50–51 (my translation).

20 Kittler, 1999, p. 154.

21 Marshall McLuhan. *The Gutenberg Galaxy: The Making of Typographic Man*. London: Routledge & Kegan Paul 1962.

22 McLuhan, 1962, p. 56.

23 McLuhan, 1962, p. 20.

24 McLuhan, 1962, p. 23.

25 McLuhan, 1962, p. 45.

26 McLuhan, 1962, p. 45.

27 Edgar Allan Poe. *Upptäckter under Hypnos.* Lund: Ellerströms Förlag 2001, pp. 95–112.

28 McLuhan, 1962, pp. 36–38.

29 McLuhan, 1962, pp. 15–18.

30 McLuhan, 1962, p. 26.

31 McLuhan, 1962, p. 40.

32 Edmond de Goncourt. *La Maison d'un artiste.* Paris: Charpentier 1881, tome I, p. 3: (my translation).

33 Margaret Morse. *Virtualities: Television, Media, Art, and Cyberculture* (Theories of Contemporary Culture, Center for Twentieth Century studies, University of Wisconsin-Milwaukee). Bloomington & Indianapolis: Indiana University Press 1998, p. 17.

34 N. Katherine Hayles. *How we Became Posthuman: Virtual Bodies in Cybernetics, Literature, and Informatics*. Chicago & London: The University of Chicago Press 1999, p. 5.

35 Hayles, 1999, p. 38.

36 Hayles, 1999, p. 49.

37 Walter Benjamin. *Paris, 1800-talets huvudstad. Passagearbetet.* (*Das Passagen-Werk* 1927–29, 1935, 1939) Stockholm & Stehag: Brutus Östlings Bokförlag Symposion 1992. (English title: *Paris: Capital of the 19th Century*).

38 Janell Watson. *Literature and Material Culture from Balzac to Proust: the Collection and Consumption of Curiosities.* Cambridge: Cambridge University Press 1999.

39 Rosalind Williams. *Dream Worlds: Mass Consumption in Late Nineteenth Century France.* Berkeley & Los Angeles: University of California Press 1982.

40 Watson, 1999, p. 133.

41 Watson, 1999, p. 132.

42 Watson, 1999, p. 140.

43 Anne Friedberg. *Window Shopping – Cinema and the Postmodern*. Berkeley & Oxford: University of California Press 1993.

44 Charles Musser. *History of the American Cinema, Vol. I: The Emergence of Cinema: the American screen to* 1907. (Charles Harpole, Gen. Ed.). New York & Oxford: Maxwell Macmillan International 1990.

45 David Robinson. *From Peep Show to Palace: The Birth of American Film.* New York: Columbia University Press 1996.

46 David A. Cook. *A History of Narrative Film.* New York & London: W. W. Norton & Company 1990.

47 Marta Braun. *Picturing Time: The Work of Etienne-Jules Marey (*1830–1904*)*. Chicago & London: The University of Chicago Press 1992.

48 Maurice Bardèche & Robert Brasillach. *Histoire du cinéma*. Paris: Les Sept Couleurs 1964.

49 David Bordwell & Kristin Thompson. *Film Art: an Introduction*. (4th ed.) (1979). New York: McGraw-Hill 1993.

50 Jennifer Bloomer. *Architecture and the Text: The (S)crypts of Joyce and Piranesi.* New Haven & London: Yale University Press 1993, p. 146.

51 Roy Eriksen. *The Building in the Text – Alberti to Shakespeare and Milton*. Pennsylvania: Pennsylvania State University Press 2001.

52 Eriksen, 2001, p. xiv.

53 Eriksen, 2001, p. 13.

54 Janet H. Murray. *Hamlet on the Holodeck – The Future of Narrative in Cyberspace* (1997). 3rd printing, 2000. Cambridge, Massachusetts: The MIT Press 2000, p. 29.

55 Murray, 2000, p. 9.

56 Murray, 2000, pp.99–100.

57 Murray, 2000, p. 29.

58 Murray, 2000, p.71.

59 See also: George P. Landow (Ed.). *Hyper/text/theory*. Baltimore & London: The Johns Hopkins University Press 1994, and Espen J. Aarseth: *Cybertext: Perspectives on Ergodic Literature*. Baltimore & London: The Johns Hopkins University Press 1997.

60 Marie-Laure Ryan. *Narrative as Virtual Reality – Immersion and Interactivity in Literature and Electronic Media*. Baltimore & London: The Johns Hopkins University Press 2001, p. 12.

61 Ryan, 2001, p. 11.

62 Ryan, 2001, p. 12.

63 Ryan, 2001, pp. 120–171.

64 Ryan, 2001, pp. 44–47.

65 Ryan, 2001, pp. 45–46.

66 Murray, 2000, pp. 121–122.

67 Ryan, 2001, pp. 332–345.

68 Ryan, 2001, p. 340.

CHAPTER ONE

1 Edmond de Goncourt (1822–1896). *La Maison d'un artiste*. Paris: Charpentier 1881. The Goncourts bought the house in 1868, and it still exists on 67, Bvd. Montmorency; the original street number 53 changed to 67 after the renumbering of the street in 1890.

2 Joris-Karl Huysmans (1848–1907). *Against Nature*. London: Penguin Classics 1959. (Robert Baldick, Trans.) Original title: *A Rebours*. First published in Paris: Charpentier 1884. (A variation of the English title is *Against the Grain*).

3 Hyperæsthesia: *The Oxford English Dictionary*. 2nd ed. 1989. OED Online. Oxford University Press. Retrieved 8 Oct. 2005. <http://dictionary.oed.com/cgi/entry/50110293>: "*Path.* Excessive and morbid sensitiveness of the nerves or nerve-centres. *Also: transf.* Excessive sensibility or sensitiveness (in general)."
Hyperaesthetic, a.: *The Oxford English Dictionary*. 2nd ed. 1989. OED Online. Oxford University Press. Retrieved 8 Oct. 2005.<http://dictionary.oed.com/cgi/entry/50110295>: "Affected with hyperæsthesia; excessively or morbidly sensitive; Excessively æsthetic." Hyperæsthesia was in the 19th century known as a nervous condition connected to the overstimulation caused by the modern urban environment. The term has been applied to the symbolists who let their senses overflow in artistic expression.

4 Malin Zimm. "The Dying Dreamer - Looking into Huysmans' Virtual Worlds", in Neil Spiller (Ed.) vol. 72, nr 3: 2002: *AD Architectural Design: Reflexive Architecture*. London: Wiley & Sons Ltd., pp. 14–19. Project webpage: http://www.arch.kth.se/~zimm.

5 Janell Watson. *The Literature and Material Culture from Balzac to Proust: The Collection and Consumption of Curiosities* (Cambridge Studies in French). Cambridge: Cambridge University Press 1999, pp. 109–142.

6 Goncourt, 1881, "Préface", *tome I*, n.p.: "En ce temps où les choses, dont le poète latin a signalé la mélancolique vie latente, sont associées si largement par la description littéraire moderne à l'Histoire de l'Humanité, pourquoi n'écrirait-on pas les mémoires des choses, au milieu desquelles s'est écoulée une existence d'homme?" (my translation).

7 Joris-Karl Huysmans. "Préface écrit vingt ans après le roman", in *A Rebours*. Paris: Garnier-Flammarion 1978, p. 55. (Translation from: "Preface Written Twenty Years After the Novel", *Against the Grain*: New York: Dover Publications, Inc. 1969, n.p., 8 Oct. 2005. <http://www.eldritchpress.org/jkh/rpf.html>). The entire novel *Against the Grain* is available at <http://www.eldritchpress.org/jkh/rebours.html>: scanned in 1997 from the Dover edition, an unabridged republication of the English translation published by New York: Three Sirens Press 1951 (no longer under copyright).

8 Deborah L. Silverman, *Art Nouveau in Fin-de-Siècle France: Politics, Psychology and Style*. Maarssen & The Hague: Gary Schwartz 1989, pp. 20–24.

9 Goncourt, 1881, "Préambule", *tome I*, p.3: "Ce sont ces causes, et incontestablement l´éducation de l´œil des gens du XIXe siècle, et encore un sentiment tout nouveau, la tendresse presque humaine pour les choses… " (my translation).

10 In the novel that precedes Joris-Karl Huysmans' *A Rebours*: *A vau-l'eau* (*With the Flow*, 1882), Huysmans brings the reader to a Paris where the misantrope bachelor Folantin tries to find happiness from the simple things in life, but finds himself unable to realise any of his moderate wishes – a decent meal or an exciting meeting – in the new city of Paris that exerts all his energy and fills him with boredom. Folantin is presented as a frustrated flâneur whose walks through Paris used to take him to derelict areas and forgotten, provincial streets, all these calm and silent environments destroyed. In *A vau-l'eau,* Huysmans' response to the social conditions of the Paris was the naturalist approach that appealed to him at the beginning of his career as a fiction writer, when he made Emile Zola his advisor and mentor. The joyless and unsatisfied character of Folantin is a predecessor to Baron des Esseintes in *A Rebours*, communicating Huysmans' critique of the process that erased his familiar Paris in front of him. In contrast to Folantin, des Esseintes' experimental lifestyle is financially and fantasmagorically unlimited, restlessly seeking sensations like Folantin, but infinitely more cultured and refined. Folantin's lifestyle is more similar to Huysmans'own, living on a civil servant's salary. Yet the excessive Baron and the state secretary share the same destiny: there is no satisfaction in life, there is no consolation in nature, nor in the city. There is nowhere to hide from modern life with its disappearing stimuli and vanishing plots.

11 Emile Zola described the world of the Department Store in his novel *Au Bonheur des dames*, published in 1884, as a female social sphere. In many ways, this novel is the opposite of Huysmans' *A Rebours*. Zola introduces a young ambitious woman to a career in the core of Paris, Huysmans retires the jaded Baron des Esseintes from the city to countryside isolation. The department store is a social scene for women, the Baron's mansion provides the ultimate privacy for a hyperaesthete hermit. What Huysmans and Zola have in common is the theme of *spaces of desire*. Both the department store and the mansion support mind travelling; the department store is decorated so as to encompass all exotic and fantasmagoric thrills of illusory travelling under one roof. The department store, a hybrid space between the public square and the private domain, was not just a new type of commercial space, but the trope for an entirely new type of consumer, a buyosphere, a natural environment for the modern urban individual.

12 Goncourt, 1881, *tome II*, p. 349: "A l'heure présente, c'est bizarre, quand je me prépare à écrire un morceau, un morceau quelconque, un morceau où il n'entre pas le moindre bric-à-brac, pour m'entraîner, pour me monter, pour faire jaillir le styliste, /…/ j'ai besoin de passer une heure dans ce cabinet et ce boudoir de l' Orient". Goncourt responded physically to this chamber, and claimed that this inspiration was crucial to any writing activity of his: "…je sens mon pouls s'élever, et tout doucement venir en moi cette petite fièvre de la cervelle, sans laquelle je ne puis rien écrire qui vaille." (my translation).

13 Goncourt, 1881, *tome I*, pp. 25–26 (my translation).

14 Goncourt, 1881, *tome I*, p. 25: "Faire une pièce dans ma maison: voilà presque toujours, après la publication d'un livre et avec l'argent qu'il rapporte, la récréation, la récompense que je me donne." (my translation).

15 Goncourt, 1881, *tome I*, p. 25: " un inventeur d'intérieurs pour gens riches" (my translation).

16 Oscar Wilde. *The Picture of Dorian Gray* (1890). London: Penguin Classics 1994, p. 145: (At the end of chapter ten, Mr. Gray is handed a yellow book which will have a devastating influence on him. Although never mentioned by name, the book in question is J-K Huysmans' *Against Nature*:) "It was a novel without a plot, and with only one character, being, indeed, simply a psychological study of a certain young Parisian, who spent his life trying to realise in the nineteenth century all the passions and modes of thought that belonged to every century except his own. /…/ It was a poisonous book."

17 Huysmans, 1978, "Préface écrit vingt ans après le roman", pp. 47–48: "le désir de qui m'appréhendait de secouer les préjugés, de briser les limites du roman, d'y faire entrer l'art, la science, l'histoire, de ne plus se servir, en un mot, de cette forme que comme d'un cadre pour y insérer de plus sérieux travaux." (Translation from: "Preface Written Twenty Years After the Novel", *Against the Grain*: New York: Dover Publications, Inc. 1969, n.p., 8 Oct. 2005. <http://www.eldritchpress.org/jkh/rpf.html>): "There were many things Zola could not understand; in the first place, the craving I felt to open the windows, to escape from surroundings that were stifling me; secondly, the desire that filled me to shake off preconceived ideas, to break the limitations of the novel, to introduce into it art, science, history; in a word not to use this form of literature except as a frame in which to put more serious kinds of work. For my part, the thing that seemed to me most indispensable at that period was to do away with the traditional plot of intrigue, even to eliminate love and woman altogether, to concentrate the ray of light on a single character, to strike out a new line at any price."

18 Silverman, 1989, p. 38.

19 Walter Benjamin. *Paris: 1800–talets huvudstad*. Stockholm & Stehag: Brutus Östling Förlag Symposion 1992, pp. 48–49.

20 Huysmans, 1959, p. 24.

21 Huysmans, 1959, p. 146.

22 Goncourt, 1881, *tome I*, pp. 238–357.

23 Goncourt, 1881, *tome I*, pp. 364–365.

24 Huysmans, 1959, pp. 180–181.

25 Huysmans, 1959, p. 183.

26 Huysmans, 1959, p. 35.

27 Xavier de Maistre. *A Journey around my Room and A Nocturnal Expedition around my Room.* (Andrew Brown, Trans.) London: Hesperus Classics 2004, ch. 4, p. 7.

28 De Maistre, 2004, ch. 1, p. 3.

29 De Maistre, 2004, ch. 6, p. 9: (Maistre's emphasis). De Maistre's attitude differs from Huysmans' in the respect that the Baron goes beyond experiencing painting and literature; he actually indulges in sensory experiences such as perfumery, so to say perfecting the organs of the beast.

30 De Maistre, *A Journey around my Room*, 2004, ch. 6, p. 10.

31 De Maistre, *A Journey around my Room*, 2004, ch. 4, p. 7.

32 De Maistre, *A Journey around my Room*, 2004, ch. 4, p. 7.

33 De Maistre, *A Journey around my Room*, 2004, ch. 10, p. 14.

34 De Maistre, *A Journey around my Room*, 2004, ch. 6, p. 10.

35 De Maistre, *A Journey around my Room*, 2004, ch. 31, p. 44.

36 De Maistre, *A Journey around my Room*, 2004, ch. 36, p. 51.

37 De Maistre, *A Journey around my Room*, 2004, ch. 8, p. 12.

38 De Maistre, *A Journey around my Room*, 2004, ch. 29, p. 41.

39 De Maistre, *A Journey around my Room*, 2004, ch. 42, p. 62.

40 De Maistre, *A Journey around my Room*, 2004, ch. 42, p. 66.

41 De Maistre, *A Journey around my Room*, 2004, ch. 42, p. 67.

42 De Maistre, *Nocturnal Expedition around my Room*, ch. 5, p. 80.

43 Paul Virilio. *Försvinnandets estetik* (*The Aesthetics of Disappearance*, 1989). Göteborg: Bokförlaget Korpen 1996, p. 36.

44 Walter Benjamin. "Unpacking my Library – A Talk about Book Collecting" in *Illuminations.* (Hannah Arendt, Ed.) London: Pimlico/Random House 1999, p. 69.

CHAPTER TWO

1 Walter Benjamin. "The Work of Art in the Age of Mechanical Reproduction" (orig. published in Zeitschrift fü Sozialforschung 1936), in *Illuminations*. (Hannah Arendt, Ed.) London: Pimlico/ Random House 1999, p. 233.

2 Henri Bergson. *L'Evolution créatrice*. Paris: Félix Alcan 1907.

3 Bergson, 1907, p. 331: "le méchanisme de notre connaissance usuelle est de nature cinématographique". (English translation from *Creative Evolution.* Arthur Mitchell, Trans. London: Macmillan 1911).

4 Benjamin, "The Work of Art in the Age of Mechanical Reproduction", 1999, p. 215.

5 Benjamin, "The Work of Art in the Age of Mechanical Reproduction", 1999, p. 214.

6 Benjamin, "The Work of Art in the Age of Mechanical Reproduction", 1999, p. 216.

7 Walter Benjamin. "A Small History of Photography" in *One-Way Street and Other Writings* (1928). London & New York: Verso 1979, pp. 240–257.

8 Jonathan Crary. *Techniques of the Observer: On Vision and Modernity in the Nineteenth Century* (1992). Cambridge, Massachusetts & London, England: The MIT Press 1999, p. 3.

9 Crary, 1999, p. 19.

10 Crary, 1999, p. 19.

11 Crary, 1999, p. 113.

12 Crary, 1999, p. 14.

13 Charles Musser. *History of the American Cinema, Vol. I: The Emergence of Cinema: the American screen to* 1907 (Charles Harpole, Gen. Ed.). New York & Oxford: Maxwell Macmillan International 1990, p.75: The Kinetoscope account showed the expense of "Revolving photograph building: $637.67" of the total amount of $24118.04 spent on the kinetograph project by April 1893. The largest post of $21736.25 was spent on the kinetoscope experiments.

14 Musser, 1990, p. 72.

15 In relation to the invention of a "heliotropic building", it may be thought-provoking to consider Benjamin's use of the analogy of heliotropism to illustrate the tendency to adjust history from what is seen as history: "As flowers turn toward the sun, by dint of a secret heliotropism the past strives to turn toward that sun which is rising in the sky of history." (Walter Benjamin. "Theses on the Philosophy of History" in *Illuminations.* (Hannah Arendt, Ed.) London: Pimlico/ Random House 1999, p. 246).

16 "Paddy" (as in "Paddy wagon") is a slang nickname for Irishman, almost synonymous with "drunk troublemaker" in the late American 19th century.

17 "The Wizard of Menlo Park". *The New York Daily Graphic.* New York, July 9, 1879.

18 William Croffut. "An afternoon with Edison, the Inventor of the Talking Machines". *The New York Daily Graphic.* New York, April 2, 1878: Reprinted in Ronald W Clark. Edison – the man who made the future. New York: G. P. Putnam & Sons 1977, p. 213.

19 Thomas A. Edison. *The Papers of Thomas A. Edison: Research to Development at Menlo Park, January 1879–March 1881, Vol. V.* Paul B. Israel, Louis Carlat, David Hochfelder & Keith A. Nier (Eds.). Baltimore & London: The Johns Hopkins University Press 2004, p. 880.

20 The "Edisonade", often a dime-novel adventure featuring Edison as a hero inventor, popular in the 1890s, as a variation of the "Robinsonade" adventure novel, modelled after Daniel Defoe's castaway narrative from1719.

21 Auguste Villiers de l'Isle-Adam. *L'Eve future*. Paris: GF-Flammarion 1992.

22 Martha Braun. *Picturing Time: The Work of Etienne-Jules Marey (*1830–1904*)*. Chicago & London: The University of Chicago Press 1992, pp. 231–232.

23 Braun, 1992, p. 187.

24 David Robinson. *From Peep show to Palace: The Birth of American Film*. New York: Columbia University Press 1996, p. 23: Edison declared in description filed with the Patents Office on October 17, 1888: "I am experimenting upon an instrument which does for the Eye what the phonograph does for the Ear, which is the recording and reproduction of things in motion…".

25 Gordon Hendricks. *The Edison Motion Picture Myth*. Berkeley & Los Angeles: University of California Press 1961, pp. 144–145: Letter of February 17, 1879 reprinted in "Appendix A: A biographical sketch of W.K.L. Dickson".

26 Hendricks, 1961, p. 149.

27 Hendricks, 1961, p. 151.

28 Robinson, 1996, p. 23.

29 Braun, 1992, p. 57.

30 Braun, 1992, p. 61.

31 Braun, 1992, p. 104.

32 Braun, 1992, p. 189.

33 The camera eye has often been declared as neutral and objective (strangely enough objective is also a technical name for the lens in the camera), yet in postmodern theory on visual culture the camera eye almost metonymously serves the subjective point of view: the role of the author is questioned, as is the genius, and the actor has entered the role of experimenter of perception of objectivity in an effort of turning the tables in the powerplay of film and photography (e.g. Cindy Sherman).

34 Crary, 1999, p. 133: A stereoscope is a handheld device that displays a still scene from a set of double photographs, called stereographs, manipulated and mounted to create illusory depth.

35 Crary, 1999, pp. 105–118.

36 Crary, 1999, pp. 118–124.

37 Robinson, 1996, p. 39.

38 Musser, 1990, p. 72.

39 Hendricks, 1961, p. 108.

40 Hendricks, 1961, p. 111: The visit took place on the 20th May and was recorded in *The Orange Chronicle*. New Jersey, May 23, 1891.

41 Hendricks, 1961, p. 113: Quoted from *The New York Sun*. New York, May 26, 1891.

42 Musser, 1990, p.75.

43 Musser, 1990, p. 81.

44 Musser, 1990, p. 88.

45 A projector is essentially a reversed camera: the lens used to compress and focus the light onto a sensitive film inside the camera,

is in the reversed condition used to spread the light and focus on a surface outside of the camera.

46 Marshall McLuhan. *The Gutenberg Galaxy: The Making of Typographic Man.* London: Routledge & Kegan Paul 1962, p. 56.

47"The Jazz Singer" from 1927 is attributed as the first "talkie": a sound film with dialogue. See also: Talkie: Wikipedia: The Free Encyclopedia. 8 Oct. 2005. <http://en.wikipedia.org/wiki/Talkie>

48 Crary, 1999, p. 29.

49 Crary, 1999, p. 39.

50 Gordon Hendricks. *The Edison Motion Picture Myth.* Berkeley & Los Angeles: University of California Press 1961.

51 Robinson, 1996, p. 65.

52 Musser, 1990, pp. 109–111.

53 Musser, 1990, p. 118.

54 Musser, 1990, p. 352.

55 Musser, 1990, p. 68.

56 Benjamin, "The Work of Art in the Age of Mechanical Reproduction", 1999, p. 215.

57 Paul Douglass. "Bergson and Cinema: Friends or Foes" in John Mullarkey (Ed.). *The New Bergson.* Manchester, UK: Manchester University Press 1999, p. 222: Bergson quoted from Mind and Energy (1919).

58 Douglass, 1999, p. 222.

59 Douglass, 1999, p. 222.

60 Musser, 1990, p. 78.

61 Walter Benjamin. "The Storyteller", in *Illuminations.* (Hannah Arendt, Ed.) London: Pimlico/Random House 1999, p. 99: "A man listening to a story is in the company of the storyteller; even a man reading one shares his companionship. The reader of a novel, however, is isolated, more so than any other reader".

62 Benjamin, "The Work of Art in the Age of Mechanical Reproduction", 1999, p. 232.

63 Benjamin, "The Work of Art in the Age of Mechanical Reproduction", 1999, p. 233.

64 Maurice Bardèche & Robert Brasillach. *Histoire du Cinéma.* Paris: Les Sept Couleurs 1964, p. 10.

65 Bardèche & Brasillach, 1964, p. 9.

66 Bardèche & Brasillach, 1964, p. 12.

67 Robinson, 1996, p. 41.

68 Musser, 1990, p. 118.

69 Musser, 1990, p. 120.

70 Robinson, 1996, p. 47.

71 Musser, 1990, p. 82.

72 Terry Ramsaye. *A Million and One Nights: A History of the Motion Picture Through* 1925. New York: Touchstone Books 1986: ch. 9. Retrieved 8 Oct. 2005. <http://www.acmi.net.au/AIC/LATHAM_RAMSAYE.html>: Russell Naughton (Web page Ed.). Adventures in Cybersound, 1998: In 1894, Norman C. Raff (of Raff & Gammon, contractors of the Kinetoscope Company) approach Edison regarding the rumours of competitors' experimenting on "wall projection" of moving images. Edison's reply was: "No, if we make this screen machine that you are asking for, it will spoil everything. We are making these peep show machines and selling a lot of them at a good profit. If we put out a screen machine there will be a use for maybe about ten of them in the whole United States. With that many screen machines you could show the pictures to everybody in the country – and then it would be done. Let's not kill the goose that lays the golden egg."

73 Ramsaye, 1925, ch. 9.

74 Robinson, 1996, p. 53.

75 Benjamin, "The Work of Art in the Age of Mechanical Reproduction", 1999, p. 229.

76 Benjamin, "The Work of Art in the Age of Mechanical Reproduction", 1999, p. 231.

77 Benjamin, "The Work of Art in the Age of Mechanical Reproduction", 1999, p. 222.

78 Benjamin, "The Work of Art in the Age of Mechanical Reproduction", 1999, p. 224.

79 Benjamin, "The Work of Art in the Age of Mechanical Reproduction", 1999, p. 214

80 Bergson, 1907, p. 330.

81 Douglass, 1999, p. 220.

82 Henri Bergson. *Creative Evolution.* (Arthur Mitchell, Trans.) London: Macmillan 1911, p. 750.

83 Joel Silver (Producer) & Andy Wachowski, Larry Wachowski (Directors). "The Matrix" (Motion Picture). United States: Warner Bros. 1999. See also: Bullet time: Wikipedia: The Free Encyclopedia. 8 Oct. 2005. <http://en.wikipedia.org/wiki/Bullet_time>

84 Benjamin, "The Work of Art in the Age of Mechanical Reproduction", 1999, p. 229

85 Walter Benjamin. *Paris: 1800-talets huvudstad.* Stockholm & Stehag: Brutus Östling Förlag Symposion 1992, p. 212.

86 Benjamin, 1992, p. 746.

87 Benjamin, 1992, p. 117.

88 Benjamin, "The Work of Art in the Age of Mechanical Reproduction", 1999, p. 225.

89 Benjamin, "The Work of Art in the Age of Mechanical Reproduction", 1999, pp. 225–226.

CHAPTER THREE

1 Elizabeth Grosz. *Architecture from the Outside: Essays on Virtual and Real Space*. Cambridge, Massachusetts & London, England: The MIT Press 2001, p. 130.

2 Virtual, a.: *The Oxford English Dictionary*. 2nd ed. 1989. OED Online. Oxford University Press. 8 Oct. 2005. <http://dictionary.oed.com/cgi/entry/50278111>.

3 Grosz, 2001, p. 129.

4 Edouard Le Roy. *A New Philosophy: Henri Bergson* (*Une Philosophie nouvelle: Henri Bergson*, 1912). (Vincent Benson, Trans. 1913) Retrieved 8 Oct. 2005. Project Gutenberg: <http://digital.library.upenn.edu/webbin/gutbook/lookup?num=1347>.

5 Malin Zimm. "The Dying Dreamer – Looking into Huysmans' Virtual Worlds" in *The Dying Dreamer – Architecture of Parallel Realities*. Stockholm: KTH TRITA-ARK-Forskningspublikationer 2003, pp. 44–65.

6 Zimm, 2003, p. 46.

7 Henri Bergson. *Matter and Memory* (*Matière et Mémoire*, 1896). (Nancy M. Paul & W. Scott Palmer, Trans.) New York: The MIT Press, Zone Books 1991, p. 173.

8 Bergson, 1991, p. 25.

9 Keith Ansell-Pearson. *Philosophy and the Adventure of the Virtual: Bergson and the time of life*. London & New York: Routledge 2002, p. 150.

10 Bergson, 1991, p. 220.

11 The specific meaning of *virtual memory*, a term used for a certain type of software memory system, would have been of interest to Bergson, denoting a computer system memory that appears to be internal although most of it is external, made possible by an unnoticable transfer between the two memory modes. See also: Virtual, a.: *The Oxford English Dictionary*. 2nd ed. 1989. OED Online. Oxford University Press. 8 Oct. 2005. <http://dictionary.oed.com/cgi/entry/50278111>: "*Computers. spec.* applied to memory that appears to be internal although most of it is external, transfer between the two being made automatically as required."

12 Grosz, 2001, p. 121.

13 Bergson, 1991, p. 233.

14 Zimm, 2003, p. 60.

15 Bergson, 1991, p. 189.

16 Grosz, 2001, p. 119.

17 Grosz, 2001, p. 117.

18 Bergson, Henri. *Introduktion till Metafysiken* (*Introduction à la métaphysique* 1903). Lysekil: Pontes 1992, pp. 58–59.

19 Bergson, 1992, p. 61.

20 Bergson, 1992, pp. 59–60.

21 Walter Benjamin. *Illuminations*. (Hannah Arendt, Ed.) London: Pimlico/Random House 1999.

22 Bergson, 1992, p. 61.

23 Joris-Karl Huysmans. *Against Nature* (*A Rebours* 1884). (Robert Baldick, Trans.) London: Penguin Classics 1959, p. 84.

24 Charles Baudelaire. "The Double Room", V, in *Paris Spleen*. ("La Chambre double", poems written 1855–1867, first published as *Le Spleen de Paris*. Paris: Asselineau et Banville 1869) (Louise Varèse, Transl.) New York: New Directions Publishing Corporation 1970, pp. 5–7.

25 Avatar: *The Oxford English Dictionary*. 2nd ed. 1989. OED Online. Oxford University Press. 8 Oct. 2005. <http://dictionary.oed.com/cgi/entry/50015367>: sanskrit *avatara* – descent. (f. *ava-* down + *tar-* to pass over) 1. *Hindu Myth.* The descent of a deity to the earth in an incarnate form. 2. Manifestation in human form; incarnation.

26 Huysmans, 1959, pp. 123–125.

27 Bergson, 1991, p. 9.

28 Bergson, 1991, pp. 220–221.

29 Bergson, 1991, p. 221.

30 Bergson, 1991, p. 222.

31 Neal Stephenson. *The Diamond Age*. (first published in the US: Bantam Books in 1995), London & New York: Penguin Books 1996, pp. 92–93.

32 Stephenson, 1996, p. 62.

33 Stephenson, 1996, p. 107.

34 Stephenson, 1996, p. 46.

35 Bergson's discussion about the virtual in *L'Evolution créatrice* (1907) takes place on a more organic level in relation to his unconventional approach to the notion of creation, involving his philosophy of evolution and the *élan vital*, the biological impulse.

36 Marie-Laure Ryan. *Narrative as Virtual Reality – Immersion and Interactivity in Literature and Electronic Media*. Baltimore & London: The Johns Hopkins University Press 2001, p. 26: *Virtus* – in scholastic Latin, the philosophical concept of virtus as force or power.

37 The Hierarchy of Needs: The Baron, in contrast to Nell, is taking the Maslow staircase down after reaching the topmost step of æsthetizisation. He needs to return to the first step of ensuring physiological needs neglected while he preferred to remain in the direct creation of his mind. See also: Abraham Maslow. *Motivation and Personality* (1954). 2nd ed. New York: Harper & Row 1970.

38 Stephenson, 1996, pp. 232–238.

39 Stephenson, 1996, p. 61.

40 Stephenson, 1996, p. 263.

41 Stephenson, 1996, p. 78.

42 Stephenson, 1996, p. 107.

43 Stephenson, 1996, p. 107.

44 Stephenson, 1996, p. 106: Stephenson might have the folktale research of Vladimir Propp in mind for this "database".

45 Stephenson, 1996, p. 135.

46 Ryan, 2001, p. 9.

47 Stephenson, 1996, p. 90.

48 Stephenson, 1996, pp. 97–98.

49 Stephenson, 1996, p. 89.

50 Marshall McLuhan. *The Gutenberg Galaxy: The Making of Typographic Man*. London: Routledge & Kegan Paul 1962

51 Ryan, 2001, pp. 120–162: The criteria of immersion: spatial immersion, represented by the setting, temporal immersion represented by the plot, and emotional immersion represented by character.

52 N. Katherine Hayles. *How we Became Posthuman: Virtual Bodies in Cybernetics, Literature, and Informatics.* Chicago & London: The University of Chicago Press 1999, p. 49.

53 William W. Braham. "A Wall of Books", in *Journal of Architectural Education* vol. 53, nr 1: 1999, pp. 4–14.

54 Steampunk: *Wikipedia: The Free Encyclopedia*. 23 Apr. 2005. <http://en.wikipedia.org/wiki/Steampunk>: "Inspired by the *Scientific Romances, Voyages Extraordinaires* and *Edisonades* of the Victorian and Edwardian eras, Steampunk as a genre developed in the 1980s as an offshoot of, or reaction to, Cyberpunk."

55 Susan Stewart. *On Longing – Narratives of the Miniature, the Gigantic, the Souvenir, the Collection*. Durham & London: Duke University Press 1993, p. 68.

56 Stephenson, 1996, p. 31.

57 Ann Gustafsson. "Nanoforskare härmar naturen" (*Nano-researchers mimicking nature*), in *Dagens Nyheter*. 10 Apr. 2005. pp. 26–27.

58 The 19th century recognized the term *virtual* from scholastic Latin since the Mediaeval Ages. Derived from prehistoric language, the etymological root of the word is *wiros* meaning man. The term was transformed in primitive Latin to *"vir"* (man, hero, husband, warrior), from where the word *virilis* ("a thing proper of man", virility, magistrate) developed. Saint Augustine launched in *De Magistro* an account of *virtualis* that approaches the contemporary meaning of the word: "he who has in himself the power to do, to make something". Saint Augustine assigned the meaning "potentiality" and "free will" to the Latin *virtus*, the right use of freedom of choice. Thomas ab Aquino simply transformed it to "power" – later assimilated by Foucault who related power to information. The translation in our days of *virtualis* into "absence" and "parallel reality" from the initial meaning "man" is a semantic mutation. The root of *"vir"* may even seem contradictory in its variations: *"virtual"* meaning "in effect, though not in fact, almost, nearly", parodically next to *"virtuous"* for "morally good, blameless" and *"virtuality*" signifying "essential nature". All these interpretations are far from the contemporary definition that makes virtuality almost synonymous with "*cyberspace*" (a notional environment in which electronic communication occurs, space generated by a computer system without real existence). Etymology compiled from: Emanuel Dimas de Melo Pimenta. "Virtual Architecture" in *Transformers*. Retrieved 8 Oct, 2005. < http://www.asa-art.com/virtus/idea.htm>.

59 Janell Watson. *Literature and Material Culture from Balzac to Proust: the Collection and Consumption of Curiosities*. Cambridge: Cambridge University Press 1999, pp. 109–142.

60 Baudrillard quoted in Ryan, 2001, pp. 27–28.

61 Hayles, 1999, p. 47.

62 Hayles, 1999, p. 22.

63 Hayles, 1999, p. 283.

64 Walter Benjamin. "The Work of Art in the Age of Mechanical Reproduction", in *Illuminations*. (Hannah Arendt, Ed.) London: Pimlico/Random House 1999, p. 228.

65 Walter Benjamin. "The Storyteller", in *Illuminations*. (Hannah Arendt, Ed.) London: Pimlico/Random House 1999, p. 99.

66 Walter Benjamin. "On some Motifs in Baudelaire", in *Illuminations*. (Hannah Arendt, Ed.) London: Pimlico/Random House 1999, pp. 155–156.

67 Janet H. Murray. *Hamlet on the Holodeck – The Future of Narrative in Cyberspace* (1997). Third Printing, 2000. Cambridge, Massachusetts: The MIT Press, 2000, pp.152–153.

68 Alvin Toffler. *Future Shock*. London: Pan books 1970, p. 210.

69 Murray, 2000, p. 161.

70 Murray, 2000, p. 86.

71 Ian Eller. "World of Warcraft Population Hits New Highs", in *RPGamer News Bulletin*, 30 Aug. 2005. Retrieved 8 Oct. 2005. <http://www.rpgamer.com/news/Q3-2005/083005b.html>.

72 Murray, 2000, p. 174.

73 Murray, 2000, p. 141.

74 iToy: A gesture/motion-detector for game interaction ("eye-toy", interactive toy) developed for Playstation 2: video game device for the PS2 console, released by Sony in 2002.

75 Walter Benjamin. *Paris, 1800-talets huvudstad. Passagearbetet.* (*Das Passagen-Werk* 1927–29, 1935, 1939) Stockholm & Stehag: Brutus Östlings Bokförlag Symposion 1992. (English title: *Paris: Capital of the 19th Century*), p. 53.

76 Benjamin, 1992, p. 23.

77 Benjamin, 1992, p. 132.

78 Benjamin, 1992, p. 422: Benjamin quotes Edouard Gourdon: I live a hundred lives in one. If I embark on a journey it takes place in the same way as an electric spark travels… (my translation)

79 Benjamin, 1992, p. 429.

80 Benjamin, 1992, pp. 429–430: Game as an activity was the priviledge of the feudal class, but in the 19th century, the bourgeoisie became gamers since time is liberated from not being part of the production process. The game was also a substitute and pastime allowed by the state to keep in check subversive forces in society.

81 Hayles, 1999, p. 288.

82 Hayles, 1999, p. 288.

EPILOGUE

1 Excite: *The Oxford English Dictionary*. 2nd ed. 1989. OED Online. Oxford University Press. 8 Oct. 2005. <http://dictionary.oed.com/cgi/entry/50079615>: From Middle French exciter, from Latin excitare, from ex- + citare: to set in motion, awaken, call forth, instigate, incite.

2 Neal Stephenson. *The Diamond Age* (1995). London & New York: Penguin Books 1996, p. 294: Example of use: "Gwendolyn /.../ sat down at an escritoire to work her way through some pending correspondence."

3 Gerald M. Edelman and Giulio Tononi. *Consciouness: How Matter Becomes Imagination*. Harmondsworth, England: The Penguin Press 2000, pp. 40–41.

4 The neologism *excitoir* is used by Alain Barbier Sainte Marie. "La Maison d´un artiste: à revisiter": Review of the republication of Edmond de Goncourt, *La Maison d›un artiste.* (Dijon: L›Échelle de Jacob, 2003). Article published online July 12, 2003. Retrieved Sept. 28, 2005.<http://membres.lycos.fr/goncourt/maisonechelledej/absmaison.htm> Site founded in 2001 by Paul Adamy & Alain Barbier Sainte Marie (Eds.).

5 Experience: *The Oxford English Dictionary*. 2nd ed. 1989. OED Online. Oxford University Press. 8 Oct. 2005. <http://dictionary.oed.com/cgi/entry/50080399>: From Latin *experientia*: To make trial or experiment of; to put to the test; to test, try. A tentative procedure; an operation performed in order to ascertain or illustrate some truth; an experiment.

6 Neal Stephenson. *The Diamond Age*. London & New York: Penguin Books 1996, p. 428.

7 N. Katherine Hayles. *How we Became Posthuman: Virtual Bodies in Cybernetics, Literature, and Informatics.* Chicago & London: The University of Chicago Press 1999, p. 287.

8 Hayles, 1999, p. 48.

9 Walter Benjamin. "On Some Motifs in Baudelaire", in *Illuminations*. (Hannah Arendt, Ed.) London: Pimlico/Random House 1999, p. 155

10 Benjamin, "On Some Motifs in Baudelaire", 1999, p. 154.

11 Joris-Karl Huysmans. *Against Nature* (*A Rebours*, 1884). (Robert Baldick, Trans.). London: Penguin Classics 1959.

12 Aristotle. *Physics* (350 BC), book II, part 1& 2. (R. P. Hardie & R. K. Gaye, Trans.) 8 Oct. 2005. <http://classics.mit.edu/Aristotle/physics.2.ii.html>: A property of Nature's subjects is the inherent principle of motion and change. An artificial product, according to Aristotle, has not in itself the source of its own production: a chair does not grow from a seed, but the tree that provides the material does.

13 Benjamin, "On Some Motifs in Baudelaire", 1999, p. 157.

14 Benjamin, "On Some Motifs in Baudelaire", 1999, p. 153.

15 Benjamin, "On Some Motifs in Baudelaire", 1999, p. 187.

16 Benjamin, "On Some Motifs in Baudelaire", 1999, p. 155.

17 Benjamin, "On Some Motifs in Baudelaire", 1999, p. 184.

18 Benjamin, "On Some Motifs in Baudelaire", 1999, p. 184.

19 Henri Bergson. *Matter and Memory* (*Matière et Mémoire*, 1896). (Nancy M. Paul & W. Scott Palmer, Trans.) New York: The MIT Press, Zone Books 1991, pp. 234–235.

20 Bergson, 1991, p. 25.

21 Bergson, 1991, p. 151.

22 Bergson, 1991, p. 183.

23 Bergson, 1991, p. 184.

24 Bergson, 1991, p. 184.

25 Antoine de Saint-Exupéry. *Le Petit Prince* (1943). Original illustrations by Saint-Exupéry. San Diego, New York & London: Harvest HBJ Publishers 1971, p. 12.

26 Hayles, 1999, p. 288.

27 Janet H. Murray. *Hamlet on the Holodeck – The Future of Narrative in Cyberspace* (1997). Cambridge, Massachusetts: The MIT Press 2000, p. 65: Stirring panic or not, the film shown was "Arrival of a Train at Ciotat station", reeled before a Paris audience on Dec. 28, 1895.

28 Black box: *The Oxford English Dictionary*. 2nd ed. 1989. OED Online. Oxford University Press. 8 Oct. 2005. <http://dictionary.oed.com/cgi/entry/50022922/50022922se83>: "orig. Royal Air Force slang for a navigational instrument in an aeroplane; later extended to denote any automatic apparatus performing intricate functions."

29 Black box: *The Oxford English Dictionary*. 2nd ed. 1989. OED Online. Oxford University Press. 8 Oct. 2005. <http://dictionary.oed.com/cgi/entry/50022922/50022922se83>: "W. R. Ashby. *Introd. Cybernetics.* 1956. vi. 86. Black Box theory is even wider in application than these professional studies. *Ibid.*, In our daily lives we are confronted at every turn with systems whose internal mechanisms are not fully open to inspection, and which must be treated by the methods appropriate to the Black Box."

30 Black box: *Wikipedia: The Free Encyclopedia*. 3 Oct. 2005. <http://en.wikipedia.org/wiki/Black_box>."In computing in general, a 'black box program' is one where the user cannot see its inner workings."

31 Black box theory: *Wikipedia: The Free Encyclopedia*. 3 Oct. 2005. <http://en.wikipedia.org/wiki/black_box_theory>.

32 Black box: *The Oxford English Dictionary*. 2nd ed. 1989. OED Online. Oxford University Press. 8 Oct. 2005. <http://dictionary.oed.com/cgi/entry/50022922>: "1674 R. Godfrey. *Inj. & Ab. Physic.* 71. She had been in the black Box (meaning the Coffin)."

33 Walter Benjamin. "The storyteller", in *Illuminations*. London: Pimlico/Random House 1999, p. 93.

34 Margaret Morse. *Virtualities: Television, Media, Art, and Cyberculture*. Bloomington & Indianapolis: Indiana University Press 1998, p. 4.

35 Plato. *The Republic*, book VII. (B. Jowett, Trans.) 8 Oct. 2005. Project Gutenberg: <http://www.gutenberg.org/etext/1497>.

36 Rosalind Williams. *Dream Worlds: Mass Consumption in Late Nineteenth Century France.* Berkeley & Los Angeles: University of California Press 1982.

37 Weblog: *The Oxford English Dictionary*. Draft Entry Mar. 2003. OED Online. Oxford University Press. 8 Aug. 2005. <http://dictionary.oed.com/cgi/entry/00319399>: "A frequently updated web site

consisting of personal observations, excerpts from other sources, etc., typically run by a single person, and usually with hyperlinks to other sites; an online journal or diary." The internet as an electronic media is suitable for hypertext, while also supporting the form of individual temporal succession in the form of the personal "blog".

38 Peter Brooks. *Reading for the Plot – Design and Intention in Narrative*. Oxford: Clarendon Press 1984, p. 4.

39 Brooks, 1984, p. 6.

40 The plot engine as writing software serves the construction of a narrative plot, not to be confused with the plot engine as an automated drawing machine or plotter, an instrument for drawing graphs and plots on plans or maps, utilised before CAD in design practises like architecture and engineering.

41 McLuhan. *Understanding Media*. New York & London: McGraw–Hill Book Company 1965, p. 242.

42 Jean-François Lyotard. *The Postmodern Condition- A Report on Knowledge* (1979) Manchester: Manchester University Press 1992.

43 Jennifer Bloomer. *Architecture and the Text: The (S)crypts of Joyce and Piranesi*. New Haven & London: Yale University Press 1993, p. 144.

44 Friedrich A. Kittler. *Gramophone, Film, Typewriter* (1986). Stanford, California: Stanford University Press 1999, p. 161.

45 Bloomer, 1993, p. 145.

46 Victor Hugo. *Notre-Dame De Paris* (1831). BOOK FIFTH, chapter II, This will Kill That. Retrieved 8 Oct. 2005. <http://www.gutenberg.org/etext/2610>: "The archdeacon gazed at the gigantic edifice for some time in silence, then extending his right hand, with a sigh, towards the printed book which lay open on the table, and his left towards Notre-Dame, and turning a sad glance from the book to the church, 'Alas,' he said, 'this will kill that.' /.../ Is it because it is printed?' 'You have said it,' replied Claude, who seemed absorbed in a profound meditation, and stood resting, his forefinger bent backward on the folio which had come from the famous press of Nuremberg. Then he added these mysterious words: 'Alas! alas! small things come at the end of great things; a tooth triumphs over a mass. The Nile rat kills the crocodile, the swordfish kills the whale, the book will kill the edifice.' "

47 David Robinson. *From Peep show to Palace: The Birth of American Film*. New York: Columbia University Press 1996, p. 23: Edison declared in description filed with the Patents Office on October 17, 1888: "I am experimenting upon an instrument which does for the Eye what the phonograph does for the Ear, which is the recording and reproduction of things in motion...".

48 McLuhan, 19

CHAPTER ONE

Fig. 1 Illustration of des Esseintes' fish tank window in his diningroom, designed as a ship's cabin. An aquarium occupies the space between the real window in the real house-wall and a port-hole window on the other side. The aquarium is furnished with artificial seaweed and mechanical fish and crabs driven by clockwork. The water of the tank, illuminated by the window behind it, can be tinted with coloured essences to create different atmospheres in the room. (See also: Huysmans' *Against Nature*, pp. 33–34). Collage by Malin Zimm 2005.

Fig. 2 The former room of Jules de Goncourt, redecorated to host *le Salon Grenier*, where the first meeting was held on February 1, 1885. Photograph by Fernand Lochard, who documented the main spaces of Goncourt's residence in 1883 and 1886. (Paris: Académie Goncourt).

Fig. 3 The library and a corner of Goncourt's desk in the writing studio – *cabinet de travail* – in "*La Maison d'un artiste*", Auteuil. Photograph by Fernand Lochard, 1883–1886. (Paris: Harlingue-Violet).

Fig. 4 Goncourt's bookcase. Photograph by Fernand Lochard, 1886. (Paris: Académie Goncourt).

Fig. 5: Huysmans by the fireplace. Photographer and date unknown.

CHAPTER TWO

Fig. 1 The Black Maria (Edison Kinetographic Theatre). West Orange, NJ. Photograph by William K. L. Dickson, 1893. (US Library of Congress).

Fig. 2 Interior of the Black Maria: Heise directing the set, phonograph for experimental purposes visible at the left side of the image. *Century Magazine*, June 1894.

Fig. 3 The Black Maria (Edison Kinetographic Theatre). West Orange, NJ. Photograph by William K. L. Dickson, late 1894. (US Library of Congress).

Fig. 4 The Black Maria, ca. 1894. (The Edison Institute: Henry Ford Collection).

Fig. 5 The police department's patrol wagon "Black Maria", ca. 1880. (Photo Credit: Seattle Times).

Fig. 6 "The Wizard of Menlo Park". *The New York Daily Graphic*. New York: July 9, 1879.

Fig. 7 Eadweard Muybridge's outdoor studio for the photographic animal locomotion studies, constructed in 1884 on the University campus, Pennsylvania. (University of Pennsylvania Archives, Eadweard Muybridge Collection).

Fig. 8 Etienne-Jules Marey's *Fusil Photographique* (Chronophotographic gun). *La Nature*, April 1882. (New York Public Library).

Fig. 9 Etienne-Jules Marey's *Station Physiologique*, Bois-de-Boulogne. *La Nature*, Sept. 8, 1883.

Fig. 10 Marey's mobile camera wagon, *Station Physiologique*, Bois-de-Boulogne. *La Nature*, Sept. 8, 1883.

Fig. 11 Marey's circular rail track for mobile camera, *Station Physiologique*, Bois-de-Boulogne. *La Nature*, Sept. 8, 1883.

Fig. 12 Interior view of kinetoscope (Dickson & Edison, 1894). The 35 mm film travelled continuously over a bank of rollers, each picture being viewed briefly through a narrow slot in the revolving shutter. (US Library of Congress).

Fig. 13 Exterior view of kinetoscope (Dickson & Edison, 1894). Electrically-driven peepshow machine for films produced with kinetograph camera, 1894. (US Library of Congress).

Fig. 14 Strip from motion picture "Dickson greeting": Experimental film fragment made with the Edison/Dickson/Heise experimental horizontal-feed kinetograph camera and viewer. W.K.L. Dickson & William Heise (Prod.), William Heise (Camera), W.K.L. Dickson (Performer), May 20, 1891, in the Photographic Building at the Edison Laboratory, West Orange, New Jersey. (Library of Congress Motion Picture, Broadcasting and Recorded Sound Division, Washington, D. C.) See also: This and other Edison motion pictures filmed in the Black Maria are available for viewing online (Library of Congress motion picture archives): <http://memory.loc.gov/ammem/edhtml/edmvchrn.html>.

Fig. 15 Cartoon by George du Maurier in *Punch's Almanac for 1879*. Dec. 9, 1878: "Edison's Telephonoscope (transmits light as well as sound)."

Fig. 16 Strip from motion picture "Dickson experimental sound film". Film made for Edison's kinetophone in the Black Maria studio ca. Sept. 1894 to April 2, 1895. Thomas A. Edison, Inc. & W.K.L. Dickson. (Prod.) Edison Manufacturing Co. 1895. (Library of Congress Motion Picture, Broadcasting and Recorded Sound Division, Washington, D. C.).

Fig. 17 The kinetophone (Man Viewing a Kinetoscope Which Is Equipped with Synchronized Sound). (Dickson & Edison, 1895). Kinetophone: kinetoscope with phonograph cylinder audio player built in and earphones. (US Library of Congress).

Fig. 18 Etienne-Jules Marey. "Pole vaulting": chronophotographic caption, *Station Physiologique*, 1890–91. (Collège de France).

Fig. 19 Still image of "Sandow" or "Sandow, the modern Hercules". Thomas A. Edison, Inc. & W. K. L. Dickson (Prod.), William Heise (Camera), Eugen Sandow (aka Friedrich Muller) (Performer), March 6, 1894, in Edison's Black Maria studio. Edison Manufacturing Co. 1894. (Library of Congress Motion Picture, Broadcasting and Recorded Sound Division, Washington, D. C.).

Fig. 20 Rendering of the Black Maria, West Orange, New Jersey. Unknown date and artist. (Library of Congress Motion Picture, Broadcasting and Recorded Sound Division, Washington, D. C.).

Fig. 21 *Peter Bacigalupi's Kinetoscope, Phonograph, and Gramophone Arcade*; San Francisco, CA, 1895. (Library of Congress Motion Picture, Broadcasting and Recorded Sound Division, Washington, D. C.).

Fig. 22 *Peter Bacigalupi's Kinetoscope, Phonograph, and Gramophone Arcade*; San Francisco, CA, 1895. (Library of Congress Motion Picture, Broadcasting and Recorded Sound Division, Washington, D. C.).

Fig. 23 Strip from motion picture "Edison Kinetoscopic Record of a Sneeze" or "Fred Ott's Sneeze" (Film made for publicity purposes, as a series of still photographs to accompany an article in Harper's weekly). Thomas A. Edison, Inc. (Prod.), William Heise (Camera), Fred Ott (Performer), ca January 2–7, 1894, in Edison's Black Maria studio at the Edison Laboratory, West Orange, New Jersey. Edison Manufacturing Co. 1894. (Library of Congress Motion Picture, Broadcasting and Recorded Sound Division, Washington, D. C.).

Fig. 24 Strip from motion picture "The Boxing Cats (Prof. Welton's)". Thomas A. Edison, Inc. & W. K. L. Dickson (Prod.), William Heise (Camera), Henry Welton & cats (Performers), ca July 1894, in Edison's Black Maria studio at the Edison Laboratory, West Orange, New Jersey. Edison Manufacturing Co. 1894. (Library of Congress Motion Picture, Broadcasting and Recorded Sound Division, Washington, D. C.).

Fig. 25 Strip from motion picture "May Irwin Kiss" (Scene from the New York stage comedy, "The Widow Jones", in which Irwin and Rice starred). According to Edison film historian C. Musser, the actors staged their kiss for the camera at the request of the *New York World* newspaper, and the resulting film was the most popular Edison Vitascope film in 1896. From Edison films catalog: "By May Irwin and John Rice. They get ready to kiss, begin to kiss, and kiss and kiss and kiss in a way that brings down the house every time"). Thomas A. Edison, Inc. & *New York World* (Prod.), William Heise (Camera), May Irwin & John Rice (Performers), April 1896, in Edison's Black Maria studio at the Edison Laboratory, West Orange, New Jersey. Edison Manufacturing Co. 1896. (Library of Congress Motion Picture, Broadcasting and Recorded Sound Division, Washington, D. C.).

Fig. 26 Strip from motion picture "Carmencita" (According to Edison film historian C. Musser, Spanish dancer Carmencita was the first woman to appear in front of an Edison motion picture camera). Thomas A. Edison, Inc. & W. K. L. Dickson (Prod.), William Heise (Camera), Carmencita (Performer), ca March 10–16, 1894, in Edison's Black Maria studio at the Edison Laboratory, West Orange, New Jersey. Edison Manufacturing Co. 1894. (Library of Congress Motion Picture, Broadcasting and Recorded Sound Division, Washington, D. C.).

Fig. 27 Strip from motion picture "Annie Oakley" (From Raff & Gammon price list: "The 'Little Sure Shot' of the 'Wild West', exhibition of rifle shooting at glass balls, etc.). Thomas A. Edison, Inc. (Prod.), William Heise (Camera), Annie Oakley (Performer), November 1, 1894, in Edison's Black Maria studio at the Edison Laboratory, West Orange, New Jersey. Edison Manufacturing Co. 1894. (Library of Congress Motion Picture, Broadcasting and Recorded Sound Division, Washington, D. C.).

Fig. 28 Strip from motion picture "Leonard-Cushing fight" (From Edison films catalogue: "An actual six-round contest between Mike Leonard, commonly called the 'Beau Brummel' of pugilism, and Jack Cushing. Full of hard fighting, clever hits, punches, leads, dodges, body blows and some slugging. Sold by rounds.) Thomas A. Edison, Inc. & W. K. L. Dickson. (Prod.), William Heise (Camera), Mike Leonard & Jack Cushing (Performers), June 14, 1894, in Edison's Black Maria studio at the Edison Laboratory, West Orange, New Jersey. Kinetoscope Exhibiting Co., 1894. (Library of Congress Motion Picture, Broadcasting and Recorded Sound Division, Washington, D. C.).

Fig. 29 Still image of Charles H. Kayser with the Kinetograph, ca 1889, in Edison's Black Maria studio at the Edison Laboratory, West Orange, New Jersey. Kinetoscope Exhibiting Co., 1894. (Library of Congress Motion Picture, Broadcasting and Recorded Sound Division, Washington, D. C.).

Fig. 30 Strip from motion picture "Three Acrobats", (Alternative title: "The Wall"), 1899. Thomas A. Edison, Inc. (Prod.), Produced for Edison Kinetoscope Exhibiting Co., 1899. (Library of Congress Motion Picture, Broadcasting and Recorded Sound Division, Washington, D. C.).

Fig. 31 Strip from motion picture "The Enchanted Drawing". Stuart Blackton sketching and interacting with his drawing, Nov. 16, 1900. Thomas A. Edison, Inc. (Prod.), Produced for Edison Kinetoscope Exhibiting Co., 1899. (Library of Congress Motion Picture, Broadcasting and Recorded Sound Division, Washington, D. C.).

Fig. 32 Rendering of the Black Maria, West Orange, New Jersey. Unknown date and artist. (British Film Institute): <http://www.victorian-cinema.net/technical.htm>.

Fig. 33 Exterior of the Black Maria replica (showing rails and roof shutter supporting structure), constructed in 1954, Edison National Historic Site. Photographer and date unknown. Retrieved 8 Oct. 2005: <http://www.nps.gov/edis/edisonia/virtual%20tour/blackmaria/blackmaria.htm>.

Fig. 34 Exterior of the Black Maria replica (showing long side of building), constructed in 1954, Edison National Historic Site. Photographer and date unknown. Retrieved 8 Oct. 2005: <http://www.nps.gov/edis/edisonia/virtual%20tour/blackmaria/blackmaria.htm>.

EPILOGUE

Fig. 1 *The Excitoir.* Illustration by Malin Zimm.

Fig. 2 *The White Screen.* Illustration by Malin Zimm.

Fig. 3 Original illustration by Saint-Exupéry in Antoine de Saint-Exupéry. *Le Petit Prince* (1943). San Diego, New York & London: Harvest HBJ Publishers 1971, p. 12.

Fig. 4 *Book Camera Obscura.* Théatre de l´Univers, France, ca 1750. (Los Angeles, Getty Research Institute, Werner Nekes Collection).

CHAPTER FOUR

Page 51: Queen of the United Kingdom of Great Britain and Ireland, Empress of India. *Portrait of Queen Victoria* by Alexander Bassano, 1887. (National Portrait Gallery, London).

Page 55: Still image from "Mary Shelley's Frankenstein", 1910 Thomas A. Edison, Inc.: The first movie adaptation of this novel was just 14 minutes long and starred Charles Ogle as the monster. It is considered a lost film, but rumours circulate about a copy in private possession. Some stills of Ogle's make-up remain, like this photograph. (Library of Congress Motion Picture, Broadcasting and Recorded Sound Division, Washington, D. C.).

Page 57: The *Difference Engine*: calculating machine designed by Charles Babbage in 1821 (this portion of the engine assembled by Joseph Clement in 1832). (Science Museum/ Science & Society Picture Library, London). Ada Lovelace quoted from "Notes" in her translation of Menebrea's paper on Babbage's Analytical Engine. Selection and Adaptation From Ada's Notes found in Betty A. Toole Ed. *Ada, The Enchantress of Numbers*. Los Angeles: Strawberry Press 1998.

Page 62: "*Point de vue pris d'une fenêtre du Gras à Saint-Loup-de-Varennes*", photograph by Nicéphore Niepce, 1826: The view from his study window in Gras, taken with an exposure time of about eight hours. This photograph is often mentioned as the first photographic picture ever taken.

Page 65: Interior view of *The Colosseum*, Regent's Park, Marylebone, London, 1829. The Panorama was created in 1827, with a panoramic painting by Thomas Hornor showing the city of London viewed from the top of St. Paul's Cathedral. (Corporation of London Libraries and Guildhall Art Gallery).

Page 68: The *Kaiser Panorama*, created by August Fuhrmann, showing stereoscopic images, ca 1910. (Stadtmuseum Wels).

Page 73: Firework displays outside Joseph Paxton's *Crystal Palace*. Since 1865, pyrotechnist competitions were organised by *Brock's Firework Company* in the Crystal Palace Park. The palace burnt to the ground on Nov. 30, 1936: all attempts to reconstruct the building have failed.

Page 87: Illustration by Grandville (Jean Ignace Isidore Gérard). *Un autre monde*. Paris: H. Fournier 1844.

Page 95: Illustration by Albert Robida. "La vie électrique" ("The Electric Life") in *Le XXème siècle*, 1890.

Page 99: Illustration by Albert Robida. "La Guerre au XXème siècle" ("Visions of Future Warfare") in *Le XXème siècle*, 1887. Quotes from John Ruskin. "The Storm-Cloud of the 19th Century", essay from 1884, from a lecture given on 11 February 1884. See also: Michael Wheeler (Ed.). *Ruskin and Environment : The Storm-Cloud of the 19th Century*. Manchester: Manchester University Press 1995.

Page 116: *Looping the Loop,* Coney Island, New York City, ca 1910. (Library of Congress, Washington, D. C.).

Page 122: Still image from "Wax-works" (Das Wachsfigurenkabinett), motion picture 1924 directed by Paul Leni (Filmmuseum Berlin/Deutsche Kinemathek).

Page 125: Vintage photo of a bearded lady, circa 1900. Photographer and date unknown.

Page 127: Houdini poses in restraints for a publicity photo, ca 1918. (The Sidney H. Radner Collection, Houdini Historical Center, Appleton, WI.)

Page 130: *La Crinolimanie*. Caricature, unknown artist, ca 1860.

Page 132: A postcard view of the West Pier, Brighton, ca 1920.

Page 134: *Dreamland*, Coney Island, 1912. Photographer unknown.

Page 135: Georges-Eugène Baron Haussmann (1809–1891), *Préfet de la Seine* 1853–1870. (Bibliothèque Nationale de France, BNF, Estampes & Photographie).

Page 137: "Les Travaux de nuit sur la Butte-des-Moulins", night work to make way for Avenue de l'Opéra, 1876. (Bibliothèque Nationale de France, BNF, Estampes & Photographie).

Page 140: "Horse Smashed Cable Car Window", *The New York World* 1897.

Page 143: Interior photographs of the *Statue of Liberty*, February 1984. (The HABS/HAER Collections, LC's Historical Collections, National Digital Library, US).

Page 144: Lamarcus Thompson's *Switchback Railroad* ("The world's first roller coaster", opened June 13, 1884), ca 1884–1885. Photographer unknown.

Page 147: Paul Nipkow: *The Nipkow disk*, ca 1884. Photographer unknown.

Page 149: Illustration by Grandville (Jean Ignace Isidore Gérard). *Un autre monde*. Paris: H. Fournier 1844.

Page 150: "In the Wake of a Cable Car" (cartoon rendering of the feared Metropolitan Street Railway's "Dead Man's Curve"). *New York Life*, 1895.

Page 152: *Au Bon Marché*, 1872. (Bibliothèque Nationale de France, BNF, Estampes & Photographie).

Page 155: "Le Grand Escalier Centrale", *Au Bon Marché*, 1879. (Bibliothèque Nationale de France, BNF, Estampes & Photographie).

Page 157: American one-dollar bill. First issued by the Federal Government in 1862. The Latin reads: *annuit coeptis* – "God has favoured our undertaking", and *novus ordo seclorum* – "a new order has begun". (Photo credit: Audrius Tomonis)

Page 158: *Aspirin*. Photographer and date unknown.

Page 161: "On donne á l´oeil" (We Serve the Eye) Advertisement for Imprimeries Rouchton, 1864.

Page 162: Edison invited to Gustave Eiffel in relation to the Paris exposition universelle, 1889. Waxwork scene in the 3rd Floor office, La Tour Eiffel. Photographer and date unknown.

Page 165: Dignitaries visiting the construction site of the Eiffel tower, 1889. (Photo credit Musée Grévin)

Page 166: *Boilerplate and Lily Campion gaze southeast from the roof of the Manufacturers' Building* (Boilerplate was a mechanical man created by Professor Archibald Campion) World's Fair in Chicago, Illinois, 1893.

Page 168: Emblem with corset that reads *Fashion Vanity: A la Mode – A la Mort* (unknown origin). In addition to the sense of the word demi-monde for courtesan, a literary demi-monde is a derogatory term for the a writer of the lowest kind.

Page 170: Henry Van der Weyde: "*Mr. Mansfield*". Albumen print cabinet card, ca 1895. (The American Museum of Photography).

Page 172: Wilhelm Konrad Roentgen. *X-ray picture* (*radiograph*), 1895. Published Jan. 5, 1896 in an Austrian newspaper. (University of Würzburg).

Page 173: Freud's divan in ground-floor study, 1997 (preserved environment in Freud's last residence, now the *Freud Museum*, 20 Maresfield Gardens, London. Photographer umknown.

WORKS CITED

Espen J. Aarseth. *Cybertext: Perspectives on Ergodic Literature.* Baltimore & London: The Johns Hopkins University Press 1997

Ansell-Pearson, Keith (Ed.). *Philosophy and the adventure of the virtual: Bergson and the time of life.* London & New York: Routledge 2002

Aristotle. *Physics.* (R. P. Hardie & R. K. Gaye, Trans.) <http://classics.mit.edu/Aristotle/physics.2.ii.html>

Aristotle. *Poetics.* (Malcolm Heath, Trans.) London: Penguin Classics 1996

Roy Ascott (Ed.). *Transmodalities: Art, Technology, Consciousness- mind@large.* Bristol, UK: Intellect Books 2000

Barry Atkins. *More than a Game: The Computer Game as Fictional Form.* Manchester & New York: Manchester University Press 2003

Gaston Bachelard. *The Poetics of Space* (*La Poétique de l'éspace,* 1958). Boston: Beacon Press 1994

M.M. Bakhtin. *The Dialogic Imagination: Four Essays by M.M. Bakhtin.* (Caryl Emerson & Michael Holquist, Trans.) Houston: University of Texas Press 1981

Robert Baldick. *The Life of J-K Huysmans.* Oxford: Clarendon Press 1955

Maurice Bardèche & Robert Brasillach. *Histoire du cinéma.* Paris: Les Sept Couleurs 1964

Charles Baudelaire. *Paris Spleen.* (Louise Varèse, Trans.) New York: New Directions Publishing Corporation 1970

Walter Benjamin. *Illuminations.* (Hannah Arendt, Ed.) London: Pimlico/Random House 1999

Walter Benjamin. *One-Way Street and Other Writings.* London & New York: Verso 1979

Walter Benjamin. *Paris, 1800-talets huvudstad. Passagearbetet.* Stockholm & Stehag: Brutus Östlings Bokförlag Symposion 1992

Henri Bergson. *Creative Evolution.* (Arthur Mitchell, Trans.) London: Macmillan 1911

Henri Bergson. *L'Evolution créatrice.* Paris: Félix Alcan 1907

Henri Bergson. *Introduktion till Metafysiken* (*Introduction à la métaphysique 1903*). (Margareta Marin, Trans.) Lysekil: Pontes 1992

Henri Bergson. *Matter and Memory* (*Matière et Mémoire* 1896). (Nancy M. Paul & W. Scott Palmer, Trans.) Cambridge, Massachusetts & London, England: The MIT Press, Zone Books 1991

Henri Bergson. *Tiden och den Fria Viljan – en undersökning av de omedelbara medvetenhetsfakta (Essai sur les Données Immédiates de la Conscience 1889).* Nora: Nya Doxa 1992

Jennifer Bloomer. *Architecture and the Text: The (S)crypts of Joyce and Piranesi.* New Haven & London: Yale University Press 1993

David Bordwell & Kristin Thompson. *Film Art: an Introduction* (1979). (4th Ed.) New York: McGraw-Hill 1993

Marta Braun. *Picturing Time: The work of Etienne-Jules Marey (*1830–1904*).* Chicago & London: The University of Chicago Press 1992

Peter Brooks. *Reading for the Plot – Design and Intention in Narrative.*

Ronald W. Clark. *Edison – The Man who Made the Future.* New York: G. P. Putnam & Sons 1977 Oxford: Clarendon Press 1984

David A. Cook. *A History of Narrative Film.* New York & London: W.W. Norton & Company 1990

Jonathan Crary. *Techniques of the Observer: On Vision and Modernity in the Nineteenth Century* (1992). Cambridge, Massachusetts & London, England: The MIT Press 1999

Tales from the Thousand and One Nights. (N. J. Dawood, Trans.) London: Penguin Classics 1973

Umberto Eco. *Travels in Hyperreality.* (William Weaver, Trans.) New York & London: Harvest Book, Harcourt Inc. 1986

Gerald M. Edelman and Giulio Tononi. *Consciouness: How Matter Becomes Imagination.* Harmondsworth, England: The Penguin Press 2000

Thomas A. Edison. *The Papers of Thomas A. Edison: Research to Development at Menlo Park, January 1879–March 1881, Vol. V.* Paul B. Israel, Louis Carlat, David Hochfelder & Keith A. Nier (Eds.). Baltimore & London: The Johns Hopkins University Press 2004

Roy Eriksen. *The Building in the Text – Alberti to Shakespeare and Milton.* Pennsylvania: Pennsylvania State University Press 2001

Robin Evans. *Translations from Drawing to Building and other Essays.* London: AA Documents 1997

Anne Friedberg. *Window Shopping – Cinema and the Postmodern.* Berkeley & Oxford: University of California Press 1993

Edmond de Goncourt. *La Maison d'un artiste (tome I&II).* Paris: Charpentier 1881

Helen Grace (Ed.). *Aesthesia and the Economy of the Senses.* Sydney: UWS Nepean, University of Western Sydney 1996

Elizabeth Grosz. *Architecture from the Outside: Essays on Virtual and Real Space.* Cambridge, Massachusetts & London, England: The MIT Press 2001

Robert Harbison. *Eccentric Spaces* (1977). London: The MIT Press 2000

N. Katherine Hayles. *How we Became Posthuman: Virtual Bodies in Cybernetics, Literature, and Informatics.* Chicago & London: The University of Chicago Press 1999

Gordon Hendricks. *The Edison Motion Picture Myth.* Berkeley & Los Angeles: University of California Press 1961

Herman Hesse. *Glass Bead Game (Magister Ludi)* (1943). New York: Henry Holt & Company 1990

Victor Hugo. *Notre-Dame De Paris* (1831). <http://www.gutenberg.org/etext/2610>

Joris-Karl Huysmans. *Against Nature.* (Robert Baldick, Trans.) London: Penguin Classics 1959

Joris-Karl Huysmans. *A Rebours* (1884). Paris: Garnier-Flammarion 1978

Joris-Karl Huysmans. *With the Flow* (*A Vau-l'eau 1882*). (Andrew Brown, Trans.) London: Hesperus Press Limited 2003.

Friedrich A. Kittler. *Gramophone, Film, Typewriter* (1986). Stanford, California: Stanford University Press 1999

Friedrich A. Kittler. *Discourse networks 1800/1900* (1985). Stanford, California: Stanford University Press 1990

Friedrich A. Kittler. *Maskinskrifter – Essäer om medier och litteratur.* Gråbo: Bokförlaget Anthropos 2003

George P. Landow (Ed.). *Hyper/text/theory.* Baltimore & London: The Johns Hopkins University Press 1994

Edouard Le Roy. *A New Philosophy: Henri Bergson* (*Une Philosophie nouvelle: Henri Bergson*, 1912). (Vincent Benson, Transl. 1913) Project Gutenberg: <http://digital.library.upenn.edu/webbin/gutbook/lookup?num=1347>

Michel de Lézinier. *Avec Huysmans: Promenades et Souvenirs.* Paris: André Delpeuch Libraire-Editeur 1928

Jean-François Lyotard. *The Postmodern Condition– A Report on Knowledge* (1979). Manchester: Manchester University Press 1992

Xavier de Maistre. *A Journey around my Room and A Nocturnal Expedition around my Room.* (Andrew Brown, Trans.) London: Hesperus Classics 2004

Abraham Maslow. *Motivation and Personality* (1954). 2nd Ed. New York: Harper & Row 1970

Marshall McLuhan. *The Gutenberg Galaxy: The Making of Typographic Man.* London: Routledge & Kegan Paul 1962

Marshall McLuhan. *Understanding Media.* New York & London: McGraw Hill Book Company 1965

Margaret Morse. *Virtualities: Television, Media, Art, and Cyberculture.* Bloomington & Indianapolis: Indiana University Press 1998

John Mullarkey (Ed.). *The New Bergson.* Manchester & New York: Manchester University Press 1999

Janet H. Murray. *Hamlet on the Holodeck – The Future of Narrative in Cyberspace* (1997). Cambridge, Massachusetts: The MIT Press 2000

Charles Musser. *History of the American Cinema, Vol. I: The Emergence of Cinema: the American screen to 1907* (Charles Harpole, Gen. Ed.). New York & Oxford: Maxwell Macmillan International 1990

Sadie Plant. *Zeros + Ones.* London: Fourth Estate 1997

Plato. *The Republic.* (B. Jowett, Trans.) <http://www.gutenberg.org/etext/1497>

Edgar Allan Poe. *Upptäckter under Hypnos.* Lund: Ellerströms Förlag 2001

Steven Poole. *Trigger Happy: The Inner Life of Videogames.* London: Fourth Estate 2000

Vladimir Propp. *Morphology of the Folk Tale* (1928). University of Texas Press 1968

Marcel Proust. *À la recherche du temps perdu* (1913-1922). (Jean-Yves. Tadié, Ed.) Paris: collection Pléiade, Gallimard 1987-1989

Terry Ramsaye. *A Million and One Nights: A History of the Motion Picture Through 1925.* New York: Touchstone Books 1986

Joanna Richardson. *La vie Parisienne 1852–1870.* New York: Viking Press 1971

David Robinson. *From Peep Show to Palace: The Birth of American Film.* New York: Columbia University Press 1996

Marie-Laure Ryan. *Narrative as Virtual Reality – Immersion and Interactivity in Literature and Electronic Media.* Baltimore & London: The Johns Hopkins University Press 2001

Antoine de Saint-Exupéry. *Le Petit Prince* (1943). San Diego, New York & London: Harvest HBJ Publishers 1971

Deborah L. Silverman. *Art Nouveau in Fin-de-Siècle France: Politics, Psychology and Style.* Maarssen & The Hague: Gary Schwartz 1989

Barbara Maria Stafford & Frances Tepak. *Devices of Wonder: From the World in a Box to Images on a Screen.* Los Angeles: Getty Research Institute 2001

Neal Stephenson. *The Diamond Age* (1995). London & New York: Penguin Books 1996

Susan Stewart. *Crimes of Writing- Problems in the Containment of Representation.* Durham & London: Duke University Press 1994

Susan Stewart. *On Longing – Narratives of the Miniature, the Gigantic, the Souvenir, the Collection.* Durham & London: Duke University Press 1993

Alvin Toffler. *Future Shock.* London: Pan Books, 1970

Betty A. Toole Ed. *Ada, The Enchantress of Numbers.* Los Angeles: Strawberry Press 1998

Anthony Vidler. *The Architectural Uncanny: essays in the modern unhomely.* Boston, Massachusetts: The MIT Press 1992

Auguste Villiers de l'Isle Adam. *L'Eve Future.* Paris: GF Flammarion 1992

Paul Virilio. *Försvinnandets estetik (The Aesthetics of Disappearance 1989).* Göteborg: Bokförlaget Korpen 1996

Janell Watson. *The Literature and Material Culture from Balzac to Proust: The Collection and Consumption of Curiosities.* Cambridge: Cambridge University Press 1999

Michael Wheeler (Ed.). *Ruskin and Environment : The Storm-Cloud of the 19th Century.* Manchester: Manchester University Press 1995

Oscar Wilde. *The Picture of Dorian Gray* (1890). London: Penguin Popular Classics 1994

Rosalind Williams. *Dream Worlds: Mass Consumption in Late Nineteenth Century France.* Berkeley & Los Angeles: University of California Press 1982

Gaby Wood. *Edison's Eve: A Magical History of the Quest for Mechanical Life.* New York: Anchor Books 2003

Malin Zimm. *The Dying Dreamer – Architecture of Parallel Realities.* Stockholm: KTH TRITA-ARK-Forskningspublikationer 2003

Emile Zola. *Au bonheur des dames* (1883). (Robin Buss, Trans.) London: Penguin Classics 2001

CITED ARTICLES AND ESSENTIAL WEB PAGES

Web page article: Alain Barbier Sainte Marie. "La Maison d'un artiste: à revisiter". Review published July 12, 2003 on site founded in 2001 by Paul Adamy & Alain Barbier Sainte Marie (Eds.). <http://membres.lycos.fr/goncourt/maisonechelledej/absmaison.htm>

Article: William W. Braham. "A Wall of Books", in *Journal of Architectural Education* vol. 53, nr 1: 1999, pp. 4-14

Web page article: Emanuel Dimas de Melo Pimenta. "Virtual Architecture" in *Transformers.* Retrieved 8 Oct, 2005. < http://www.asa-art.com/virtus/idea.htm>.

Web page article: Ian Eller. "World of Warcraft Population Hits New Highs", in *RPGamer News Bulletin*, 30 Aug. 2005. <http://www.rpgamer.com/news/Q3-2005/083005b.html>

Web page: Russell Naughton (Web page Ed.). *Adventures in Cybersound*, 1998. <http://www.acmi.net.au/AIC/LATHAM_RAMSAYE.html>

Web page: *The Oxford English Dictionary*. OED Online. Oxford University Press. <http://dictionary.oed.com>

Article: Charles Rice. "Rethinking Histories of the Interior" in *The Journal of Architecture*, vol. 9, nr 3: 2004 pp. 275-287

Web page: Edison National Historic Site, West Orange, New Jersey, US. Official web page. <http://www.nps.gov/edis/edisonia/virtual%20tour/blackmaria/blackmaria.htm>

Web page: US Library of Congress *Motion picture archives,* Broadcasting and Recorded Sound Division. <http://memory.loc.gov/ammem/edhtml/edmvchrn.html>

Web page: *Wikipedia: The Free Encyclopedia.* <http://en.wikipedia.org>